Emotional Wellbeing:

Emotional Attachments Shape Our Lives

By

Professor Dr Nazir Ahmad

M.Phil. (London) PhD (London), DBMS, MCILIP (Manchester)
Ex-Professor Dept. of Information Science &
Knowledge Management
Faculty of Arts & Humanities
King Abdul Aziz University, Jeddah, Saudi Arabia

Illustrated By:
Aqeel Nazir Ahmad
MSc. (UK), BSc. (Hons) U.K.

SHL
WITHDRAWN

Radiant Valley
West Midlands, U.K.

Emotional Wellbeing:
Emotional Attachments Shape Our Lives

Copyright © 2021 Dr Nazir Ahmad

First Published in the United Kingdom: 2021/ 1443 A.H.

Published & Distributed by

Radiant Valley,
Castle Bromwich, B36 8EU
West Midlands, United Kingdom

Website: www.radiant-valley.com
Email: info@radiant-valley.com
drnahmad3@hotmail.com

[Place direct orders for this book]

Printed and bound in the United Kingdom

Ahmad, Nazir
Emotional Wellbeing: Emotional Attachments Shape Our Lives.
West Midlands: Radiant Valley, 2021.
Contains Citations & Plates
DDC 155.234

Cataloguing in Publication Data for this book is available from:

The British Library, United Kingdom.

ISBN: 978-0-9957147-1-7

Emotional Wellbeing:
Emotional Attachments Shape Our Lives

DEDICATED TO

Dr Adeel Nazir Ahmad
MBBS, MRCGP (UK), DRCOG (UK), MSc Sports & Exercise
Medicine (UK), CPHQ (USA), FRCGP (UK)

Medical Director, Consultant, and Head of Family Medicine
KAUST Health
King Abdullah University of Science and Technology
Western Province, Kingdom of Saudi Arabia
and my daughter-in-law, Gull Adeel

In The Name of Allah, The Most
Gracious The Most Merciful

TABLE OF CONTENTS

FOREWARD

It is a great pleasure to reflect on the emotionally electrifying and gripping narrative of Dr Nazir Ahmad. Youth wellbeing, knowledge sharing, and the intricate web of interconnections ultimately shape young lives. I am well aware of the significance of social, physiological, and cognitive aspects of human beings. All these areas have captured the author's attention.

How individuals create social identities through cyberspace, initiating intimacy, developing infatuation, and enjoying hilarity? The author's classroom affiliation with multicultural university and college students delineates youth relationships, poignant expressions, and pleasant encounters. His beautifully composed poems in almost every chapter of the book make it an impressive piece of literature that invigorates the reader to smile, enliven memory, and energise psychological health. Naturally intended for teenagers, but pleasantly reminds adults of what they once experienced themselves, experimented, and derived elation. Anna Freud's insights, Hall's views, and Durkheim's assessments make it exceedingly enjoyable to understand human feelings.

Our emotions are the perceptions of body states under the prefrontal cortex and organismic control, responsive to actions. With variations, emotions are universal across all cultures, biological in origin, genetic in nature, and social in outlook. Children equipped with social skills better tackle delicate and dicey scenarios. The author discusses campus-based university development programmes to promote dexterities, acuities, and attachments for fostering trusting lifelong links. It is interesting to know that the Dutch broods are the happiest in Europe.

My exposure to thousands of British patients in the United Kingdom and Saudi patients at King Abdullah University of Science and Technology has enabled me to visualise the emotional aspects of multicultural communities in multilingual societies. Dr Nazir has diligently portrayed the feelings and perceptions of youngsters in Western and Eastern populations, mainly covering their college and university relationships and everlasting impact on shaping social lives.

The author specifies Turkish government measures to improve the social and learning situation in the country. He narrates productive closeness, mutual fondness, and youth rapport for lifelong relationships with meaningful intimacy and sentimental affection. Smiles and laughter in social interactions, humour, and jokes in interpersonal communications carry cognitive health benefits. Concerning youngsters' feelings and acuities, the author delineates Cannon-Bard (1927), James-Lang, and Schachter & Singer (1962) theories with examples from William James (1884), Hall (1904), and Anna Freud's (1969) thoughtful outlooks on psychological wellness and social adventures.

The present work reaffirms his penetrating style of motivating readers to study 'Emotional Wellbeing' to enhance their knowledge and seek guidance for shaping youth lives. Feel is the gasoline just as sense is the firewood that will make the young ablaze, activating emotional power, stimulating reading habit, and instigating learning appetite. Beautifully composed poems make this book exceedingly intriguing and captivating.

This book epitomises knowledge sharing in an emotionally charged educational environment that facilitates learning on the one hand and socialisation on the other. Emotional wellbeing is worthy of study to acquire the evocative meaning of young lives, garner awareness of powerful media impact, and desirability of adopting measures for shaping teenagers' future.

Finally, I am honoured to be able to write a foreword for this timely produced outstanding publication that I believe, is a need of the day. With pandemic surrounding the entire world, far fewer people can access the printed version, but the digital form would be specifically useful for the universal readership.

Dr Mudassar Habib
MBBS, MRCGP(UK), FRCGP (UK),
Chief of Staff & Consultant Family Medicine,
KAUST Health (Operated by Fakeeh Care)
King Abdullah University of Science & Technology

PREFACE

This work is a far-reaching addition to socio-psychological literature that already exists, albeit every individual attempt opens up fresh avenues to understand human beings' psychological functioning. Our emotions are at the forefront of all significant episodes occurring during the development of mental powers. Any fiction or non-fiction book can be a good read for some but less exciting for others. Some meaningful writings, including prose and poetry, stir readers' thoughts either positively or less progressively.

This book stimulates your perceptions and shows a new angle for depicting paternal and maternal sentiments. It is interesting to know the real-life reflections of Anne Freud, the daughter of a world-renowned psychologist. The author has utilised personal teaching and academic rapport with students to underline teenage attachments' social mechanisms. The exciting youth tenure begins with university entrance where links are created and friendships formed. On-campus culture is a breath-taking experience for youngsters paving the way for sharing thoughts and feelings. They formulate knowledge alliance for knowledge enhancement and self-discovery. Once they get to know each other, companionships prosper as intimate relationships are fashioned. The students while pursuing academic careers, compete in finding mates matching their taste. Unsurprisingly, girls are deeply absorbed in their physical metaphors, facial features, and bodily perfections.

The young university students evaluate their feelings for others, learn the meanings of smiles, the application, and social value of keep smiling. Their personalities grow while learning the difference between laughing at and laughing with friends and peers. They equally discover the hidden magnetic power of laughter. There are some interesting episodes in this book for light hilarity and graceful amusement.

The last two chapters of this book are exclusively devoted to humour that heels hearts, moods, and compassions. It links buddies, connects chums, and proliferates excitements, kicks, and thrills. Dr Nazir Ahmad is instrumental in tracing how the British, French, German, and Turkish comedians entertain and amuse the masses through harmless puns for fun and exhilaration. Academic life demands focus and concentration, and in the absence of palpable buzz, boredom creeps into youngsters' lives. Those youth studying literary works are aware of the wittiness in English and European literature but may not have found time to enjoy stage dramas and theatrical performances illustrating jokes, jests, and wits. German graphic has been trendy among university students across the country. The author quite rightly asserts that many Western universities with substantial international student intake organise comedy shows to entertain youngsters with spoofs, pranks, and caricatures. Fifteen poems that Dr Nazir Ahmad has gleefully composed reflect several aspects of emotional pleasure, happiness, and psychological health.

There is great excitement in making new friends, conducting joint experiments, and constructing knowledge. Collaborative learning continues to fascinate boys and girls in their on-campus and online educational endeavours. The cooperative learning captivates the freshman in a learner-centred approach reclaiming approbation from all quarters. In an activity-based knowledge sharing, the faculty offers backup while each participant unreservedly contributes to augment learning, inspire discovery, and motivate exploration.

It is an informative book for young adult readers to find our emotions' realities in practical situations. Sometimes we are hurt and, on other occasions, overjoyed due to the environment and our surroundings. The student life in universities and colleges evolves learning, gaining knowledge, and pursuing worthwhile careers. In academic institutes, we meet people from all hues, create attachments, choose partners, and select friends. In short, coordinated learning creates an engaging, interactive setting that promotes the spirit of team-work, triggering inventiveness, and eliciting imagination.

The author could have expanded some areas in this study, such as meaningful intimacy and socialisation, further with examples from the less developed countries. However, it is fascinating to understand how different students from emerging economies behave, intermingle, and interact during higher education at Western universities. The book is a useful read for parents, students, teachers, sociologists, and psychologists. A comprehensive list of citations offers the researchers and scholars an opportunity to investigate relevant topics and expand their knowledge horizons.

Professor Nikolaos Hadji Christidis. PhD
Distinguished Professor Chemical Science, Physical Science, & Engineering Division,
King Abdullah University of Science and Technology,
Kingdom of Saudi Arabia
Email:Nikolaos.hadjichristidis@kaust.edu.sa

INTRODUCTION

Healthy attachment is an emotional bond connecting two individuals amicably and sharing common perceptions, insights, and acuities. Feeling appreciated, unique, cherished, and flattered fills a void in the life of an individual. If you are attached to a person, you do not emotionally blackmail, manipulate, or dominate him/her. Sensitive youth are vulnerable to sensory stimulation in their environment and become easily absorbed into their way of life. Female teens are relatively shy but open-minded, boys comparatively abrupt, hasty in their approach, and not always emotionally expressive. Infants' fundamental essentials are met by their loving parents, who implicitly contribute to attachment strategy throughout their lives. Excessive emotional attachment believes to be unhealthy, especially when it unsettles your normal activities. It can be invasive in life as it amounts to co-dependency, resulting in reliance on others. Any sort of relationship's interdependence does more harm than good in building mutual decency and dignity. Attachment is a need for someone to fill a vacuum in your life and feel that someone cares. If you have little in stock and the other person pesters and criticises you a lot about trivial things, you should demonstrate courage, be bold, keep sailing, and even on your own; you will weather the storm. Couples continue living together to see their kids through to college, but some struggle staying under one roof for children making it to adulthood. Acquaintances with neighbours, associations with working colleagues, links with mentors, contacts with families, interactions with people at train stations, conversations with strangers on the train, bus, and aeroplane predictably wield a certain degree of emotional influence on our lives. Even a simple reference enquiry at the reader's services desk of a university, college, or public library might arouse mutual interest for a consecutive meeting between two individuals. Exchange of a simple dialogue at a theatre, golf club, tennis court, art gallery, or Trafalgar Square can inadvertently spur social get-together due to emotional attractiveness. Emotions are convoluted and intricate twiddle of interwoven, tangled, incompatible notions and feelings; we experience various times in pleasant and sometimes in embarrassing situations. For example, I compose poems with an emotional touch, hoping to draw the readers' attention, stir and engender his/her own emotions.

We entrench values in our youngsters and make them understand the world around us. In the U.K., U.S.A., Australia, and New Zealand, virtues and principles take precedence over other activities. The public or school library is considered a place of contact, friendship, and dialogue. The principals and teachers cooperate with families in promoting positive culture between home and school. The school librarian acts as a tutor librarian engaging pupils to use the library before class and during lunchtime. He/she promotes parent-teacher rapport, making the school library a pupil's second home. The public library complements in-school education and cultural behaviours. Flexible learning and talking environment improve pupils' attitudes and syllabus engagement, minimising the accomplishment gap, supports fairness, and increases parity in education. School and public libraries in Europe, Australia, and New Zealand create better opportunities for socialisation, romance, and companionships. Informal interactions occur during pupils' visits to museums, art galleries, ancient sites, impacting pupils' thinking, feelings, and values, and eventually help shape their emotional attachments. They learn how to question thoughts and express ideas while parents offer guidance to recover when their social steps are vacillated. Pupils from diverse cultures have different stances, manners, and moods, which they display in educational settings. The school librarian can provide the right books to read, moulding their sensitivities and generating flexibility in their temperament. Present writer's tenure at Rutherford School, London witnessed some pupils' coming at lunch break to meet the librarian, confide in him, seek solace and consolation. This trust helps cement turbulent relationships among school fellows.

New Zealand Education Act 1989, Bill of Rights Act 1990, and Harmful Digital Communication Act 2015 has helped reduce school-based teasing, mocking, and bantering among pupils, visibly improving social, psychological, and academic atmosphere across all school in the country. Netsafe's cooperation with the education sector has considerably improved cyber safety, permitting students to develop interpersonal relationships.

The emotional wellbeing programme for Liverpool 2015-2020 has achieved admirable success in making youth mental health 'Everybody's business'. It is important the way we think and feel about ourselves and others. The authorities addressed disorders related to social divide, puberty, hormone, and emotional needs. British Worth-It organisation supports workshops, coaching sessions, lessons, and events for young people for promoting resilience. Complimentary psychology workshops have now become Positive Education hubs in schools. In February 2019, the government started a 'Measuring National Wellbeing Programme' focusing on overall satisfaction with life. It was recognised that a positive relationship is a single significant factor in shaping people's personal wellbeing. Young people feel lonely due to a lack of get-togethers and inadequate social connectedness. Covid-19 has exacerbated the situation for people causing emotional distress. There has been rapid decrease in leisure activities due to self-imposed lockdown, creating increased isolation for teenagers. Under the current climate, there is an immense need to create opportunities for youngsters to socially meet and greet, invigorate emotional attachments for better health.

In the shaping of emotional life, relationships, feelings, and numerous situational factors come into play that brings together two different individuals at various stages of adolescent growth. Social relations generate feelings of desire, warmth and create closeness between two souls. Emotions are intensely personal mindsets. It is an indisputably delicate topic for the researchers who advance their theories and experiences gained in culturally diverse situations, dissimilar surroundings, and discrete ambiences. Emotions are feelings, but feelings are not real emotions since our pleasant memories arouse considerable emotions, and we become aware of inner emotional dynamics. The researcher can merely describe what he/she might have felt about past spasmodic relationships with either school or college peers. You might recall someone's mesmerising smile, enthralling grin, and hypnotic wink. Sweet recollections result from pleasurable experiments and unforgettable episodes in early college days, where students enthusiastically make cherished connections. The researcher being a university professor, scientifically observed students' social behaviour without asking any questions about their relationships. For instance, if we follow two teens as they intimately communicate on the university premises, we may say they are emotionally connected. If we notice a young couple at the far end of the playground arguing or shouting, we would assume that one or both of them are emotionally disturbed. One of the said encounters is pleasant, whereas the other face-to-face meeting is profoundly shocking and decidedly perturbing.

The choice of friends determines the quality of interaction that leaves a substantial impact on youth morality. Social learning allows everyone to add, discuss, and gain awareness about the vital aspects of life. Psychologically, each emotion accentuates a specific element's unique fragments, such as shame, pleasure, anger, and happiness. Sensory feedback from bodily actions supports warm feelings, whereas facial expressions and gaze patterns can contribute to the attribute, feature, and strength of emotional experience. Initial emotion instigates action and preparation for an intended action or, in certain instances, inaction. Psychological activities lead directly to our feelings. Passionate, positive emotions are love, compassion, sympathy, and euphoria, arousing thoughts for expression. Social psychology is interlaced in youth emotions impacting behaviour and perceptions, intentions, and objective. Jealousy of our relationship with others reflects negativity, whereas loneliness or belonging is based on the nature of being connected. Lack of self-restraint, display of anger, and resentment towards the inner circle are indications of being emotional, losing temper, becoming irritated, and showing irrationality. Laughter and hilarity, humour and comedy are means of youth interaction, permitting informal connections, socialisation, and companionships. Emotions are understandably the products of socialisation evolving psychological, mental, and bodily symptoms. Each chapter of this book unfolds deeply searched knowledge, vibrant fresh thoughts, and authors' reflections on human feelings, emotions, connotations, social undertones, exciting intimacies, and inviting relationships.

In the process of writing this book, the present writer has imaginatively composed fifteen meaningful poems to amplify the text.

Reader's Emotions (POEM)

When emotional smoke rises higher
Our tender feelings are on fire

Coronavirus has taken people by storm
Impacted civilisations, dismantled norm

Doctors' grapple boldly, grief and laugh a little
Ventilators inadequate, surgical masks brittle

Many doctors and medics sacrificed their lives
Leaving behind children, spouses and wives

COVID-19 is a tragedy on a global scale
Neither we condemn nor we assail
Pray to our Lord, ask for bail
Efforts of Medics, in UK we hail

Banging at windows, pots and pans
Doctors admired, we are your fans

Multiple health centres in UK sprang
The NHS arranged for us, tests, and scans

Public in Britain, on doorsteps they cheer
Nurses and doctors are saviours and dear

Chemicals in the air cause pollution
Infections occur, what is the solution?

Sooth muscles, exercise, relieve stress
Remain hugely optimistic, despair less

Viruses invade, stay well clear
Don't be afraid, God is near

Two yards away, you might hear
Dangers surround us, intent sincere

I aspire to stimulate readers' emotions
Stir compassions and tickle their notions

My words and phrases, induce in readers
Dramatic reactions produce in leaders

Some may admire and others despise
Emotional inducement, is a big surprise

Multifaceted emotions, divergent voice
How you perceive, is the readers' choice

[Composed by Dr Nazir Ahmad,
 January 12, 2021/
Jamadi Al-Awwal 28 , 1442 Hijra, Tuesday]

CHAPTER I - PATERNAL AND MATERNAL EMOTIONS

Maternal love is known to be transcendent, noble, and sanctified for her progeny. She goes through the painful process of gravidity and agonising procedure of childbirth, sometimes even alone. Paternal love is equally generous, decent, holy, and unmatched for kids, albeit more affectionate towards daughters. Daughters are a blessing in Western cultures, although the birth of a girl is disliked in some societies. There are some amazingly incredible tales of daughter-father pure love and adoration. In many environments, grown-up daughters are known to be implausibly sensitive and profoundly caring towards papas. The girls are emotionally attached and deeply perceptive to their fathers and are relatively less prone to experiencing psychological problems due to paternal warmth and support. The emotional attachment induces girls' social and psychosomatic growth in their rapport with mothers and fathers. An exciting story of daughter-father emotional proximity appears in the 'Nine Books of Memorable Acts and Sayings of the Ancient Romans' vividly penned by Valerius Maximus. We can view an impressive statue at Botermarkt 17 in Ghent, Belgium. It is a sculpture on top of a building that initially used to be an entrance to the prison and the warden's residence. The jail at Lakenhelle accommodated inmates between 1742 and 1902. A magnificent hugely expensive and famous painting of daughter and father (Pero and Simon) made by Hans

Sebald Beham portrays how Pero is breastfeeding her dad Simon in a prison cell behind bars regularly to prolong his life span. On account of the crime, he was condemned to death by starving. The correctional officer discovered reality resulting in a new hearing in which the court released the father on compassionate grounds. The painting in possession of Roman Charity depicts the natural empathy of a copiously adorable daughter whose determination and daring stance saved her father at a highly critical juncture.

Emotional Brainpower

The children learn the fundamentals of emotional brainpower at home and ascertain the meaning of deprivation, thirstiness, and starvation. Parents instil in their children critical thinking skills such as understanding and control of disturbing thoughts. An affectionate father is thrilled to see when his daughter smiles and begins talking, demands attention and expects to cuddle. According to Daniel Goleman and also, John Gottman, emotion-coaching parents become emotionally intelligent, and they can better regulate their emotional states. (p.16). Some parents are inspirational trainers, whereas others are dreadful. The present writer has a 3-year old granddaughter who 'loves me dearly, plays with me, and keeps me engaged in various innocent activities. An emotional attachment makes me listen to her eagerly, respond compassionately, give her drink if thirsty, and feed her if she is hungry. I respect her choice of food and act accordingly – it is my kind-hearted words that offer this innocent little angel, emotional happiness, and sentimental cheerfulness. I attempt to fulfil her trivial desires with feelings of acceptance. She makes colourful sketches and describes these to me in a commendable manner expecting positive feedback which she wholeheartedly and unswervingly receives'.

Emotional coaching plays an indispensable role in shaping the emotional strength of children. John Gottman and his colleagues researched in 1986 at Champaign, Illinois, involving 56 married couples employing questionnaires, interviews, and live observations. All of them had children aged 4-5 years, and researchers asked about their emotional expression with their kids' feelings of sadness, happiness, and anxiety. Unsurprisingly, the kids of emotion-coaching parents were performing well academically and socially, expressing fewer negative emotions and were relaxed, possessing good health. Emotion-coaching necessitates self-emotional awareness and the resilience to pay attention to the child's basic needs. We should be encouraging children to express their feelings of joy and excitement, desolation, and gloom. There is a genuine need to accept negative and positive emotional expressions without reservation and undue cross-questioning. It is utterly undesirable to poke fun at the kid's pleasant or unpleasant phrases. Parents who wish to expand their practical knowledge of emotion-coaching would benefit reading books produced by two female intellectuals Adele Faber and Elaine Mazlish (1925-2017). Of particular interest is the publication entitled 'How to talk so kids will listen and listen so kids will talk' and 'Liberated parents/Liberated children.' The authors guide you through helping children deal with their feelings; engaging cooperation, an alternative to punishment, encouraging autonomy, praising good work and strengthening their self-image.

The parents should worry and interfere less but use conventional wisdom to deal with emotional issues. Perhaps, reading 'Queen bees' wannabes' by Rosalind Wiseman would help understand the taxonomy of teenage girls who adapt well and learn through fun and exploration. Haim Ginott (1972), in his work 'Teacher and Child: a book for parents and teachers' offers inspirational guidance to cultivate changes within the hearts of boys and girls. Mothers closely watch and nurture constructive emotions in their daughters. Mother is the cradle of primary training. (Ahmad, 2020, p. 221) and even the grandparents help kids learn discipline, regulations, and boundaries (p. 264).

A sensible mother simultaneously identifies gifts in offspring to promote strengths and enhance buoyancy. Dr Harriet Tenenbaum of the University of Surrey proclaims that mother-daughter dialogue is excessively sensitive, exhibiting an advanced level of emotional literacy as compared to young boys. In mother-daughter communication, inspirational words are frequently used, which indicates better emotional intelligence.

While growing up, girls feel confident in making productive choices, making the right decisions, addressing social issues, and facing emotional challenges. Between the age of 9 to 14 is a crucial stage of development in the lives of girls since they undergo psychological, cognitive, biological, and emotional changes. They build up physiognomies based on self-discovery, parental guidance, and media exposure. Domestically, a daughter will experience a sense of control and management if the mother permits her to choose clothes, shoes, literary books, biographies of achievers, and time to relax and reflect. Online screen time and social media exposure should be minimised and monitored to prevent inappropriate influence on her sensitivities and perceptions. The mother-daughter relationship relies on a close affinity, trustworthiness, and constancy. Besides, the following measures would be ideal in building emotional competencies in your daughters:

Active engagement in important domestic tasks

Encourage thoughtfulness and reflection

Allow experimentation under moderate supervision

Inspire creativity and inventiveness

Instigate discussion on critical topics

Entertain her ideas with resilience

Appreciate constructive viewpoints

Be a compassionate listener

Find time to sit down and listen attentively

Pay particular attention to her feedback

Let her air grievances and complaints

Do not criticise and evaluate her grumbles

Lend a sympathetic ear and make polite suggestions

Act as a discussion board and invite proposals

Give the self-confidence to face emotional tests

Stimulate gifted daughter to excel in STEM

Help her form social strengths and powers

Build analytical skills to assess peers' intentions

Motivate her to reject deception & duplicity

Guide her in choosing friends and peers

Transmit productive family values

Recreational undertakings are beneficial for both girls and boys as long as such activities are either supervised by parents, teachers foster guardians or carers. They need to have fun in harmless adventures, pleasurable ventures, and short journeys, which tend to be exciting and stimulating and also revitalise youth energies. They require refreshments and treats such as ice-creams, chocolates, lollies, and toffees, but obesity must be discouraged for the sake of robust health. The youngsters in higher secondary schools and colleges are thrill-seekers, crack jokes, laugh wildly, and smile spontaneously. Laughter occurs impulsively in their regular interactions and relationships. Admittedly, healthy figures possess healthy cognitive powers, and healthy brains have smart and fit bodies. Two significant features are related to routine physical exercise and secondly 'watch what you eat and drink'? Including the quality and quantity of food you consume.

Gain Knowledge, Unlock Potential (POEM)

Gain knowledge, unlock your potential
Emotional brainpower absolutely Essential

Then will you attain, treatment preferential
Uniqueness makes you, a genius and influential

Whenever you reach university or college
Develop your spheres, acquire greater knowledge

Plough the fields of transcendent knowledge
Read ibn arabi, al-biruni and rumi while at college

Share with roommates, insights you gain
Intuitions, acumens, are learnt with pain

We should never make any futile noise
Forceful reasoning, with sturdy voice

Ideas stem from the ideals we hold
Habits are innate; as such we cannot mould

Adaptations count in human relations
Imitations are called mere sensations

False parodies are simple vibrations
Self-worth exhibits dignity of nations

Values in children, virtues are essential
Smooth nurturing to unlock potential

Cultivate individuality, show differential
Nurture empathy, become instrumental

Youth think inversely with dreaming mind
Imaginary situations, one may well find

Towards enthralments, they are inclined
Deceitful enchantments must be declined

You give and return moderate favours
Relish the delight but add no flavours

Fantasy world might be a charming illusion
Precautionary measures for right conclusion

Fertilise intellectual soil with finest seeds
Let the talent blossom, remove the weeds

Ibn-khaldun, khwarizmi left literary deeds
Al-ghazali, al-shuraim fulfil spiritual needs

Split open brain cells and view the skies
Pause and think, who made those butterflies

Still, you are profane, an utter disgrace
Waste no time, true faith you embrace

Almighty God will take you into heaven

The layers of skies are altogether seven

(Composed by Dr Nazir Ahmad,
October 2, 2020/ Safar 14, 1442 Hijra, Friday]

Buoyant Emotions Impact Academic Progress

The impact might be positive or negative, depending on the emotional atmosphere prevalent in the household, school, and society. Parents, caregivers, teachers, and classmates effectively contribute to shaping youth lives, perceptions, and outlooks.

Emotional resilience pays off rich dividends, enabling youth to better concentrate on academic lessons, navigate knowledge, and untangle intricate problems. Domestic and school atmosphere creates the right conditions for youngsters to explore, evaluate, experiment, and share personal space and adventures with school mates. Suppleness in shared learning and pliability in collective explorations promotes self-esteem and compassionate feelings for others. The combined experience of buoyant emotions through social play and mutual affection creates pleasantness and amiability. Kelvinside Academy, Scotland, under its former Rector Ian Munro, excelled in developing conditions suited to the school population's aspirations. Munro rightly remarked that "Outdoor learning is one of our core philosophies and opening a Wilderness Campus in the Cairngorm National Park can provide a better outcome than when confined to a classroom." (Muir, 2018).

Through the Forest School programme, their educational strategy was meant to empower kids to guide their own learning, instead of telling them "what they should do, or how should do it", says Esther Henderson, leader of the initiative. She observed the children in the woodland environment, following their own curiosity, while planting trees and building dens. Long hours in the classroom cause monotony for children who lose focus, diminishing their creativity. Away from the school settings, kids use ingenuity, trust their instinct, and learn risk management. (Scottish Field, 1st October 2018). Positive emotions facilitate creative thinking, whereas romantic feelings are associated with inherent enjoyment.

Changes in distinctive thought and behaviour displays transpire during constructive emotions. Outside the formal educational venues, youngsters feel exhilaration, mirth, and amusement in imaginative, playful activities, discovering new things, fooling around, and engaging in fun-loving tricks. While developing social skills, kids generate feelings of involvement, gaining untested emotional experience with another person. Physical education creates the urge to play and be playful, broadening the scope of interpersonal relations and positive personal experience. Such feelings offer latitude of attention, thinking, and action, optimising chances of enhanced pleasure and contentment. Satisfaction is an effective response to meeting biological needs. When teenagers try to extend the play attitude beyond its natural limits, they may encounter negative emotional reaction from mates. The desire to indulge can be an unintentional fervent rejoinder to a passionate gesture stemming from another person's yearning for adoration.

Pupils' emotional wellbeing cannot be measured as we do with the accuracy of spellings. An emotionally optimistic classroom augments learning and develops motivation. Emotions do exist, and realistically, we cannot modify them. We should seek to establish self-control forms among students and staff that embolden indulgent non-disruptive emitting of emotion. Educational events that induce feelings, such as replications, role-playing, and joint projects, provide appropriate memory stimuli, and help youngsters recollect the information during strictly connected happenings in the real world. In schools sometimes, we practice sensitively charged fire drills without warning. Emotionally demanding school surroundings are counterproductive because they can reduce students' ability to learn. Actions that highlight social interface tend to provide the most emotional support. Collaborative learning, games, supportive projects, physical training, and field tours engage the pupils emotionally. Activities that encourage students to talk about their emotions strengthen self-control and self-esteem. For example, why did the Italian explorer Christopher Columbus settle in Valladolid, Spain, instead of asking students where Columbus finally settled? Such a conversation among students converts towards emotions.

Emotions play an indispensable role in educational settings, shaping leadership strategies, facilitating curriculum delivery, and influencing social relationships. A visionary headteacher leads the team to equip youth with hope, inspiration, and resilience to accept challenges and make a difference in others' lives. A distinguished British intellectual Ian Munro, the youngest headteacher in the world, has accentuated "the significance of the precious relationship with pupils, parents, and colleagues," underscoring the fact that "these relationships are strongly influenced by emotions."

Rector of a world-renowned Dollar Academy in Scotland, Ian Munro, has diligently described in his article "My emotional journey to the heart of headship" the necessity of teachers to be visible in both the classroom and the playground, addressing pastoral concerns and creating the veracious environments for learning. Given the epidemic scenario, Munro has meticulously launched the "Dollar Discovers" initiative to benefit all pupils across Scotland, preparing them for " life beyond the classroom and better understand the world." Free online access for all kids is a brainchild of Munro to instigate learning, activate curiosity, and arouse critical thinking. His initiative of turning homes into a classroom where pupils stay connected, do group work, and collaborate in homework receives approbation from educators in the U.K. Some schools efficaciously use blogs as thinking tools, polishing pupils' written communication and imagination. We need to pay attention to youth's social and psychological development as well as moral maturity.

The experience of positive emotions is fundamental to pupils' nature and contributes to the quality of their lives. Emotions contain motivational components and sway cognitive and adaptive functioning. (Izard et al., 2008). Emotions are crucial contributors to kids' inspiration, interpersonal resources, memory, and learning. (Lewis & Haviland-Jones, 2000).

On the contrary, emotional syndrome increases the menace of school dropouts. Positive emotions such as pride and joy in academic achievement share the Duchenne smile, i.e., raised lip corners with muscle contraction near the eyes. Buoyant emotions enhance academic proficiency, integrating diverse subject matter, and broadening potential methods of solving problems. (Fredrickson, 1998; 2001). Psychology drifts toward issues and works to solve them. It has laid emphasis on negative emotions such as sexual jealousy leading to domestic violence and sadness swelling into depression, being a foremost psychological condition. Since negative emotions generate problems, positive emotions provide solutions to the problems and inspire a desire to act in particular ways. Therefore, a tendency to act in a specific manner makes an emotion embodied. (Lazarus, 1991, p.285). While presenting a phenomenon of emotional motivation, Scarantino (2014) classifies three distinct dynamic actions: impulsive emotional actions, planned emotional actions, and reflexes emotional actions.

Emotions motivate youngsters to act and react in a given situation. There is a visible difference between emotional desires and practical desires. A youth with strong motivational desire will act on the instinct to go for a run, while the person of weaker strength would avoid such a venture. For example, if an emotional desire to meet a friend at the concert is more potent than going to the library, the individual would follow the sturdier reflex. We teach children how to exercise self-control in certain situations when they have to act contrary to their emotional desires. It would be academically beneficial to visit the library to meet the deadline for a given project rather than submitting to a socially fulfilling desire. Sometimes emotions do not conform to practical judgements, and one is unconsciously swayed towards desirable pursuits, which may be undesirable and realistically inappropriate. Innocent teenagers are oscillated by fluctuating emotional dispositions, making errors in their decisions. Lack of self-restraint and immaturity drive them to take impulsive, emotional actions rather than well planned dynamic actions.

Apart from parental love, the school provides a congenial environment for kids' emotional wellbeing. Emotions can induce exercise of self-control and prompt self-regulation in many situations. Willpower is an innate trait that helps to exert considerable self-control in a given setting. Willpower can overrule the strength of emotional desire, preventing displeasing actions and distasteful reactions. In monogamous relationships, cheating might be emotionally desirable, but morally objectionable. Under such circumstances, wilful self-restraint should prevail, removing the feelings of guilt and deceitfulness. Positive emotions stimulate positive thinking in the face of emotional desire, but decision to act in relationship scenarios depends on the strength of feelings towards the other person. The weaker the emotions, the stronger will be the self-restraint in intimate connections. Youth hankerings have an impact on the potency of emotional desires. Teenagers' drives and cravings would positively influence emotional desires in academic settings for focused attention and social situations for pleasurable activities. In interpersonal relations, sometimes there are sound reasons to support the realisation of emotional desires depending on the circumstances, while on other occasions, such treats may not be justified.

Rumours, whether real or false, about a targeted pupil cause anxiety, shame, and unpleasantness. Such negative perceptions lead to emotional damage, psychological stress, and mental strain with lingering pain. Damage can be minimised by timely intervention and sensible counselling at school or college. Also, the rumour-monger needs to exercise self-restraint, conceding the mistake and apologising to the victim. Owing to lose self-control, the perpetrator could not resist the temptation of emotional desire to inflict psychological harm to a classmate, tarnishing her reputation. Emotional desires give rise to mental actions, later transmuting into physical undertakings. Some emotional desires such as excessive drinking, drugs and heavy smoking adversely influence individual health whereas pleasant emotional pursuits bring joy, pleasure, and satisfaction. Emotional desires dictate actions when a pupil decides to remain absent from the chemistry lab and escape to the woods for thrill and excitement. Taming emotions is like calming a lion, but willpower has a crucial role to play in exercising self-control to overcome pride. The pupils usually come up with logical excuses to justify emotional actions, prompting instant execution of desirable acts. Youth often give into emotional desires unconsciously. Thoughts, feelings, and an individual's behaviour are components of self-control. Under the coronavirus, peer-to-peer socialisation has become increasingly difficult.

While posting chirps on MySpace and Facebook, teenagers do not realise that their emotional wellbeing is affected, albeit they use typical terminologies such as Activity Feeds, Thumbs Ups, Wall Posts, and Status Updates. Teens cannot pull away from internet use, spending little face-to-face time with friends and parents. Getting together in a social place permits them to share information, gossip, crack jokes, seduce, or slipup. Predators can easily lure vulnerable youth who remain glued to social websites. The display of light-hearted sensations indicates self-absorbed captivations that carry emotional risk. Revealing social exploits online for self-gratification is loathsome, especially for girls.

Self-control is vital in everyday life due to broader connections with the outside world. Can emotions traverse and exhibit a pertinent role in stimulating self-restraint? Do teenagers need to demonstrate self-control in emotionally desirable situations? It depends on the nature of desires and the moments of such occurrences because adolescents follow their instinct, preferring unrestricted access to social venues and unobstructed care free life styles. When youth get together, they find it virtually impossible to resist wayward enticements, whims, and cravings. Sometimes emotions destabilise self-restraint, allowing individuals to follow impulses and temptations. Other times, emotions augment self-control, preventing socially attractive indulgences. As of December 2020, online knowledge disbursement is a blessing in disguise for children unable to attend regular classes at school due to the latest pandemic wave. However, they are missing out on the psycho-social aspect of life pattern so vital for youngsters' emotional well-being. Almost a year in quarantine, teenagers are suffering in isolation, relying on text messaging or oral communication with their chums. Young buddies are missing out on socialisation and interpersonal relationships. Social networking sites are not a feasible alternative to outdoor recreational activities. The absence of vital opportunities to meet, greet, and intermingle, might have immense effect on youngsters' academic progress, intellectual growth, and edifying pursuits.

Female Psychologist Reflections

Emotional psychology relates to bodily sensations, gaze patterns, facial expressions, and specific proprieties of happiness, love, envy, sense of beauty, and pleasure the present writer vehemently feels that:

"Sense of Beauty is a Pure Emotion Signal of Connectivity & Insinuation"

It would be exceedingly pertinent to narrate personal and highly sensitive internal childhood experiences of a famous male psychologist and an illustrious female psychoanalyst to realistically comprehend the adolescence and inherent issues attached to the growth and development. Youth is a turbulent phase, and transition to adulthood is even more challenging given the atmospheric environment in which the kids are groomed, coached, and mentored. An Austrian-born Anna Freud (1895-1982), the youngest daughter of Sigmund Freud, is eminent for her works on psychoanalysis and her 30-years association with Hampshire Child Therapy Clinic. She developed a system of surveillance and data collection related to the psychoanalytic treatment of children. She proclaimed that parents have to cope with flashes when a child is changing. These sparkles and flickers shape the psychological wellbeing of adolescents. She commenced creative writing at the age of 13, and an article:" On adolescence," 1958 depicts her clinical experiences with children's object-relations and interpersonal interactions. It shows specific significant moments when a kid finds it impossible to tolerate frustration while possessing overwhelming desires of prompt fulfilment in social relationships.

Anna Freud out rightly spurned incestuous fantasies. She viewed adolescence as a universal period of developmental commotion that involved mayhems in drive states, in family and peer relations, in ego defences and values. (Caplan & Lebovici, 1969). Adolescence is a thread unobtrusively connecting her life to her father Sigmund Freud, with whom she claimed closeness but felt despised by her mother. Her writings portray personal turbulent childhood, altruism, daydreaming, and struggle against human exploitation. Being an unwanted child, she felt uneasy, rejected, and unimportant and, by 1922, began to analyse her adolescence, rebellion against mother, developing eating disorders. Her father wished Anna to enjoy her life what other girls want, but she inhibited her genital pleasure and dedicated herself to the joy of others. She developed a spirit of sacrifice, living an empathetic life but passionately loved her father and later translating his German works into English. She believed that most adolescents possessed core values, e.g., attaining education, justice, equality, and even spirituality, and 'these are consistent with those of their parents'. The choice of friends reflects the mutual interest and the same ideals.

Teen's Sensations and Attachments

Emotions are at the heart of human psychology, influencing teenage relationships, inspiring familiarities, stimulating feelings, stirring linkups, and exposing positive social dimensions, reactions, and reflections.

A distinguished American psychologist Granville Stanley Hall (1846-1924), portrays adolescence as a stage of "Storm and stress" in the course of which kids experience emotional turmoil before founding a steady symmetry in adulthood. The curve of despondency starts at eleven, rising steadily and rapidly till fifteen. (Hall, 1904, vol. 2, p.77). He is talking about unhappiness and hopelessness when the teens usually feel being disliked, shunned, unduly evaluated, and criticised. The social relations with friends and links with intimate partners are a common source of "depressed mood in adolescence" (Larson and Richard, 1994, p.85.). The emotional need for sensation is comparatively irrepressible during the delicate age period of a child. At this point in life, an emotion of exhilaration is enormously robust as the kids are growing up. Therefore, they "crave strong feelings and new sensation, when monotony, routine and detail are intolerable" (Hall, 1904, Vol.1, p.368.). He further asserts that specifically during adolescence, sensations are more objectified, and their pleasures and pain effects are more keenly felt. "There is a new sense of delight or enjoyment of the sensation itself for its own sake" (Hall, 1904, Vol.2, p,2.). Arnett (1994) and Zuckerman (1995) endorse the view that sensation is to be the highest in the teens. Despite the fact, no television, computer games, internet, or social media existed in those eras that might have impacted, reproduced, and intensified adolescents' pleasure-seeking adventures. Medical literature delineates that several organs and body parts have distinctive degrees of growth, with the limbs growing faster than the rest of the body in early childhood. Also, the growth surge in girls precedes that of boys. Likewise, in middle childhood, the brain forms a network of connections, and the pruning process shapes the minds which produce synapse, and the brain develops rapidly. Attachment starts at an early age when kids make an emotional connection with their parents. This interconnection shapes the wiring in mind and establishes patters for how the adolescent will develop relationships as he/she grows older. Kids who keep their calm, demonstrate self-restraint, avoid overeating are likely to ride over the wave of exciting feelings and peer pressure.

Hall describes his conversion to Christianity as the experience of being cleansed from the stain of sin because he viewed evil as a sense of limitation and imperfection. (Vol. 2, p.314) . His conversion entailed from love of self to the love of others. (Vol. 2, p.345.) Perhaps, religious example promotes higher morale and evolutionary ideals. Hall esteemed Prophet "Jesus not as the son of God but evolutionary exemplar, representing the culmination of the entire series of organic forms of existence... the Revealer of a new and higher cosmic, consciousness, and advancing the human ideal and opening the way to the higher destiny of man." (Hall,

1904, vol. 2., p.328). Unsurprisingly, Professor Hall having vast knowledge of world religions, did not mention any aspect of Islamic faith based on Divinely revealed Holy Book called Holy Qur'an. The English translations were readily available in the Library of Congress and many important University libraries in the United States.

The transition from adolescence to teens, and adulthood is the most crucial tenure for boys and girls who experience unforeseen scenarios, experiment with newly formed startling partnerships, engage in compassionate but risky relationships. Dicey human connections are untested, requiring critical competency and social skills. Decent girls are not well equipped to handle tricky social situations as they are gullible and susceptible to deception.

Innocently drawn into emotional connections, girls are known to be vulnerable, defenceless and susceptible. Youth truly need a tangible awareness of the dynamics linked with perils and how teenagers learn the social skills necessary to promote healthy growth. Biological activities and social relationships are the two significant areas in which engagements evolve errors impacting mental and emotional health and hamper consistent physical growth. Camp-based youth development programmes in the USA have positively influenced the rational abilities and social dexterities of teens. Outdoor activities such as backpacking, rock climbing help youth build physical stamina, mental power, and new social connections. They seek pleasure in competitive sports and learn to cope with setbacks but foster trusting relationships. Active participation in outdoor sports strengthens youth social and emotional assets. Relationship satisfaction and personal gratification are vital resources of teens, but interpersonal rejection is the notable cause of youth mental disorder, depression, and anxiety. Psychological dependence on an unreliable and untrustworthy peer is problematic for vulnerable kids.

John Bowlby (1907-1990), an English psychoanalyst, is the founder of the attachment theory. He proclaims that the fundamental question is that "is the attachment figure nearby, accessible and attentive and does the person feel loved, secure, and confident." Bowlby also stressed that attachment characterised human experience from the cradle to the grave. In the 1980s, both Hazan and Shaver (1987) evaluated Bowlby's ideas about romantic relationships in adults. Initial infant-parent or infant-caregiver bonding carries the features into adulthood closeness. If the initial affection were healthy, then the youth's romance would be confirmatory and emotional attachment acquiescing. Both would feel safe when the partner/peer/friend is responsive, and they would engage in close, intimate, bodily contact, share discoveries, and exhibit a mutual fascination and preoccupation with one another. Hazan and Shaver assert that adult romantic relationships are attachments.

Secure attachments with parents lead to better youth behaviour and less psychological issues. The youngsters can confidently deal with unexpected scenarios in their lives. They are adequately equipped with enhanced social skills and better coping strategies. The teenagers are well capable of making new friends and develop intimate relations. The teenagers at colleges and universities enjoy freedom and open atmosphere, feel eager to seek sensational associations. There are others primarily interested in the acquisition of new knowledge, conducting research and producing high standard work.

CHAPTER II - SOCIALISATION AND SOCIAL RELATIONS

Socialisation is among the top priorities of the young generation entering colleges and breathing the fresh air of unchallenged independence, thrilling adventures, and unrestricted freedom. Partying freely, meeting privately, and holding get together weekend escapades are fascinating electrifying activities that teenagers relish. In the 1930s, Cole Porter composed a beautiful song that conveys a lot to youth and is still enormously germane today.

"In olden days, a Glimpse of Stocking was

Looked on as something Shocking

Now Heaven Knows Anything Goes

The world has gone Mad Today, And Good is Bad Today;

And Black is White Today; And Day is Night Today;

When Most Guys Today, that Women Prize Today

Are Just Silly Gigolos".

The last several decades have witnessed uncheckable cultural revolution gripping the youngsters, chucking away conventional values, and setting entirely different decency standards and social norms. Many Western nations had little choice but to wilfully accept the exhilarating limelight in the form of parliamentary approved social laws geared to the sensual desires of the population. Until recently, the editor of a popular magazine pronounced that adolescent morality may be tumbling towards Shanghai on a sailor's holiday. The insinuation is that the ways of the 19th century and earlier were far loftier compared with the 21st century. European societies had informally developed a social system in which middle and upper-middle-class boys and girls held a casual meeting with the approval of their parents and families. It was a disgraceful act for young couples becoming intimate and giving birth to a child out of wedlock. Aspiring young men were incapable of getting married unless they possessed financial resources to support a future wife. The industrial revolution altered all previous criteria, and the romantic feelings took antecedence over all other considerations. Such feelings over time started to overshadow quantifiable deliberations in the quest for a prospective spouse. However, from the 1960s to date, teenagers entering college instantly commence explorations and social experimentation in the absence of parental or family watchful eyes. New terms came into being for describing social relationships in colleges and institutes of higher learning. Intimate interactions take place in an open and carefree climate in which words such as 'booty call' and 'friends with benefit' contain specific meaning and interpretation.

The only way of expressing emotion in the form of art says Eliot (1921), is to find a set of objects, a situation, a chain of events which shall be the formula of that particular emotion. When the external factors, terminating in sensory experience, are present, the sentiment gets evoked. As passion overlaps cognition, the difference between the feeling and its effect becomes visible. Felicity Collard and Constantina Papoulias (2010) pinpoint as pre-cognition, 'an amorphous, diffuse, and bodily experience of stimulation impinging upon and altering the body's physiology. But emotions are various structured and recognisable experiential states.' Silvan Tomkins (2008) perceives its effects are biologically based, and impact includes enjoyment-joy, interest-excitement, shame-humiliation. However, results are infectious, like a shame transferable to another person. Emotions are like a mild infection having a capacity of biological and physical transmission; also, organically communicable because the effects are fundamentally social and shared. T. S Eliot considers emotion in the form of origination and novelty and as a means of exploring new feelings. In the company of courteous friends, the senses are energised and rejuvenated.

Teenager social exploits get in the way of bio-paternity absoluteness apart from DNA testing leaving all kinds of cognitive and behavioural consequences. The machinations of 'cuckoos' between sensual encounter and birth offer ample prospects for the generation of gossip, banter, and chitchat. Roman laws and Napoleonic regulations in that era proscribed paternity suits exclusively to obliterate extramarital fathers. Former U.S. President Thomas Jefferson was not the father of the children he had with his slave Sally Hemings, his paternity officially unidentified and legitimately immaterial. In

1998, however, his descendant's DNA provided scientific proof of the president's paternity. DNA testing in France so far continues to be illegal without a particular court order. It is no different than "Discovering cuckoos or cuckoldry without compelling reason is deemed too socially disruptive, and not at all in the best interest of children." (Milanich, 2020). A nineteenth-century French Jurist once stated that 'paternity was as mysterious as the source of the Nile, concealed by an "impenetrable veil," it was a riddle to be solved,' and culture is about reckoning out how to unravel the mystery by allocating and then stabilising paternity. In partial fatherhood, a child can have multiple fathers, each of women's husband or partners contributing to the making of the child.

Interestingly, too many births out of wedlock and very young couples unplanned intimate spells in Brazil has given rise to children without a responsible father. The governmental initiatives to pin down the bloke include mobile vans roaming around rural and urban areas testing men under the sponsorship of the state. In the United States, huge vans inscribed with "who's Your Daddy"? Regularly visit New York's roads, malls and boulevards inviting people to undergo tests arousing recreational curiosity about origins. These vending tests appear as though they were ice cream for customers' enjoyment and hilarity.

The biological mother remains solely responsible for the newly born baby since the man accountable either disappears or remains aloof. George Gilder, in his "Sexual suicide', states, 'Whether automatic or not, the maternal role in the original constitution originates in the fact that only the women are necessarily present at birth. Gilder submits that only the woman has a dependable and easily identifiable connection to the child-a tie on which society can rely. This maternal feeling is the foundation of the multicultural community.

An authentic researcher and a distinguished professor Kathleen Bogle's study of 42 girls and 34 boys at two different U.S. universities, sums up the discussion about social standards. She interviewed all participants over five years and raised questions about their social experiences, how boys and girls met, got together, and formed relationships. (Bogle, 2008, p.6-11). Another female, Professor Lisa Wade, in her work "American hook-up": the new culture of sex on campus' conducted qualitative and quantitative study at the university. Participants included 75 young female students, and 26 young men described who consciously described their hopes, dreams, exposed insecurities, lamented their disappointments, and celebrated victories. Numerous social clubs help students to get socialised through inciting activities promoting knowledge-building culture. The discussion groups inspire moderation, enabling the free exchange of experience and proficiencies. In ancient times, cave drawing was etched on rocks warning people of dangerous animals. The tribal dwellers were aware of the complex beasts looking for prey, so they alerted the potential victims about the hazards through sharing their knowledge. In the United Kingdom, newspaper-based information dissemination commenced on March 11, 1702, when a single-page newspaper was published at Fleet Bridge, London. It was called "The Daily Courant," eventually merging with the "Daily Gazetteer" in 1735.

The knowledge-sharing was revolutionised in August 1991 with the inception of the World Wide Web, a global internet service. Now you can share videos, photos, podcasts, stories, blogs, and opinions. Social education media empowers you to share whatever you wish but hold back a piece of undesirable personal information.

The social feeds, live chats, and expression of ideas promote cross-cultural competencies among international students.

On-Campus Link-ups & knowledge Collaboration

Uncommitted link-ups have become gradually more entrenched in youth culture in most countries around the world. A large number of students from prosperous Arab countries and wealthy Asian families come to Western universities for higher studies. The multicultural environment has witnessed increasing liberalism among native and international students. They intermingle and form intimate relationships during their academic years at universities. Whether Harvard (established 1636), Yale (est.1701), Oxford (est.1096), Cambridge (est.1209), Edinburgh (est.1583) or Aberdeen, (est.1495), learning and social environment influences youth attitudes and behaviour. One of the university Student Experience

Surveys in the U.K. concerning good social life named Leeds (87.8), Sheffield (87.8), Newcastle (86.5), and Bath (86.2) topmost in offering a pleasant setting for young learners. Loughborough University scored higher in the provision of opportunities for academic studies and social life.

Concerning night social life, Leeds, Liverpool, and Nottingham received over 90 per cent scores. In the United States, Averno College, Milwaukee, Harding University, Arkansas, and James Madison University and Virginia are highly charged social institutes involving on-campus social clubs, late-night breakfast, and purple out activities. Likewise, California Baptist University organises social and frivolous events such as Fortuna bowl, an intramural flag football season with both male and female students. It arranges week-long events for students. Other institutes have a wide range of historical and multicultural shows. Some universities have on campus halls of residence in which faculty and students learn, live, eat, sleep, and go out together to augment fraternisation.

Newcomers feel happy and emotionally involved if they find ample chance to join extracurricular activities, participate in social and sports clubs in a friendly university environment. They like to connect with close-knit communities, go skiing, and snowboarding, work hard, and play hard. The first year is always full of challenges, thrill, and excitement in which young people seek the best quality of life, attend house parties, and feel happy. They go hard on big nights such as Halloween and New Year Eve. Arab students throw parties on religious festivals and make plenty of free food available to everyone on-campus irrespective of sex, race, or country of origin. Some universities provide learning with fun by organising comedy shows, weekend theatre evenings, and movie screenings. The students freely choose to associate with sports clubs and organise game nights, attend cake-decoration parties, and go rock climbing. There is a way for every student to get involved, go hiking, ride a bicycle, and go bowling. Fun permeates the atmosphere as students flock to festivals, visit restaurants for a delicious meal or catch up over coffee at Costa or Starbucks.

Usually, students enter universities at the age of eighteen, feeling excited about exceedingly free, fair, and open in academic surroundings. They indulge in conducting scientific, artistic, and social experiments to expand knowledge and explore undiscovered fields that provide know-how, buzz, and adventure. The first two years of university life is an exploratory escapade full of caper and enjoyment, offering opportunities for electrifying contacts and forging amorous relations with peers. More serious-minded loners are far and few but ambitious learners invest their time and energy in intellectual quests. Most students equitably divide time between academic dreams and social interests. Primarily the students club together or get hitched during semesters for experimentation and emotional satisfaction. Small minority teenagers fool around on account of the affluent background and habitual merry-making nature. It is a normal youth behaviour and instinctive urge to find new friends establishing casual or permanent relationships. Naturally, students choose universities not only for academic achievements but for glamour and fun that permeates the atmosphere. Students flock to music festivals, go for rock climbing trips and make friends. They love game nights, like to visit restaurants and cafes and join sorority clubs for pleasure and excitement.

In most universities both in the Western and Asian countries, dating for courting has considerably dwindled for the last fifty years. The personal pledge has regressed, pair-bond has become gradually typical and informally tolerable. Female teens have been empowered over decades to make independent decisions without any strings and societal moral barriers. Media has fortified youth to be free from parental accountability, encouraging them to display the uncommitted nature of behaviour. They seek gratification without any sense of responsibility and obligation, manipulating others for timely satisfaction. Temporary pair off is nothing more than the formation of unimagined feelings without being emotionally involved. The traditional form of courting has moved to more casual collaboration, becoming culturally recognised. Bradshaw and Kahn (2010) confirmed there was increased youth interest in informal hook-ups rather than profound connections.

Hatfield et al. (pp.2-3) conducted a study of university students' informative, social, and delicate involvement as well as biological features that outline young people's thoughts and readiness to join in casual meetings. Penhollow et al. (2007) remark that those who attend religious services are less likely to engage in decadent acts. The girls compete with each other in finding a partner but are more indiscriminate in their mating (Alcock, 2005). Pedersen et al. (2011) inform us that short term mating and other forms of coupling outside of pair-bonds are natural by-products of a suite of attachment. "Both men and women seek, select, create, and maintain a pair-bond"(p.639). There are a wide variety of motivations for students to hang out and intermingle for fraternity pin-ups. In a study, Garcia and Reiber (2008) revealed, eighty-nine per cent of young girls and boys considered physical gratification to be a significant aspect of personal life.

In contrast, fifty-four per cent preferred emotional indulgence to be paramount in social relationships. Campbell (2008) reported his research in Human Nature about university students who indicated positive and negative affective reactions after the occurrence. Fisher et al. (2012) made a qualitative study of Canadian university male and female students. They found that seventy-eight per cent of girls and seventy-two per cent boys admitted the unplanned encounter but registered regret after the incident wishing that it would not have happened.

The production of Hollywood films and TV shows in the past two decades has done more damage than good to the ethical behaviour of youngsters. Whether British series "Skin" (2007), the U.S. Hooking Up (2009), reality show "Jersey Shore" (2009) glorifying hooking up among strangers, friends, and acquaintances, and "Strings Attached" (2011) have liberalised youth social controls and loosened morality.

Frequently, girls become vulnerable in their naïve attempt to look desirable and attractive. The type of on-campus atmosphere shapes the desires and behaviour in which girls react to intimate social meetings with friends and peers. On the contrary, religious-minded students show self-restraint and do not willingly involve in such immoral undertakings. More importantly, competition in making new friends and peer social pressure entices them to make errors, especially if they have close links with university social groups. These individuals are often regretful after the unintentional link-up episodes. On-campus, girls feel confident in choosing a desirable mate, but risks are more significant for making the wrong judgement. In social scenarios, poor decisions cause disappointment, despair, and depression. An arbitrary choice of a life partner leads to disaster and irreparable cognitive damage. However, reproductive technologies permit girls more significant control over prioritising, choosing, and engaging in emotional connections and social experimentation.

Collaborative learning fascinates students enhancing capabilities and boosting confidence. Social interactions among students and between students and professors increase motivation for developing a topic within the university environment. A thoughtfully designed project generates desired interest and encourages student engagement who bring in fresh ideas benefitting all learners. Engaging faculty and students in an academic partnership to investigate didactic exercise is viewed as a ' threshold concept in educational development' (Cook-Sather, 2014, p.186). The students are expected to read in their leisure time and bring into the classroom, currently acquired knowledge for discussion and critical analysis. The classmates reflect on and comment with varying degree of their perceptions and capacities. This knowledge co-production portrays intellectual liberty on one hand and social freedom on the other in which new informal links are established. The professors oversee the entire collaborative learning process with considerable satisfaction offering their knowledgeable guidance for enriching students' wisdom. The students become equal learning partners as they learn about themselves and unremittingly assess and replicate upon their improvement. The recurrent creation of cooperatively produced knowledge is called "deep learning" that also involves faculty members' active contribution. Such educational pattern evolves 'different approaches to learning'. (Fullan and Langworthy, 2014, pp.3 & 7). It inspires students to learn, and they discover "how to go about learning". (Bruner, 1985, p.8). This process draws on emotional and social intelligence and power of reasoning, their individuality as well as collaboration. Their knowledge develops through joining as learning enthusiasts because such cooperation is wholly based on 'mutual respect and trust in the ability of the different students to contribute to different types of learning'. (Atweh and Clarkson, 2002, p.107).

We, the professors, spark motivation to make learning a pleasurable experience and set up an experiment designed to entertain and simultaneously educate the youth. A group of students jointly develop a specific topic inspiring curiosity, inviting attention and increasing motivation. It becomes fun to share academic knowledge, coupled with improved social interaction. Such informal communication boosts learning, heightens interpersonal contacts, facilitating pairing off. As all students are fully involved, knowledge-sharing workshops sustain interest in providing deeper awareness of a topic. It nurtures social curiosity, expedites individual's involvement, and promotes peer-to-peer socio-psychological engagement. Such collaborative learning intensifies knowledge acquisition and social engagement. The Western universities are no longer classroom-based instructional hubs, but knowledge dispensation and relationship formation academies. Innumerable social interactions are built around research topics through idea sharing activities. Their engaging participation for developing theories help students to accomplish the most demanding tasks.

The students love to indulge in outdoor adventures such as hot-air ballooning and mountaineering for letting off steam. Equally, inspirational acts include windsurfing, kitesurfing, and other water sports that are available for students to enjoy and relax after serious studies. The waterspout societies at sea resort universities provide great, fun-loving games because students get immersed in thrilling adventures. The waterspout is a column of rotating, cloud-filled wind, descending from a cumulus to an ocean or a lake. Other universities in Europe have established institutions for slacklining, caving and mountain biking to dissipate dullness in academic life. It is sometimes risky for youth to get out of the comfort zone and even more tricky to try out new things. Sensible teenagers express self-restraint about sharing personal space with grace by firmly saying no to unfavourable activities. Indulgence in unanticipated field of socialisation necessitates caution and thoughtfulness. Meeting different individuals is not harmful, but personal experimentation carries lasting ramifications for exposed and vulnerable students.

Knowledge sharing is knowledge creation, extension, and application. There is a degree of consolation in helping others and sharing new ideas. The ambitious student is always anxious to advance know-how about a particular scientific subject. It may not have any emotional excitement but might fulfil dreams and ideological goals. The quality of domestic settings and the nature of the academic environment play an indispensable part in the achievement of unwavering personal objectives. Most students welcome some fun and pleasantness in their careers through socialisation and entertainment. For example, the University of Bristol offers a course entitled "Choco logy: the science of Chocolates". A large number of students choose the option to stimulate their imagination and attain exhilaration. Such techniques improve the group performance leading to feelings of happiness, cheerfulness, and joy.

A sense of 'equal learning partnership' prevails in the classroom that turns into workshop-based experimentation and responsibility-sharing coordination. Everyone gets an opportunity to raise questions and present new ideas that are valued and fully appreciated. Especially in post-doctoral studies in Western universities, international students are no more passive learners through instruction, but active knowledge producers through research, combined study, evaluation and writing. Even the Master degree students are independent, co-construct knowledge through problem-solving projects and learn to build up confidence for creative writing. The higher the standard of their English language, the better would be the quality of writing. The professors are relatively conscious about leisure and pleasure-seeking students who exhibit the least interest in knowledge enhancement and make a nominal contribution in the co-production process. Active learners and contributors to event-based projects achieve more and leave their imprints in the academic environment. Such learners ultimately become professors, scholars, leaders, and creative writers. The international students who had studied English as the second language make substantial linguistic improvement in Western universities. Their verbal contribution to the knowledge sharing mechanism helps develop oral skills enabling them to become impressive orators and admirable debaters. Their lecturing skills are polished, and narrations are incredibly refined.

Sharing Thoughts and Feelings

Inherited social values and parental grooming impact teenagers' concept of sharing intimate feelings with friends and peers. Boys might be reluctant, but girls are too eager to engage in exchanging cherished views and cravings. Kristi Coulter (2020) from Seattle, USA, advises girls that you do not need liquor to lead a fun, carefree life because sobriety teaches you to value and prioritise honesty. You sometimes can share actual thoughts and feelings for more than one person at a time, and there is nothing wrong with that, tells her partner. But 'I cannot give you that kind of variety and newness' he replied. The readers should be aware of the fact that Seattle in the U.S.A. is on the free end of the relationship's spectrum. In social interaction, the interpersonal attraction invites friendly response related to liking. (Davis & Perkowitz, 1979). There is a close link between affective presence and social relationship because 'effect is a mediator in the attraction process'.(Clore & Byme, 1974). Responsiveness postulates the message required to actuate the mate's delicate repertoire to make others feel good. Mate choices reflect personality characteristics and physical features influencing emotions expression in a face-to-face conversation. Socially sharing emotional experience is in itself perceived as hedonically positive. Youth emotions are comparable to a socially charged football match in which the winning team supporters enthusiastically share emotions by loudly chanting slogans and delightfully singing in a triumphant mood.

Owing to massive-scale migration of Syrians and Afghan refugees into Europe, both Austria and Germany played a commendable role in accommodating these communities. In 2015, twenty-two Austrian public universities launched an initiative "MORE" for young boys and girls to integrate them into their higher education system. Ostensibly, the immigrants from Syria and Afghanistan look no different than the host society in terms of physical features, fair complexion, and facial appearance that make it easy for them to assimilate. The university authorities offer language training, grants, and scholarships to young learners .The German universities have an good programme for immigrants providing free German language courses before the transition to mainstream higher education courses in the field of medicine, literature, architecture, and humanities. There are other schemes involving Syrian and Afghan youth for participating in city walks and various sports activities. To a lesser extent, Norway's Refugee Education Post-Secondary Education initiative has been offering a scholarship to camp-refugees who anticipate higher studies at universities. Mostly German-speaking states focus on social integration covering four areas such as placement at universities, interaction with natives, cultural familiarity, and identification. They have numerous social clubs engaging migrants and natives in informal contacts, relationships, and partnerships. Austria has indeed, become a multicultural society. Still, the vast majority of local inhabitants and ethnic minorities speak the German language, share knowledge, jokes, food, accommodation, and feelings, demonstrate forbearance and show respect for diversity.

Sharing Knowledge with Mates (POEM)

Facial metaphors are natural descriptions
Picture our dreams and social prescriptions

Links we discover with meetings of choice
No cash, property nor a Rolls-Royce

Sincerity we proclaim without any noise
We study together with thrills and joys

On-campus, you view lots of fashion
Openly display their youthful passion

When two souls get together
Care little about changing weather

Bonds are built with other classmates
True to their words without any dates

Neither do you cheat nor deceive
Mutual reverence, you do perceive

In some ways, the youth are mostly imperfect
But with practice, humility, can become perfect

Whether at school, university or in college
Participative learning and shared knowledge

Higher education, you see innovations
Collaborative learning, with little isolation

When Social connections, structure your relations
Knowledge Co-construction becomes an inspiration

We share ideas and feed our intellect
We enhance learning and breed respect

[Composed by Dr Nazir Ahmad,
February 20, 2021/ Rajab 8, 1442 Hijra, Saturday]

CHAPTER III - ADOLESCENTS EMOTIONAL STRENGTH

Emotional development through recreational activities can have a lasting influence on youngsters' consistent bodily growth and reflective maturity. It is not always easy for children in their early teens to designate a vibrant occupation in a demanding field of sports in the absence of domestic reassurance and the ethical backing of family members and school teachers. Presently, no less than fifty million teenagers (National Council of Youth Sports) take part in copious national and international contests. Many athletic associations heavily rely on volunteers, financial patrons, promoters, and guides to support their ingenuities. Impassioned families get candidly involved in their children's dietary requirements, weightlifting programme, and appropriate resting itineraries. Physical and psychological fitness is a criterion for participation in dynamic training for acquiring innovative skills. Compassionate mothers and fathers calibrate their jobs and social schedules to adjust teenagers' sporting engagements. Emotional wellness is the top priority for kids to advance in their respective fields of interest. Emotional power amplifies the behaviour of children as they learn to understand the implications of choices, difficulties, and outcomes. The purpose of active involvement in a particular sport is to present an opportunity for relaxation, social interaction, and pleasure. A child has the chance of communicating freely with school and college mates and training coach.

They can discuss intrinsic personal matters and share fibs, gibes, laughs, and jeers. Learning from mistakes would prepare the youth for meeting un-anticipated moral and social challenges. One hour tennis court or racket club attendance refreshes the brain and body and improves youth educational focus.

High performers develop grand ambitions, participating in training sessions, school board meetings, and community workshops. They aspire to appear on radio and television talk shows and use Facebook, Twitter, Instagram and Snapchat to get acquainted with other youngsters. Their hesitation recedes and becomes capable of speaking at public gatherings that form part of their social and academic learning. In their late-teens, some youngsters hold youth workshops, organise sports clubs, communicate with potential sponsors to acquire financial backing for economically underprivileged players. Youth social development is a psychological process in the course of which they achieve qualitative perfection, desirable discipline, and efficacy. Intention to excel in a chosen activity leads to positive behaviour influenced by personal ambitions.

Youthful years between 13 to 19 are a sensitive time of mental growth and emotional progression as the kids acquire perceptive skills in hikes and pikes. They are in the process of traversing social affiliations and simultaneously expect motherly love and care. They are entering a complex world of countless hues, and as such, their common sense is underdeveloped. Throughout the teen years, parental guidance and consultation promotes maturity and boosts self-confidence. (Ahmad, N and Ahmad, A. N., 2020, pp.32-40).

Emotional strength building in pre-school kids commences with the block building of various shapes and sizes. Give them wooden blocks to make pillars and columns, stacking square unit to form a tower without letting it tumble. Such assembling indicates consecutive growth and highpoints of emotive strength. I have observed countless times my grandchildren have explored the physical properties of blocks, building bridges, triangles, quadrilaterals, and making tetragons, dismantling them, then recreating new shapes. Knocking a stack of blocks gives them pleasure, sustaining interest and attention, culminating brain growth. All children are enthused by indulgence, fully immersed in their play and actions. Submersed in their self-chosen games, children enjoy thrilling activities, integrating social, emotional, and psychological aspects of learning. Children feel comfortable and happy in a stimulating environment facilitating cognitive progress and emotive health. Enriched settings present kids with fertile grounds for free interaction. In primary school, teachers deploy numerous engagement strategies to retain teenagers' focus and responsiveness.

Children express their frustration if controlled and offered little choice in their academic and playful activities. They complain about the lack of comprehensive skills training such as the practice of using the header to score a goal in a soccer game. The goal-scoring expertise consists of emotional power and physical flexibility to enact specific manoeuvres in the playground. Psychological empowerment that involves efficacy and esteem is more than the perceived strength that develops knowledge, skills, and propensity. Mental liberty consists of three constituents, namely a sense of control, awareness of settings, and autonomy of action. Intrapersonal empowerment is an emotion-linked know-how of necessary tools and are resources for achieving success.

The brainpower is indispensable in the performance of balanced human activities in all spheres of life from birth to adulthood. The brain works most efficiently when periods of high levels of attentiveness are followed by periods of more mediocre levels of attention. Jensen, (1998, p.43) suggests teachers candidly engage pupils' attention only 20 per cent to forty per cent of the teaching time and then provide a choice of unusual activities designed to help the student process and absorb the information. The student classroom focus is limited to 25 minutes. For the 1st grade's, that is about six consecutive minutes; for a high school student, that is up to fifteen minutes. The remainder of the lesson time is utilised for projects, discussions, group work, partner work, self-assessment, and feedback. Part of the lesson takes the form of research, mapping, interviews, reviews, and memorisation. The scientists claim that the electrolytic balance for the proper functioning of the brain comes from water. They recommend the consumption of six to twelve glasses of water per day. Dehydration is a familiar classroom learning setback that leads to impaired cramming and reduced memorisation power.

A second significant component of brain functioning is the ample supply of oxygen for students to breathe and enjoy fresh air in the classroom with proper ventilation. A psychologist has argued about the superior brain powers of some pupils, implying that it is hereditary while others proclaim environmental factors determine the quality of human intellect. Nolan asserts that the influence of heritable vs environment on brain development is a 50-50 proposition. Classroom settings have a considerable impact on academic learning (Nolan, 1960). Socio-emotional learning occurs at school where pupils adjust to the new environment, adapt to changes, make connections, and gain knowledge. Young learners explore movements, create games, use imagination and chase each other around the playground without being closely watched.

Harriet Merrill Johnson (1933) in 'The art of block building' mentions seven stages of block play. It begins with carrying the blocks without making anything, stacking them, building bridges, enclosures, patterns and symmetry, early representational and finally late representational. In the beginning, a kid learns the physical attributes of the object and then progresses to form different shapes. In the process, he/she exhibits emotional power to make intersections, arches, elliptical curves, and squares. Lucy Mitchell, Caroline Pratt and Harriet Johnson, established the Bureau of Education Experiments in 1916 for observing how children learned. The experimentation with school children led to reforming the system that involved exciting ferryboat rides, visiting the zoo, and other places of excitement. Glasser (1990) advanced the idea of quality school and student empowerment at the Huntington Woods Elementary School in Wyoming, Michigan. As the school opens, teachers and student observe "Kids of the Week", receiving a blank copy in which to write 'All About Me', 'My Family', 'My Friends' and 'Ways I Meet My Needs'. Each pupil gets a chance to speak for five to ten minutes explaining the things he/she wishes to do, such as coin collecting and making items with clay and mud. Others cut out pictures from old magazines and mount them on the board. If any dispute arises between two pupils, they work out the solution amicably using choice theory.

Dr William Glasser, an American Chemical Engineer, turned psychiatrist and educationist, identified seven deadly habits that pollute the class atmosphere.

SEVEN DEADLY HABITS

Destructive Power of Criticism- denigrating and belittling the pupils' assignment

Blaming students – demeaning and accusing them of petty things

Complaining- focusing on the past rather than looking towards the future

Nagging- Irritating students and causing distress

Threatening- Intimidating and menacing pupils in the class

Punishing- Using various forms of harsh disciplinary actions

Bribing- Inducing and enticing with corrupt practices

Mocking - Making fun of them in the classroom. Cracking Outrageously hurtful jokes about under achievers.

Such measures and dreadful actions do little to create a pleasant and workable atmosphere for teenagers who feel scared, mocked, ridiculed, teased, mimicked, irksome, and humiliated.

Glasser equally mentions SEVEN CARING HABITS

Caring- Display attitude of compassion. Taking care of kids' needs

Listening- Attentive listening empower and make them feel worthy

Supporting- showing appreciation and getting involved

Encouraging- Infusing confidence in their abilities

Trusting- It is an unquestioning belief in pupil's honesty

Befriending- Patronising and upholding

Negotiating Differences

A teacher has the responsibility of creating a caring, safe and compassionate environment in which students feel valued and respected. They actively participate in their learning and recreational pursuits. They want to be heard, trusted and supported in all matters about social, emotional, and psychological wellbeing. They look upon the teacher as a role model and imitate what is visibly taught and practised. Their basic needs and interests vary significantly because one youngster might have high emotional urge and desire for companionship. At the same time, the other could be a sports addict and the third one disinterested in any worthwhile entity. If one child does well in a drama class, he might perform poorly in the mathematics group. We should allow adolescents to make decisions that make them feel happy. Feeling empowered helps adherence to the rules. Retribution and reprisal achieve nothing but resentment and antipathy. Antagonism makes the classroom an extremely unpleasant place for the youngsters. It is only through students' active participation in all matters; the teacher can create a shared vision of a quality classroom. Conversation on every topic ranging from fairness, honesty, trustworthiness, and sense of responsibility and self-accountability would produce an outcome for an ideal learning environment. Teenagers will begin to understand the meaning and positive consequences of delayed gratification, harmless fun, freedom, and emotional health.

Permitting kids to mark and evaluate their work and then, giving them feedback is supposed to be one of the noteworthy sources of inherent motivation. (Jensen, 1998, p.67). Undue praise and excessive appreciation of their work can increase the pressure to do well under all circumstances. (Kohn, 1993, p.98)

Emotional stability entails mindfulness and openness, empowering adolescents to be active participants in informal and formal debates and topical discussions. They would learn to reason, argue, and influence, respecting opposing views, but exercising emotional control and practising self-restraint. Relationships are the active ingredients of the environmental impact on youth psychological development. Children's direct links with parents and teachers result in academic and socio-emotional encroachment. Good relations with classmates and friends inspire cooperative learning and group play activities. Interpersonal relationships do not specifically mean intimate companionships and emotional ties but a strong collaboration, teamwork, and intellectual alliance. Pupil empowerment is about giving a chance to be heard, inviting ideals, and understanding their perspective of learning. It would mean conceding teachers' power, compromising classroom control and entertaining realistic feedback. A school atmosphere is a vital place for emotional and logical nourishment, encouraging situational demeanour which is conducive to inspired learning.

Social roots regulate childhood life-courses as the pattern of brought-up leaves psychological scars on young minds. (Bernfeld, 1892) . Social origins of childhood obesity embedded in the domestic food environment derive food choices. Bernfeld researched and presented the notion of primary education. Being a psychologist, he promoted the perception of liberalism. Infanthood to adolescence changeover transpires steadily with an adjustment of thoughts and manners, slants, and protocols. The genetic progression relates to the body, physical strength, and sturdiness. The psychological process refers to the functioning of the brain, thinking, and reacting to the environment. Stanley Hall cherished the teenager above the adult. He says, 'Youth, when properly understood, will seem to be not only the revealer of the past but of the future, for it is dimly prophetic of the best part of history which is not yet written because it is not yet transpired.' (Hall, 1904, p.233) The biological procedure forms the basis of development for youth relations and social activities. Both at school and playgrounds, peer-group socialisation dissolves family-bonds and diminishes ties between families and the youngsters. Youth transition to adolescence and adulthood is supposed to be the most significant moment for social stability. Parents at this crucial stage of grooming must pay thoughtful attention to the genuine socio-psychological needs of youth. They should initiate a shared decision-making process with complete kids' involvement and participation. Teenagers unable to comply with measurable performance goals would require increased parental support, demonstrating courage, patience, and tolerance.

Social freedom and sports passion generates interest, promotes positive conduct, and minimises negative behaviour. Positive Attitude reflects kids' discipline at school playgrounds, where they tend to get on well with classmates. Regular involvement in sports inculcates in them the habit of curiosity, the desire to educate and improve oratory skills. The refinement of sporting skills brings meaning into their lives. Their appetite to do better increases engagement and ensures presence in the sports venues. Youth sport has the potential to keep children off the street and create excitement in a safe environment. The schools can focus on giving youth a chance to join one or more indoor or outdoor games in which they can build skills, talents, and efficacy. The kids will prove their usefulness and worth with precipitous tenacity and absolute determination. The local Government's financial incentives and support to strengthen training programmes can raise the aspirations of deprived communities. The voice of young scholars should be valued in all matters about recreation and academic career choices. Kids should feel empowered and engaged, which ought to be depicted in their relaxed outlook and joyful posture.

Regular reassurance and praise motivate kids to improve their performance with obstinacy and vigour. Encouraging utterances lift children's drive, strengthen vitality, and regenerate confidence. Using sport as an outlet for amusement makes them thrilled and vibrant. The collection of memorabilia and souvenirs is a passion for most kids who earnestly obtain autographs of famous sportsmen and women. Purchase of baseball caps, shirts, and pictures of top footballers such as Ronaldo, Messi, Neymar, and Harry Kane is just proof of youngsters' craving for soccer. The photographs and paintings of the highest goal scorers on bedroom walls create thrill and joy for broods. Building emotional skills and adopting measure for strengthening emotional health, the teachers have a crucial role in the classroom where children spend a few hours a day. Kids encountering emotional issues tend to be withdrawn and less cooperative in group work. A warm, pleasant, and friendly atmosphere helps develop a teacher-pupil relationship. Everyone should feel valued, respected, and loved, finding the teacher approachable, responsive, and amicable. Even the misbehaved kid can feel obliged to reconsider disobedience towards the teacher who shows kindness and sympathy.

In a relaxed classroom setting, children are more likely to ask a question, try new tasks, and express themselves freely. (O'Connor and McCarthy, 2007). Teachers creation of close and trusting relationships with their pupils results in the improvement of emotional and academic skills. (Palermo et al., 2007). Newly trained teachers might benefit from reading guides issued by the Center on the Social and Emotional Foundations for Early Learning. Kids can learn to communicate emotions and solve problems effectively. Teachers need to develop individualised interventions for those with the most tantalising behaviour. (Hemmter et al., 2019). What Works Briefs produced by SEFEL elaborate the expression of warmth and affection to children. (Twardosz, 2005). Reading specially selected books in which characters' emotional aspects are discussed, and then, asking pupils to delineate would help them understand and relate the experience to their own. (Robert and Crawford, 2008).

For creating an emotionally charged, stimulating, and electrifying child-friendly atmosphere, the teacher applies the following formulas:

A.   Avoid Shouting and Yelling

B.   Lenient Attitude towards all kids including misbehaved ones

C.   Confidence Building Measures boost self-esteem. screaming and howling might boomerang

D.   Develop a Sense of Empowerment

E.   Encourage Physical Activities such as cycling, running, and skating. Energise Youth with Pleasant and Attentive Listening

F.   Freedom-based Class-room invigorates kids' learning

G.   Give Emotional Support to Disadvantaged children

H.   Happiness Improves Behaviour. Be Part of the Class rather than the Manager

I.   Educate on the Spot and shower Praise at small achievements

J.   Display Encouraging Outlook

K. Keep the Volume of Voice Moderate

L. Frequently use Non-Verbal Gestures in the class such as nodding the head, shaking hands, and giving thumbs-up signs

M. Acknowledge Kind and minor acts, appreciate a noble deed

N. Keep the Momentum with little jokes, magical words, and funny stories

O. Value Kids' Opinions and suggestions

P. Psychological health takes Priority with Emotional Strength

Q. Reduce tension and Inspire Learning with an emotionally engaging environment

R. Pay Particular Attention to the needs of disturbed and weak children

S. Smile and Keep Smiling. Create a Sense of Classroom Community where everyone enjoys

T. Tranquil and Soft Tone appeals to children

U. Urge Parents to Attend Meetings and Parents Evenings

V. Visual Cues Help Children's Emotional interaction. Let Children Create Games and Use Imagination

W. Maintain Focus on Psycho-social Development

X. Infuse a Spirit of Sharing and collaboration

Y.   Be prepared to answer "Why' questions with suppleness

Z.   Zoom and Increase break intervals for emotional health

Assurance enhances their optimism and revitalises commitment paving the way for setting high targets. The signs of improved focus begin to appear on his/her face, indicative of progression in the competitive environment. Mothers are ardently involved in the practical help necessary for their children to feel safe and comfortable. Mindful fathers indeed remain on board and attend to a child's genuine requirements, including the purchase of uniforms, sporting equipment, and related apparatus. They make sure on-time payment of sporting club fees and miscellaneous expenditure. If a child does not perform well initially, praise must not be withheld, and caution should be avoided under all conditions. Sporting genius is not produced overnight, but it is a slow process demanding patience and endurance. Kid's sporting stamina is built with meticulousness and diligence over time. In the sporting environment, children feel a sense of freedom and accept responsibility, learn self-control, and develop an individual identity. They make better choices and get prepared to deal with the consequences of decisions. Sportsmanship sharpens qualities of compassion, judiciousness, and care.

Teenage girls are increasingly missing out on the terrific benefits of sports due to puberty issues arising as early as at the age of ten or eleven. Participation in a football game is inspiring and rousing for girls who give incredible performances by winning trophies and shields. In European competitions, British girls bring home medals and golden plaques. They feel empowered and get emotional rewards by exhibiting splendid talents. Sports engagement fuels their sense of achievement, but sudden puberty brings emotional upheaval, causing anxiety and disengagement. The girls in the U.K. prefer to try out new things and gain experience with different activities, including baking a cake, walking in the woods, and playing hide and seek in the local parks that offers happiness and pride. Any form of self-expression is worthwhile as long as it is rewarded with emotional feedback, social and psychological satisfaction. In a survey covering America and Europe, it is revealed that more than one-third of youngsters aged 10-17 drop out of the sport due to social and psychosomatic factors. (Crane, et al. 2015). Many youngsters do not join team sports owing to personal and family circumstances (Rottenstein et al., 2013). They do not feel connected, coupled with the lack of motivation which leads them to stepping aside. Regarding drop out and sports, there are 38 published studies conducted between 1980 and 2015. Overwhelming drop out reason appears to be the disputes with coaches, pressure from peers, occupation with social life and relationships, lack of fun, and plenty of boredom. (Monteiro et al., 2017).

Surprisingly, youth participation in sports has been on the decline in Canada, owing to the coaches exerting pressure on athletes and their families to respect the training schedule. Some youth pull out of the sports due to intolerance, racism, and lack of fair play. The teenage girls withdraw from training on account of harassment and a greater emphasis on winning the competition. The Canadian coaches often complain that the parents are either over-involved or under-involved, which disrupts their programme. The kids have reported various forms of bullying, physical and mental abuse during training sessions. Amongst the most popular games are tennis, cycling, skiing, baseball, soccer, and golf. The kids often express disquiets and apprehensions that they do not like sitting on the bench for the winning team and would prefer to play for the losing side. There is a shortage of volunteers who run practices and coach games. Sport participation for children under the age of 13 have become difficult. Hyper-competitive environments and setting high standards have dissuaded the kids from remaining in training. They have stepped away before 13-years of age and have hung up their sneakers, plimsolls, and cleats for good. The coaches pick up the best players too soon, leaving low performers disgruntled and demoralised. They have no viable option but to quit altogether. A very rigid selection based on an excellent performance backfires on coaches and parents with stunningly high dreams for kids. Concerning gratuitous parental expectations, Karri Dawson, Director of the True Sport Foundation, Canada, asserts that those who excel and are seen in the Olympic teams have distinguished themselves through tremendous struggle, tenaciousness, and passion. She tells parents, "They were multi-sport athletes, they played hockey in the winter, soccer in the summer, and they participated in different sports at school. They cross-trained, and they exercised all kinds of different muscles and abilities that one day made them gifted at a particular sport". Besides, the steeply rising cost of sport dissuades most children for participation that equally demands plenty of time and distraction from serious studies.

However, during the last three years, the Canadian Government has injected funds to support the training of female coaches in hockey, soccer, and tennis and also to eliminate gender-based violence, helping increase girls' participation. Several organisations, including engagement, Motivate Canada, Physical Health Education Canada, Go KidSport, Canadian Tire Jumpstart, and Le Grand Defi Pierre Lavoie, are actively promoting participation in sport throughout the country.

For encouraging youth to choose a particular sport as a career, there is a need for youth-parent-teacher partnership. The trio affinity will co-jointly discuss, consult, and design comprehensive economically affordable programme feasible for children from diverse backgrounds and multicultural communities. During the process of implementation and training stages, youth opinions, voice, and empowerment would act as useful tools to facilitate enrolment, engagement, and practice. The more regularity is achieved at the training sessions;

the better would be the outcome, raising youth morale, interest, and cooperation.

A well-thought-out youth sports programme carries tremendous benefits for the mental, biological and psychological wellbeing of youngsters. Health benefits include the burning of calories, better hand-eye coordination, and increased enjoyment. Moreover, it expands focus and motivation, energising brainpower, embedding desire for learning. Youth become caring and helpful, accepting defeat and setbacks with forbearance. Obesity in adolescence is penetrating at a staggering rate, creating laziness and sluggishness. Idleness in the playing field impacts overweight children who do not make substantial progress in any sport. For instance, running develops bone density in female participants and prevents osteoporosis later in their lives. Physical activity positively affects the brain physiology by increasing cerebral capillary growth, oxygenation, blood flow, and better growth of nerve cells in the hippocampus. The kids become more conscientious of their fitness, follow instructions, enjoy training, and avoid using harmful drugs. They can distinguish between accurate and wrong, truth and falsehood, justice, and unfairness. They cooperate with friends and mates at school and playing field, reach out to help the injured and console the losers.

Youth athletes view sport as a positive leisure involvement leading to psychological maturity and social capital. It increases robustness and eliminates surplus body fat in boys and girls. In 1995, Borra and Colleagues conducted a Gallup Survey "Food, Physical Activity, and Fun" in which they discovered that the American children have a positive attitude about food nutrition and physical activity. Since that time, many psychologists and sociology Professors have researched youth attitudes and behaviour in the field of sports, health, and fitness.

Through sports, children can stay in shape, polish motor skills, and make new friends. Even a short walk, ride a bike or some exercise can increase levels of protein called " brain-derived neurotrophic factor" useful for good memory and thinking skills. (Allen, Victor, How even a short walk can give your memory a boost. Daily Mail, London, September10, 2020, p.29).

Young boys and girls learn endurance, capable of withstanding danger and hardships, and persevere in all weathers and conditions. The youth find a sport an outlet for socialisation and an opportunity to demonstrate sporting talent, build self-image, and enhance academic competence. Winning creates feelings of accomplishment and jubilation since competing, and getting a trophy is a hard-earned privilege. In present-day sports, victory brings fame, dignity, honour, and above all, financial reward. When youth gains world recognition, he/she becomes a role model for aspiring amateurs, acting as an inspiration. Eminence makes a youngster celebrity dishing out autographs, delivering talks, and appearing on television shows. Almost all sports commentators are sportsmen and women who have excelled in their chosen fields. They understand the true spirit of play, rules of the games, and rewards of achievements. Women participate in masculine sports and produce excellent results, winning world cup hockey and football competitions.

Young boys and girls are naturally adventure lovers and thrill seekers in mountain climbing, hot air balloon voyage, and identifying different species of birds on seaside and treetops in the green forests. Most schools and colleges organise student trips to exciting destinations.

The Young Birders of New Zealand have introduced online sessions for kids to develop their knowledge of numerous birds, migration patterns, and breeding practices. Predator-Free Motusara Island Bird Sanctuary is a bird lovers paradise and home to Blue Penguins, Kereru Bellbird, Yellow-Crowned Parakeets, N.Z. Falcon and South Island Robins. Youth bush walk tours take them on to the top of the Island, where the teenagers enjoy the viewing of white-fronted terns and Australasian Gannets. Norwegian school kids receive encouragement from parents to join officially arranged tours of coastal areas to study and watch unique birds, take down notes, and capture photographs with their smartphones. They can make sound recordings of bird sounds from a considerable distance, bring home videos for others to enjoy, and gain knowledge of ornithology. Bird watching is a breath-taking and pulsating pastime for the youngsters to broaden their perception of beautiful bird varieties, hues, and singing descriptions.

Similar Ornithological societies exist in the U.S.A., Canada, Europe, and Australia, especially for youth engagement who learn to work on academic assignments exploring the history, origin, and breeding environment of birds. Kids learn through bird watching the wonders of nature, broadening their knowledge of marvellous creations. The sight of flora and fauna and rare exotic species of seabirds revitalises youth memories and improves thinking power.

Teenagers possess remarkable concepts and breath-taking opinions requiring authentication, a sympathetic ear, and a compassionate response. The meaningful participation and sustained involvement of kids in recreational activities make them more confident, composed, and self-reliant. They like to be heard and perceived, responsible for making choices and accepting the implications of such decisions. A high degree of perfection and excellence in a sport is gracefully unpredictable. Tenacious and strenuous training energises youth technical talents, invigorates ambitions, and rejuvenates physical capacities. Accuracy in the playground develops overtime; confidence comes by surmounting hurdles and vanquishing misgivings, doubts, and hesitations. The supportive parents are logical partners in youth engagement, nurturing the strengths, abilities, and knacks. Parents, teachers, and trainers infuse trust, permeate conviction, appreciate progress, and praise achievement. Parental input in achieving educational goals injects a renewed spirit of coordination between teachers and pupils. Once asked what their children needed most to succeed in school, the vast majority notified self-esteem and self-confidence was the top priority.

The parents were sent a set of 10 components, requesting them to rate and prioritise ten educational goals concerning what they feel was most to least essential for the school to help their child to accomplish? Harris and Harris (1992) have quoted these components in their research article entitled " Glasser comes to a rural school".

Health and Physical Development. Nutrition habits; physical fitness; strength, endurance, agility, and skill in sports, games, and life activities.
Human Relations and Communication. Getting along with others, leadership, cooperation, courtesy, respect, listening, speaking, reading, and writing.

Identity and Individuality. Self-esteem, self-confidence, self-discipline, responsibility, moral character, and the development of individual talents, gifts, interests, and abilities.

Inquiry, Thinking, Learning. Curiosity, eagerness to learn, study skills and habits, problem-solving, creativity, and decision making.

Science and Mathematics. Knowledge and skill in mathematics and physical sciences.

Arts. Knowledge, skill, and appreciation for literature, music, dance, and the visual and performing arts.

Work. Initiative, self-motivation, self-direction, persistence, following through and evaluating work; understanding of attitudes, knowledge, and abilities needed for various vocations.

Responsible Citizenship. Respect for and understanding of the workings of a democracy, appreciation for political processes and free enterprise.

Environment. Respect and maintenance of personal and public property, enjoying and protecting nature.

SOURCE: Stoddard, L. (1992). Redesigning education: a guide for developing human greatness. Tucson, Arizona; Zephyr Press.

To maintain discipline in schools, the teachers act as lead-managers rather than bosses. Problem-solving is not the teacher's sole privilege, but a student-teacher shared consultative effort. A friendly atmosphere prevails at all times, every pupil is equally respected and given a chance to succeed in any field of interest, whether academic, social, educational or recreational.

We should give our children a sense of self-worth, dignity, and purpose in life, an authentic voice, and boost the courage to speak their mind without any pressure and external density. Build resilience and imbed constructive values, ethical power, and emotional effectiveness to embrace honesty and diversity, believe in justice, and empowerment to make decisions. Instil social skills and psychological autonomy, imbed self-restraint and sense of sharing intellectual capacities.

Ensure them the abode of real power lies within rather than elsewhere, give them tools for utilising emotional power and mental strength for the welfare of others.

Emotions have a significant effect on youth erudition, learning memory, and observation in various settings. They learn through reflection, having an indelible impact on sensitive response to the situation. Emotions have significant sway on attention and retention in an educational environment where the focus is paramount to absorb and retain in the memory. There are multiple views about the power of emotions interceding memory encryption and moderating memory consolidation. The scientists concede that emotions either augment or weaken learning and long-term memory retention. Recollection and remembrance are necessary features of positive emotional focus. Traditional face-to-face education in a classroom requires individual attention and personal involvement in the learning process. The online-based tutoring demands a different set of dynamic learning strategies and virtual technologies entail exceptional learning focus to digest new knowledge. The coordination of rational powers and emotional management would enhance the enrichment of learning.

The pupils with disturb thinking and shattered perceptions are unlikely to focus on gaining knowledge to advance an academic career. Emotional upheavals can have an impact on motivation, a significant component of emotion. In an education environment where teaching and learning take place, pupils habitually display facial gestures, bodily movements including finger twitching, nail-biting, daydreaming, and curling or styling hair. Youth inattentiveness is prone to cause interruptions and distraction in emotion and memory system. Just as we learn pain management and behavioural management, emotional power should be an essential aspect of formal lessons. Dynamic control aptitudes would help inspire learning and enhance remembrance proficiencies. Emotions are the psycho neural procedures that are dominant in monitoring the vitality and modelling of actions in the vigorous flow of penetrating common substitutions. Our feeling result from the interfaces of innumerable emotional structures. We feel happy if emotionally fulfilled; we feel angry due to emotional disturbance; we express pleasure when we experience emotional gratification. Emotion is elicited by physical touch, listening to soothing music or observing the beautiful object and, this, in turn, is interrelated with the permutation of feeling and motivation. Positive emotions are likely to expedite learning, whereas deleterious emotions would adversely impact memorisation and engagement.

The youngsters experiencing unease and despair, take the least interest in their educational work and find it difficult to pay attention to the lessons because they are emotionally troubled and mentally sad. Apart from psychiatric disorders, teachers identify unhappy students and offer emotional support to prevent learning regression and improve motivation. With the introduction of sophisticated methods of imparting knowledge and technological innovations to facilitate instruction, student learning cue has substantially enriched. Event-based learning and visual depiction of characters' act as an emotional inspiration for kids to remember and retain visual knowledge with ease and comfort. Memorable events are those that arouse our emotions, e.g. wedding functions, university award ceremonies and degree convocations and unique holiday spots. These activities become engrossed in our memory and immersed in our thoughts throughout our lives owing to overwhelming emotional involvement and sentimental attachment.

The school is a discernible pitch for health interpolations, and emotional learning can take place in the classroom where expert psychology teacher uses multiple cognitive methods to help pupils improve self-control and self-awareness. But youth need to know the positive and negative portrayal of people and personalities and be able to express themselves without fear or constraint. A famous female Arsenal team English footballer Alex Scott in her talk to one hundred and thirty 14-to-18-year schoolgirls from London Inner City advised them to break the mould and overcome life's troubles. She emphasised that girls should stay true to themselves because she has learned how to communicate with emotions. There will always be struggle and failure along the way. But the critical point is that you deal with it. Ms Scott finally recommended and encouraged girls to be open and support each other. (Scott, 2020) In a survey of

2,324 university students from eight countries including USA, Germany, Ghana and Poland, the authors probed students' nature of emotions. What made them happy is the feelings they anticipated and the feelings they experienced in their lives. The results indicated that most partakers desired to experience more pleasant emotions and less unpleasant emotions. (Best, S. August 14, 2017, Mail Online) For example, Columbian female student is emotional uniquely within the optimistic sense, looking wonderful so are the young Venezuelan girls who are empathetic and credible in fulfilling your expectancies. They are known to have positive feelings towards their partners and hold emotionally optimistic perceptions.

Likewise, Argentinians have their exclusive manners of expressing emotions and developing social relationships. Trompenaars in 'Riding the waves of culture' describes the emotional aspect of young girls who accord welcome with a big smile and also people, in general, relate to one another. Personal space, body language and signals are ethnically determined. Argentinians youth feel no restraint in freely displaying their emotions in public, such as touching each other, laughing and talking aloud. If you are from U.K. or Norway and visit Argentina where you happen to attend a social function and meet a local girl, she might kiss you on the cheek as a gesture of graciousness rather than flirtation. Emotional intimacy will develop slowly and consistently. Portenos have their usual cultural standards on how to socialise and build relationships. Brazilian women are equally fun-loving, broadminded, passionate and devoted. They are outgoing, care about their physical fitness and openly discuss all personal secrets. They are also dependable and trustworthy in their communication with acquaintances, friends and strangers.

Youngsters Psychological Development

Sigmund Freud argued that adolescent and adult development was shaped by early psychosexual development while other psychologists stressed the impact of social environment on emotional health. On the other hand, the psychosocial theory of Erikson portrayed the significance of relationships at each stage of youth character development. Youth can attain happiness, pleasure and gratification by personal efforts and set goals that lead to a good life. Seligman confirms this view stating youngsters can pursue happiness and fulfilment through their own decisions. Individual differences in youth disposition aptitudes are associated with psychosocial performances. Each teenager behaves differently in a social setting bringing in his/her own childhood experiences. They do have the capacity to change and accept the social norms incompatible with personal characteristics. Social interactions are quite often interpenetrating and casual since youth are equally responsible for their development, character strengths and social tolerance. Young girls habitually develop personality traits in their small groups, communicate freely but resist and loathe criticism directed at their looks, features and complexions.

Benson et al. suggested 40 developmental assets, including social relationships and personal experiences and interactions. There were two categories internal and external, both sharing 20 assets each. Youth domestic assets pertain to their learning pledge, engaged studies, reading for pleasure, belief in personal abilities, forming relationships, able to face challenging situations, self-restraint and resistant skills. External assets relate to emotional support, care and acceptance by peers and people around him/her, supportive family and caring neighbourhood, caring school environment and time management. Research scholars have asserted that 'adolescents with more personal and social assets have a higher chance of wellbeing and future success. Academic competence is essential for the youth career that reflects attendance record, work habits, and exam grades. Catalano proposed 15 youth assets, including emotional skill, social expertise, resilience, bonding, moral competence and positive behaviour. Complimentary Youth Development programme can only be effective if schools, communities and parents or caregivers (for children in foster care) are practically and consistently involved in youth-focused activities.

Conrad and Hedin (1981) surveyed 4000 students studying in thirty educational environments and reported that experiential programmes had a strong influence on their moral reasoning and social development. There was a dramatic improvement in developing social relationships in colleges. Lerner et al. (2013) researched the impact of youth development surveying 7000 teenagers. Growth was apparent in their assertiveness, social acceptance, parental trust, attendance, and self-control. We believe the evaluation of youth development programmes helps to improve emotional wellness.

Two significant assets are the youths' ability to adapt to new situations (resilience) and identifying one's own and others' emotions. Greenberg (1996) have suggested 'Providing Alternative Thinking Strategies that instigate youth to ruminate optimistically and cultivate collaborative problem-solving skills. In Sweden, they teach Social and Emotional Training programmes to grade 1 to 9 school pupils in real-life community venues. During 2001-2002, a study involving pupils from eight schools within the Stockholm metropolitan area surveyed the functions of the students' self-awareness, social competence, motivation, empathy and managing one's emotions. The students were required to complete 399 class-based exercises and tasks to improve their social, emotional and psychological skills and perceptions. They were asked about handling strong emotions, appreciating similarities and differences, managing conflicts, interpreting pictures, repelling peer pressure, being able to say no, knowing what one feels, what makes them feel good, recognising people and situations. Assigned tasks equipped students with special social skills; dynamically cultivating in them the art of unravelling photo images on internet platforms. Also, building self-confidence to say no to spiteful encroachments, robustly stand up to peer insistence to perform undesirable chores, understand the feeling of others, become capable of identifying intimate friends and be able to evaluate challenging situations. These solicitously premeditated exercises wielded a positive influence on students' thinking power and evaluative abilities. It had enormously valuable outcome for youth mental health and social behaviour.

Emotional Impact on Perceptions

Emotion has extensive sway on the intellectual progressions in individuals. How people think, behave or solve problems depends mostly on their sensory perceptions. Patterns of thoughtfulness affect memory and recollection processes equally shaping attentiveness and concentration. Emotions have considerable sway on our long term retention of information. Positive emotions can nurture our memory, cultivate our perception, and stimulate creativity. Given the Coronavirus pandemic, live classroom-based learning has shifted towards virtual online-oriented education for our kids. The school closures during the 2020s have developed revitalised youth thinking and changed priorities relating to home-based self-learning and remote online instructions. A brief mention of the world's ancient institutions reminds us about the significance of learning in earlier times. The oldest one is the University of Al-Qarawiyyin (al-Karueein) established (859 A.D.) in Fez, Morocco. It was founded by Fatima Al-Fihri, daughter of Muhammad Al Fihri, a wealthy merchant. Al-Azhar University (970 A.D.), Cairo, Egypt, is the second one followed by University of Bologna

(1088 A.D.), Italy, University of Oxford (1096 A.D.), University of Salamanca (1134 A.D.), Spain, University of Paris (1160 A.D.), the University of Cambridge (1209), and Al-Mustansiriya University, (1227), Baghdad, Iraq.

We learn pain management and behaviour control, and we also need to deploy emotional control skills to navigate online courses. Our routine interactions evolve subjective feelings and psychological responses, reflecting physical gestures and vocal expressions. We experience emotionally charged dysfunctions, such as anxiety and depression, impacting our mental performance. Our emotions have deep-rooted value, and each emotion exhibits a diverse feeling quality, the production of feelings stems from physical and cognitive conditions. Our usual mood has a close association with the instigation of any emotion. When a pupil does not pay attention in the classroom but twitches fingers or bites nails, the teacher asks for attentiveness and questions the individual. 'I am not in a mood to study because of domestic annoyance that has disturbed my focus, the pupil replies'. These are negative emotions negatively impacting youth learning contributing to academic regression and psychological relapse. Although focus improves understanding, perturbed motivation hampers acquisition of knowledge. We cannot deny perplexing influences of emotions on learning, whether at home or school. The pupils should have a profound incentive to self-study supported by online instructions. The curiosity to enhance erudition acts as stimulus equipping the young brain to retain information, absorb ideas and digest facts and figures. A scientific study reveals that emotional stimuli provoke a 'pop-out' effect that leads to the attentional capture of new information. If we succeed in improving the focus and attention for learning, they can robustly perceive, assess, absorb and memorise the information needed for educational and academic pursuits. The pupils should not fear exams or despise memory-based tests, but gladly welcome knowledge-based learning for scholastic quests. Cognition regulates, galvanises, and inhibits our emotions since it serves as a feedback process that automatically and freely restores pupils' state of equilibrium. Just as conditions of fear, grief, anger, and frustration, hamper learning, relaxation, confidence, and self-belief promote learning.

We can identify emotional states that enhance kids' learning performance and produce admirable learning outcomes. We can give the right direction to their activities to achieve their personal goals. The focus will stimulate them to show enthusiasm in pursuing the desired objective and attain the result. Secondly, we instigate curiosity, unquenchable thirst and yearning for new knowledge. It develops a sense of curiosity and advances their ravenous appetite for the fulfilment of a noble ambition. Emotions invigorate kids' memories consolidating brain functions. The children become skilful in identifying people, recognising facial expressions, and interpreting the meaning behind those feelings, looks, and perceptions.

Overcoming Negative Thoughts (POEM)

Think not about dark alleyways
Gloomy and miserable walkways
Unseen, unheard causeways
Vague and muddled pathways

Imagine not about obscure sidewalks
Muddled and confusing catwalks

Underestimate not inherent dangers
Friends and pals turn to strangers

Think of something that gives you hope
Brighten your thoughts and future scope

Negative emotion causes scare
Dispel the jolt with a hearty prayer

Restructure inner self, reframe your mind
Repel your dismay, with feelings refined

Positive thoughts purify your brain
A Positive outlook, remove the strain

Comical pictures will gladden your day
Optimistic roles you choose to play

Worries and concerns, do have a cure
Belief and a true faith makes you pure

Some of the hardships, we sadly endure
Freeze negativities, stay sound and secure

Challenges we have, bravely we face
Maintain dignity, and repel disgrace

Self-indulgent judgements, look for cure
Tarnished and tainted heart can't be pure

How do we dismiss, and dissipate our fear
Demonstrate goodness, keep mind clear

[Composed by Dr Nazir Ahmad,
February 14, 2021/ Rajab 2 , 1442 Hijra, Sunday]

Tranquil Garden (POEM)

Everybody needs emotional strength
But keep the worries at arm's length

Emotional nourishment seeks in the garden
Spend some time, behaving like a warden

Grow many flowers, take well care
Pruning roses, here and there

Shrubs breathe as humans inhale
Bushes sprout some, shrubs become pale

Swallow in the morning air so fresh
Cool wind removes emotional stress

Smell relieves your emotional strain
Birdsongs take away the rational pain

Slackening of the body frame relieves tension
Wonders of nature, pay some attention

Feelings of discomfort, mental anxiety
Self-heal emotions, with sobriety

Alleviate disquiet, relax brain tissues
Halt emotional distress, forget the issue

Bonds with people slip and slide
Bonds with nature, carefree ride

Remain cheerful for physical wealth
Continue smiling for emotional health

Rest in the garden, think and pray
Emotional wellness, early in the day

Pray to one God, for inner relief
Reinforce faith, nourish belief

Robin birds sing, with charming sound
Enjoy saplings, mother nature around

Believe in one God, confirm notions
He is the Creator of skies and oceans

We meditate, ruminate in our prayers
We lift our spirits with spiritual affairs

Generosity is an act of love and care
Helping destitute, hearts would repair

Gardens are heaven for joy and rest
Ease muscle tightness, doctors suggest

Sow seeds with your munificence deeds
Reach out to insolent, fulfil their needs

[Composed by Dr Nazir Ahmad,
March 23, 2021/ Sha'ban 9, 1442 Hijra, Tuesday]

Emotionally Anxious Human Capital

Best educated and rigorously trained personnel are an invaluable asset and irreplaceable human capital for a nation desirous of sustainable economic, social, psychological, and industrial progress. Young brains morally expect a reasonable reward for their intellectual and inventive contribution to society. The unfair and unjust treatment makes them emotionally anxious and fervently apprehensive, embedding thoughts of discovery and exploration. The emergence of such feelings of uneasiness and disquiet gives rise to the concept of migration. The wealthy and powerful are preoccupied with their luxurious and opulent lifestyle, strengthening, personal, and family prosperity. The ruling elite lack vision to recognise the significance of talented people as the backbone of the economy and domestic magnificence.

Brain drain familiarly known as the flight of human capital is not a new phenomenon that occurs due to wars, viruses, draughts, and other calamities. In the 1940s, many scientists, engineers, and doctors from Austria, Italy, Spain, and Germany emigrated to Scotland, Wales, England, and North America. The term brain drain was first used in 1963 by the British Royal Society for defining the migration of British scientists and technologists to the United States and Canada. Their departure at an alarming rate resulted in the acute shortage of health professionals. Unsurprisingly, the U.K. simultaneously experienced both the outflow and inflow of human capital that maintained the favourable momentous of development. Between 1960 and 1980, a considerable number of doctors from South Asia and Europe migrated to Australia, Canada, U.K., and the U.S.A. Many doctors acquiring postgraduate training in France, Germany, and the U.K. never returned to their countries of origin. On the other hand, thousands of Polish (E.U. membership 2004) and Romanian (E.U. membership 2007) doctors and nurses came to Britain immediately after both countries were admitted to the European Union. Currently, there are 3.6 million E.U. born people in the U.K.; among them, the highest percentage belongs to Poland, followed by Romania and Ireland.

Emotional anxiety is the root cause of human capital loss, which is a brain gain for the stimulating economy but a brain waste for the losing nation. Educated youth feel undervalued due to depleted respect, scarcity of equal status, and insensitive governmental attitude towards capable individuals. Emotionally strained skilled youngsters anxiously explore pathways to get away from unfavourable conditions grabbing the promising opportunities abroad. The enormity of brain drain is such that emerging countries remain underdeveloped and in colossal debt. Implications of brain drain, and the flight of human capital are gigantic for the losing nations such as:

Stifling and Oppressing Innovation and Modernisation

Hampering Improvement of National Infrastructure

Impeding Scientific Research and Development

Debilitating Intellectual Inspiration

Incapacitation Thoughtfulness and Reflection

Draining General Economic Progress

Creating a Shortage of Doctors and Engineers

Widening Gap Between Capability and Incompetence

Discouraging The Grooming of Fresh Talents

Reversing The Fiscal gains

Breeding Corruption and Exploitation.

Proliferating Profiteering

Flourishing Sleaze and Perversion

When knowledge migrates, ignorance creeps in and takes over meaningful fields of human progress, causing upheaval, instigating confusion, and increasing nepotism, snowballing greed, and prescribing recipe for downslide. Imaginative minds are not valued, and an ingenious segment of society becomes insignificant. Economic crises, least progression chances, reduced wages, and mistreatment of brilliant youngsters in their native states are some of the constraining factors influencing an individual's decision to seek green pastures. Infertile national policies discourage home trained talents to collaborate in the nation-building programme effectively. German media giant Bertelsmann develops and retains local skilled professionals by fulfilling their aspirations and meeting their expectations.

Human capital retention necessitates the provision of conditions that entice brains to remain rather than leave to attain a tangible reward and well-deserved remuneration. Discontented youth are dissatisfied with the prevailing circumstances, and therefore, unhappiness turns into emotional uneasiness instigating thoughts of travel into foreign pastures. Sustainable economic growth in the West tempts professionally qualified and intellectually enlightened brains to apply for higher studies, gain scholarships and grants through international technical aid programmes. Emotionally depressed youth are sometimes indecisive due to family attachments and responsibilities. However, bright career prospects enable them to accept the challenges of resettlement, improve living conditions, and enrich personal knowledge. In Europe and the U.S.A., scientists and engineers exhibit potential, gain appreciation, and professional recognition. Medical school graduates and fully qualified nurses are in high demand in many industrialised countries where the standard of living is comparatively high, quality of life is better, salaries are generous, and progression chances are bright. Capable expatriates feel rewarded and deploy their knowledge, skills, and abilities for enhancing the personal image and providing the best education to their children. Medical doctors and chemical engineers enjoy scientific experimentation in well-equipped sophisticated labs at Western universities. Enlightened researchers in the favourable settings create productive knowledge and share the scholarly outcome with their professors and colleagues.

In July 2020, Boris Johnson, the British Prime Minister, announced that two hundred thousand people from Hong Kong would be allowed into the United Kingdom, permitting them to apply for British citizenship. (Mikhailova, 2020). It is a wonderful breakthrough for the well qualified brilliant youngsters, most of whom are likely to welcome this generous offer of living in a free democratic society. For Hong Kong, the brain will be a "typical problem" (Adams, 2003) because medical doctors are increasingly mobile due to the attractiveness of global careers. (Habti and Elo, 2018). Retaining educated people is a significant concern for Hong Kong, as pointed out previously by UNESCO (2018). Many intelligent individuals from Hong Kong would "contemplate leaving their home country" (Carling and Schewel, 2018) for liberty and academic progression. Economic advantages are associated with migration. (Alleyne and Solan, 2019). Career building chances for young boys and girls are no longer "typical incentives" in their homeland. (Glick and Salazar, 2013). The Young Hong Kong population, at present, feel emotionally perturbed due to oppressive policies, diminishing press freedom, least job opportunities, and uncertainty of living conditions. They hold demonstration, face detention and censorship, but boldly state that "If we shut up, then we lose completely." (Financial Times, 3 July 2020). David Roche told CNBC on 31 May 2020, that

"For young people in Hong Kong, the future is elsewhere" (Huang, 2020). Roche gave a clear warning of expected mass migration. Many young people would presumably leave Hong Kong and settle abroad for better careers and human freedom.

Taiwan has also made a very generous offer to the people to migrate for their betterment. (Tan, 2020). Tsai Ing-Wen, the President of Taiwan, declared that his government is devising a comprehensive programme evolving, residential arrangements, job opportunities and placements, and promising life in the host country. They shall warmly welcome people from Hong Kong to enjoy living in a democratic society.

Human capital is a positive spillover effect that stimulates economic growth (Romer, 1986; Lucas, 1988). Both economic factors and socio-political features prompt bright people from less developed states to migrate (Lee, 1966). Emigration on a large scale of highly competent and skilful youngsters adversely affects the prosperity of the home economy by impeding progress (Watanabe, 1969). Brain drain sways the dispersal of educational opportunities in third world countries. (Webb, 1985) and creates political pressure on governance. The affected countries have to invest heavily in the education sector to train more and more skilled workforce and scientists to meet the shortfall caused by the flight of human capital. The expatriate engineers and doctors in the Western countries get high remuneration than their peers back home in the state of origin.

Secondly, in European, American, and Australian universities, ample chances for improvement and transmission of advanced knowledge do exist. Intellectual progression is an outstanding motivation for inventive and creative individuals.

Apart from most industrialised countries, some Far Eastern and African states have partially succeeded in retaining their super brains due to robust incentives and moral support. Among those states offering material enticements to medical professionals are Japan, Singapore, Malaysia, the Philippines, and Tanzania. Relocation decisions are interwoven with emotions and surrounded judiciousness. Doctors from Close-Knit families feel the emotional pain of migration when moving away and navigating farthest lands. Some doctors may be prompted by a specific purpose to alleviate poverty through remittances as it would be a window of opportunity to rejuvenate parental economic conditions and help educate minors.

On the contrary, Tanzanian doctors prefer to stay back in their country of origin and serve local communities despite arduous conditions and average salaries. The government and the faith hospitals offer dual incentives to their medical professionals. Inducements include respectable jobs for spouses, subsidised kids' education, and postings for close family members. Owing to ethical association with Christian faith, doctors feel obliged to deploy their knowledge and skills for the treatment of natives in the homeland. Fertile grounds for scientific experimentation in technologically equipped medical and engineering labs do exist in Singapore. They lose some talented people, but quickly get a replacement with similar calibre creating a robust environment. Doctors and engineers are very well paid who lead comfortable lives. Malaysia has not been able to stem the flight of medical professional and top engineers. Best professionals are working in Brunei, Singapore, Australia, and Canada, and newly qualified PhD's continue to look for equitable job opportunities in the U.S.A. and Europe.

To curb the loss of medical personnel, the Philippines has issued guidelines to limit the outflow of doctors. One of the noteworthy incentives is the provision of free medical education linked to an obligation of serving for a few years. Thailand's medical graduates are required to serve the country for three years before migration. Vietnam has made it mandatory for doctors to stay in the country and accept placement in rural areas. In a competitive world, the best brains with emotional strength excel, perform, and endure.

The departure of doctors and nurses drains the healthcare system of developing countries. Millions of patients look towards private clinics, incompetent medical helpers, unqualified paramedical staff, and illiterate herbalists. In many African and Asian countries, sorcerers, magicians, phoney spiritual healers, and fake dispensers rob innocent citizens of their cash by offering unfounded medical treatment. Every government must set aside sufficient funds for looking after the health and education sector rather than channelling resources to those with guaranteed comfort, luxury, and power. Retention of human capital for any state is virtually difficult to ensure in an interconnected world. Even partial solution necessitates the creation of tempting infrastructure, enticing working conditions, and alluring permanent accommodation.

Virus Affects Emotions

An unprecedented number of infections (over six million as of 3 September, 2020), and fatalities exceeding one hundred and eighty thousand, the resumption of formal schooling is not insight in the U.S.A. The emotional insinuations for kids and job losses for parents have ripped apart family structures. Dan Levin (New York Times, 20 May 2020) reports that the coronavirus is taking a toll on young people's psychological health. Pupils have no classroom-based communication with their teachers due to school closures. There is no replacement for face-to-face contact between teachers and kids; neither can they meet friends and classmates. Teachers try to look after the emotional wellbeing of their pupils by conducting video classes, and school psychologists are holding online therapy sessions. Younger people are experiencing negative emotions, such as anxiety, gloom, frustration, and apprehension.

Pollak, the current Director of the Child Emotion Lab at the University of Wisconsin-Madison has categorically asserted that 'not every kid can be online and a confidential conversation about how things are going at home with parents in earshot.' Emily Fox, a social, emotional specialist at a primary school in Ohio, uses zoom to meet her pupils and delivers lunch to deprived students. Many teenagers are isolated and feel lonely due to inactivity and the complete absence of social relationships. They cannot hang out with friends or go to the local shops for fear of catching this disease.

There is evidence of irresponsible behaviour, paranoia, resentful attitudes, and outbursts of racism and stigmatisation. This severe and acute respiratory syndrome is spreading across many continents, causing irreparable psychological damage and psychosocial emergency. Unpretentious fear of contracting and infecting relatives at an increasing rate has compounded trepidation. Anger and frustration grips the front line health professionals. One cannot disregard the psychological effect of post quarantine experience of people who travelled abroad and returned home to face fortnight isolation. "I predict that the next major outbreak – whether of a highly fatal strain of influenza or something else – will not be due to a lack of preventive technologies. Instead, emotional contagion, digitally enabled, could erode trust in vaccines so much as to render them moot" (Larson, 2018). A large number of medical personnel, local security forces, and bank staff have been exposed to Coronavirus-19, and a fair percentage have perished.

Separation or divorce harms kid's mental health, causing interruptions in smooth education and leisure pursuits. Troublesome and anxious conduct is apparent in the classrooms, and their teachers often report studying difficulties. Estrangement very frequently leads to relocation of single mothers with children to new neighbourhoods. It is stressful for kids to form new relationships, emotionally disturbing to make trusting links, and psychologically cumbersome to feel comfortable in peculiar surroundings. Moving from a spacious house to a small compact tiny apartment adds to the traumatic experience of economic suffering. Many private legal firms help in making available co-parenting coordinator to minimise emotional damage by resolving day-to-day issues arising out of family breakdowns. The influence of income disparity on the psychological wellbeing of children is a matter of great concern for the state. A study of 1725 Hong Kong Kids showed that they exhibit low self-esteem and carry symptoms of depression. (Ho et al., 2015). The type of diet and housing choice were other contributing factors in causing such symptoms in children. Mothers buy frozen vegetables and canned food containing excessive sodium and cholesterol and purchase bakery products with more sugar and low fibre. Lack of resources hampered children's participation in extracurricular activities at school. Low-income family kids are not welcomed in the group of resourceful children who feel superior and proudly move in their upper-class circles. Feelings of inferiority have a damaging effect on the emotional health of deprived kids. They become lazy and eat cheap junk food, building undesirable body fat. Depressive attitude ((Teychenne et al. 2010) and extremely low-self-esteem (Asare and Danquah, 2015) are the results of such feelings in the broods of low-income families.

The Coronavirus pandemic has adversely affected underprivileged children, says Marta Colombo (U.S. News America 2020, 9, April 2020). It is emotionally challenging for innocent kids to live in cramped ten by ten feet accommodation where movement is minimal, and they cannot be allowed to play outside for fear of being hurt, injured, or kidnapped. While confined to a tiny room without natural light, a chair, and a desk, children cannot do homework or take online courses. An unhealthy residential space causes excessive emotional pressure on mother and child. University students are also stressed, and the suicide rate has continuously been rising among youngsters. (Benitz, 2018)

The ordinary family or single parent children can uplift their temperament by indulging in simple, pleasurable activities at home such as hide and seek, cross puzzles, and making paper boats and kites. They can sing a song, use the flute and play with marbles or recreate images of footballers, jugglers, and magicians. These activities may be negligible, but give pleasure and boost self-confidence. Reading motivational stories, real tales, and joyful episodes also promote emotional health. Hong Kong Adventist Hospital has introduced Play Therapy for children demonstrating depressive emotions, encouraging them to express their feelings of anxiety, nervousness, and fretfulness through playful activities. Yet again, the poor children cannot afford an expensive treatment that appears to be targeting upper-middle-class families. This hospital-based practical programme helps kids develop creativity, imagination, and boost concentration. Youth are talented, and professionals are competent, hardworking, and innovative.

Youngsters are surrounded by pleasant or unpleasant emotions all the time, whether at university, recreational hub, or home. Some feelings prompt them to study hard and attempt to excel in their peer group in the face of competition. Other times, negative emotions dissuade them from taking a focused interest in science subjects involving chemistry equations, metallurgic engineering, quantum gravity, plasma physics, or algebraic formulas. Excitement seekers choose drama, music, fine arts, and acting as a career that never bores or causes weariness. Exhaustion and tiredness occur in solving complicated mathematical sums and learning problem-solving techniques requiring innovation. One has to be reflective of making a connection between various aspects of mathematical modelling that leads to predictions and solutions. Learning about Newton's Laws of Motion, trigonometry, differential equations, kinematics, probability, and statistical analysis demands in-depth academic commitment and urge to grasp cumbersome fields of knowledge. Comparatively pleasurable stress-free disciplines attract a vast majority of male and female students who equally become valuable members of the society.

Environmental interaction influences youth emotions either positively or negatively depending on the nature of the interface, college settings, and home setup. Angry youngsters prefer courses related to gratifying activities. Motivational progressions are related to their educational achievement, but if they feel upset or restless, shy, or nervous, progress slows down as they show little interest in classroom lectures. Naturally, the joy of learning and the pleasure of social life are two different entities, but still, both units are interconnected and complement each other. One derives emotional pleasure out of knowledge acquisition, simultaneously enjoying a social life with some boundaries and fetters. Emotional expressions are central to many aspects of cognitive functioning and academic advancement. Emotional self-knowledge helps them regulate their emotions for making educational progress and achieving better academic results. The more engaged they are in traditional classroom lessons, the more productive would be the learning outcome. Just as sports provide psychological, physical, and social strength, the study of educational disciplines such as pure and applied sciences ensures intellectual progression. In both instances, emotions play a considerable part in making headway either winning medals at Olympics or earning Nobel Prize. As we have seen in many parts of the world, talents migrate from developing countries to the industrialised world for enhanced carrier prospects and higher knowledge. A healthy brain needs a healthy body, and therefore, the significance of participation in a chosen sport is crucial for the emotional wellbeing of adolescents.

Coronavirus was intensified again in December 2020 through January 2021, creating fear and panic among the young population in the USA, UK, and New Zealand. However, the speedy vaccination of millions of citizens greatly helped to control the virus spreading further. The rapid rise was causing anxiety and panic, further isolating the college and university students. Sir Peter Gluckman, Professor Richie Poulton and Rochelle Menzies raised concern about its adverse impact on youth mental health. (Foon, 2020). The University of Auckland study identifies excessive use of drugs, alcohol, and misuse of social media as the main factors affecting youth's emotional wellbeing. The youngsters lack social connectivity and fun-loving activities. The New Zealand government and private organisations have set up various platforms, Rural Support Trust Helpline, Rainbow Youth, Youth Line, and Online Chat for social and counselling services. I have composed the following poem in this regard portraying people becoming obese, losing jobs, halting trade, and obscuring their plans.

Between Fear and Hope (POEM)

Hope for the best, oh my dear
Creeping in slowly, typical fear

Coronavirus spreads, like wildfire
Mobility restricted, no one desire

Public is housebound, just like a jail
Once a day, still arrives royal mail

People are obese, physically weak
Virus yet again might reach peak

Jobs have perished, morals' are low
Halted trade, economies are slow

For snooty & conceited, heaviest blow
Darkened their plans, removed glow

Boy comes home and askes his mum
Why do we live in an indecent slum
It is the best place, my dear son
Houses are small, obstacles to overcome

I shall sing songs with my lovely voice
Music is my career, I have made a choice

Musicians are many; singers are few
People admire songs, that are new

Films are made for public to view

Outside cinemas, youngsters queue
Jack lemon movies are long overdue
People Still watch all the way through

Amusement receded, gloom has endured
Entertainment declined, despair matured
Film actors jobless, pilots not restored
Millions lost living, poor are ignored

Slowly but quietly now, power slips
Largest economy, dreadfully dips

Great shall remain great, no one knows
Unseen disasters ahead, virus shows
Flattened and trampled, as wind blows
Nothing withstands, hurricane throws

The situation is such, no one is sure
Imminent is closure of megastore

Who shall weather safely storm
Time will tell, without any harm

Those who survive, will see it through
Ships will sail perhaps without any crew

Planes are grounded, pilots sacked
Internet polluted, many are hacked

Buses wait for passengers to arrive
People are confused, how to survive

No longer crammed, trains in operation

People have lost, trail of destination
Travelling was once, a big sensation
Feelings of despair, stifled stimulation

Lockdowns lifted, then imposed
Games of thorns are being exposed

Unjust acts have destroyed the weak
Beg for survival and justice they seek

God has heard the innocent themes
Moans, howls, whines, and screams

Retribution for haughty, not far-removed
Laws of nature have apparently moved

Our optimism anyhow, must not fade
Natural calamities, we cannot evade

[Composed by Dr Nazir Ahmad,
March 5, 2021/ Rajab 21, 1442 Friday]

CHAPTER IV - MEANINGFUL INTIMACY

Friendly interpersonal behaviour falls into the sphere of intimacy, beginning with an acquaintance, familiarity, associate to just friend, casual contact, a bit frank companion, best chum, expedient friendship, beneficial friend, and mutually convenient mate. Two individuals might have a joking relationship, transitory, inalienable fellowship, differentiated friendship, and common affection. They could have immutable intimacy, desirable intimacy, passionate intimacy, and obsessive intimacy. A relationship is a combination of multiple attributes, matching traits, reciprocal attractiveness, harmonising desirability, and biological magnetism. When two teenagers enter university, expecting jolly settings and delightful like-minded classmates, surprises do happen beyond imagination, especially in interpersonal connections. In an academic environment, the terms close friends or intimate friends are frequently used and applied in social communication. Interpersonal relationships are vital for societies to exist wherever a group of people are in reciprocal links. (Simmel, 1921, p.348). Intimacy is the closest voluntary relationship between two individuals, characterised by mutual openness, confidence, and fondness.

Liberal culture in the West offers youth freedom in forming intimate links, encouraging meaningful close relationships. The Oxford University English Dictionary (1937, p.1034) defines intimacy as 'closeness of observation, knowledge, and the like.' Desmond Morris published a book Intimate Behaviour in 1971, the earliest publication in this field to be recognised. Chum relationship is converted into deep intimacy (Sullivan, 1953, p.245) as the friendship progresses over time. Latin word Intimus implies intimacy, and in German, it is Innigkeit. Psychological intimacy implies the interpretation of selves and personalities. (Bensman & Lilienfeld (1979, p.99).

Paine (1974, p.118) rightfully believes that specific human needs are universal, and intimacy is one of them, but friendships fulfil these wants. Some fundamental natural human desires are related to intimate relationships. However, friendship and intimacy are two similar but different connotations in different cultures. In the West, the wife of a friend is also your acquaintance and workmate, but she will be your sister with whom informal rapport would be prohibited in the East. A sociological luxury is a form of social bonding between two people who meet up infrequently for everyday social adventures. They are usually considered mates who share privacy and private space to laugh and joke, invoking understanding and empathy. They have ordinary virtues and many similarities and share exceptional characteristics that keep them together in an academic and social environment.

Such friends have virtually one soul, making a friend a second half because a decent young man would have one genuine friend (Smith, 1935, pp. 27-43). It is rightly acknowledged that one friend in a lifetime is much; two are many; three are hardly possible. (Reisman, 1979. P.20). This kind of friendship is a virtue and not merely a social relationship. (Smith, 1935. P.39). Harmony comprises a wide gamut of relations ranging from 'best friends to buddies' (Du Bois, 1974. P.16). In 1958, Naegele (p.234) interviewed ten boys and ten girls from a high school, asking them about the meaning of friendship. He concluded that these youngsters felt 'friendship implies some kind of reciprocal closeness between two or more people.' Before this survey, Simmel (1950, p. 236) had observed that friendship is the degree of invasion and reserve within the relationship. Such linkage is based on openness, mutual pleasure, and preference. They are free to reveal their relationship or keep it private with no external pressure.

Manipulative contact between college boys and girls is a casual friendship that does not last as they move on to make new friends. They can be called less serious college chums, willingly or unenthusiastically staying together to enjoy a social life. These are not the ideal type of interpersonal relationships. After every few decades, we can witness new cultural norms in various societies affecting youth behaviour. In the modern academic settings in institutes of learning, social bonding transforms into emotional intimacy. Consensual validation of physiological aspects of bonding arises from the need for self-fulfilment. Sincere friendship is a lasting relationship centred on deep fondness motivated by the quest for combined ideals. The close friendship has emotional and social elements that enhance bonds of intimacy.

In reciprocal intimacy, mutual loyalty, affection, and love consistently develop, creating durable likeness and resilient feelings. The casual linkage is a chance intimacy, psychologically enriching both individual's social connectivity and somatic proximity. In the working-class environment, social activities are considered essential for cognitive and physical wellness. They strongly believe in the friendships of convenience to minimise wearisome in their daily strenuous working lives. They meet regularly, especially at weekends, laugh, joke, and share fibs and make each other happy. Social relationships and intimacy consist of standard psycho-social rudiments. Intimacy is the beholding of each other in an essential depth, adoring him or her in high esteem, knowing reciprocal innermost with unrestrained indulgence.

Friends and Mates (POEM)

In universities reside friends and mates
On a casual basis, they hold debates
Temporary links without love or hate
Under no compulsion to fix a date

Often, they have casual friends
Casual friends become special friends

Affectionate intimacy, clue they intend
Noble intentions, is the message they send
Accommodate mates, rules they bend

In earnestness, one must not pretend

Good-natured youth get on well
Tranquillity on faces, you can tell
Plenty of time, they jointly spend
Amicable they are, do not offend

Affect attention, their smiles, and flairs
Frequently they are seen in pairs

Sober and kind feelings they show
On darkest nights, bright stars glow

A few of them smile through eyes
In the rose garden, like butterflies

Their smiles convey, sense of compassion
And soberness exerts a lasting impression
Let me give you a humble suggestion
Exercise restraint for undue obsession

Academic settings are an ideal place
When two individuals come face-to-face
Opposite viewpoints, selflessly embrace
Never make decisions in speed and haste

Quick actions could spoil actual grace
Sugary conversations have a bitter taste
Capture vital moments, do not waste
Move with the tide, but do not disgrace

In-class or student guild, moods they share
Enjoy companionship, unique and rare
Genuine discernments, they openly declare
Substantial obligations with love and care

Search begins in dreams without a clue
Getting together is a union of two
Flaws and slip-ups, one can go through
Truth predominates if you remain true

[Composed by Dr Nazir Ahmad,
August 12, 2021/Muharram 3,
1443 Hijra, Thursday]

Open Societies Liberal Values

Since the 1960s, we have witnessed a restructured change in the social connotation of interpersonal lovingness and rationalised intimacy. Modifications in the interpretation of social values of privacy have been brought about by the industrialisation of economies. There has been increased demand for girls to work side-by-side with the male workforce in the textile, travel, catering, airline, and entertainment industries. The societies are more open, permitting freedom of thought, enhanced openness, and autonomy. Social media and on-the-counter protective pills have helped accelerate liberalisation and augment socialisation. Now the state laws offer better protection to women, allowing independence, social freedom, and empowerment. Hard-earned emancipation has made women strong and confident, brave and assertive. Intimate relations have a broader scope for the youngsters, whereas historically acclaimed love is linked explicitly to moral and lasting compassionate commitment. Such adoration and affection narrow the latitude of social exploration. Even the meaning of morality has undergone momentous alterations.

Davis (1973, p.xiii-xviii) categorises intimacy into love being a psychological concept and intimate relations being a sociological concept but coins a new terminology Philemics. He says, it is an ongoing social interaction between two individuals, involving the internal movement of the mind and the external actions of the body. Intimacy is a positive interlocking of personalities. (Berne, 1961, p.86). Intimacy, according to some scholars denotes sexual relations between two people (Mazur, 1973), corroborated by Freud (1949, p.71) and Reisman (1979, p.50). intimacy contains a potential sexual element along with intellectual, social, and emotional components. (Ramey, 1976, p.87). It is not easy to sustain psychological intimacy for a long time without physical intimacy. (Bensman and Lilienfeld, 1979, p.143). Lovers can be intimate friends, but not all friends are intimate lovers because casual mates and termly chums like two or three semesters in a year are beneficial friends. However, an intimate physical relationship is termed as a diploma without an education (Oden, 1974, p.33). Kilpatrick (1975, p.15) utterly bemoans an intimacy in which lovemaking without love is practised.

Howard and Charlotte Clinebell, (1970, 37-38) discuss twelve types of intimacies namely sexual (erotic); emotional (turning on), intellectual,(sharing ideas) aesthetic, (appealing to each other), creative (sharing creativity), work, crisis, conflict, commitment, spiritual and communication intimacy. The authors have ignored psychological intimacy without the involvement of sexual relationships. In Dahms' (1972, pp.20-21) study, emotional intimacy stands out in the three significant kinds of intimacies followed by intellectual and physical components of closeness. In the context of emotional and physical intimacies, each partner is expressively involved and passionately close to one another, comforting in times of stress and indulging in pleasurable activities. Right natured individuals enjoy being selfless dedicated to sharing their feelings with friends.

Interaction and Affection

Realistically speaking, the frequency of interaction determines the intensity of warmth and depth of feelings between two individuals who may be colleagues, classmates, or just friends. Homans (1950, p.242), in his publication 'The Human Groups, ' states that the more interaction, the more affection, and the increased affection would further augment communication. "The more frequently persons interact with one another, the higher is their liking for one another, feeling at ease in each other's company." (P.243). Twenty-four years later, Homans (1974, p.64) expertise in his field asserts that young male and female companions who interact frequently are apt to be similar in some respect. The similarity is fundamental to friendship. (Smith, 1935, p.34) because resemblance had the effect of increasing the degree of liking felt for a stranger. (Duck, 1973, p.71). Duck uses the word similarity rather than connection or parallel likeness since analogy has a strong overtone that validates an individual's self-worth and magnetises the other person. Mutual interaction determines social, physical, and psychological nearness in a cheerful atmosphere. Intimacy tends to be an expression of heartfelt affection in which images of one's private self are exposed gradually at the deeper levels. (Oden, 1974, p.12).

Friendly interactions inspire and influence a person's actions, improving wisdom, developing personal perception seeing through illusions, and understanding other's perspectives. Affection is an essential social need of an infant towards a mother, a teenager towards a classmate, and a university student towards an opposite individual that runs through the whole gamut of community life. The sentiments of fondness and affective attachment accelerate the interaction. Many interfaces create casual friendships that are not durable but are situational encounters. Some students prefer to sit next to each other in a classroom and hang around during break times. They do not necessarily develop any particular affection for each other but simply remain friends for two or more semesters and then move on to make other alliances. Initially, just friends spending more time together tend to increase the frequency of meetings. When communication grows, relationships develop into friendship. (Homans, 1974, p.65) becoming close friends (Du Bois, 1974, p.19). Researchers have discovered that there has always been enriched interaction among students of equivalent social standing in the institutes of higher education. When Riley, Cohn, and Toby (1954) undertook a study of ninth and tenth-grade female students in eight high schools across New Jersey State, they found that the members of each status received more interaction from other members of their group than from any other segment of the society. Unsurprisingly, social interaction resulted from their family background, parental economic worth, and academic standing in the community. Typically male and female students prefer to stay close to their indigenous circles within the campus. Palisi (1966, p.218) observed that most close friends happen to be of similar ethnicity.

The similarity of attitudes rather than race brings people together. Broad-minded youth from all hues warmly accommodate each other in a social context, making new friends and exploring different cultural acuities. Interpersonal attraction induces individuals to modify conservative values and develop interracial relations. Psychological affinities promote interpersonal affections as we notice commercial flights, the crewmates and shipmates at sea become close friends. Such incidental closeness interconnects two souls for the fulfilment of social needs. Mills (1967, p.129) asserts that they seek each other's company for socialisation and mutual experiences gratification. A close relationship is typified by affection, keeping ongoing interaction vibrant and animated. Such relationships often develop into lifelong attachment (Sullivan, 1953, p.245), gaining pleasure in the relationship itself and accepting each other (Douvan, 1977, p.20).

Trust in Emotional and Physical Intimacy

Physical intimacy commences in the mother's womb as a means of first intimate connection followed by birth, seeking comfort and cosiness in the lap, enjoying cuddling and snuggling. This physical touch with the mother says Morris (1971, p.13) is the initial experience of intimacy. As schooling begins, children make new friends and play together and then form likeable alliances with like-minded mates at the higher secondary level. Intimacy is a quality of openness, and complete intimacy is the ideal interpersonal relationship, sharing disclosures and caring intensely about one another (Levinger, 1977, p.138). Bensman and Lilienfeld (1979, p.156) proclaim that intimacy is shared privacy, yet not all shared privacy is intimacy. The roots of symbiotic attachments lie deep in the past social experiences. (Fromm, 1956, p.70). In young adulthood, one learns to choose compassionate and caring, sensitive, and confident friends. Chum relationships are the foundations of intimacy, enabling them to form an identity. In private lives, Erikson (1974, p.124) believes, the youth share intimacies. High ideals are the end product of intimate relationships. (Cooley, 1914, p.23). Intimacy is a necessary phenomenon for the survival of the human race because the future of this race depends on human feelings and belonging to someone. (Adler, 1964, p.55)

The intensity of physical intimacy that exists between two youngsters relates to the degree of trust between them. (Morris, 1971, p.145). A young man or woman can comfortably expose him/herself if mutual trust prevails. Trust is a precondition of intimacy, and beneath understanding, there is a depth of acceptance, love, and affection. However, intimate secrets are not revealed to non-intimate friends for fear of being exposed, bullied, and intimidated. In such relationships, both have unconditional positive regard, warmth, and acceptance for each other. (Rogers,1957). In physical intimacy, three aspects are vital says Cooley, (1902, p.152)), the imagination of our appearance to the other person, the originality of his judgement about the female acquaintance or friend, thirdly, an imputed sentiment, i.e., the feelings he holds. Physical appearance plays a significant part in the enumeration of personal qualities. Natural intimacy entails nonverbal mutual self-disclosure, whereas pleasure operates on the demand side of the intimate relationship. Fulfilment quite often is mostly contingent on the other's keenness to welcome and entertain. (Parsons, 1964, p.120)

Also, the vocal gesture is essential to any other signal. (Mead, 1934, p.65). Intimacy brings out feelings of biological empathy. Some social scientists have described an example of American people's closeness and affability attitudes towards others. The Americans act amiable too quickly but abandon those friendly relations rapidly. (Reisman, 1979, p.83). A German social psychologist Kurt Lewin resided in the United States for over a decade and expressed his opinion about American society. He said, "Compared with Germans, Americans seem to make quicker progress towards friendly relations in the beginning and with many more persons. (Reisman, 1979, pp.83-84). The same view was expressed by Cooley in 1914 (p.100) when he commented about the superficiality of American life frequently experienced by migrants from different cultures.

In underdeveloped countries, there are more opportunities for forming friendships than developing intimacies. Young men hang around in their neighbourhoods, sharing gossips, cigarettes, and drinks in the evenings. William Whyt (1943), in his Street Corner Society, throws light on these friendships. The youth formulate small gangs and, in the evenings, commit petty crimes, disturb public disorder, and intimidate others.

The intimacy literature covering the period 1940-1980 indicates that intimacy had different connotations than friendship in liberal societies. But all types of intimacies embrace closeness, affection, and adoration. Although intimate relationships were enjoyed widely by the youth, most remained private matters and not publicly recognised or commonly reported in the press. The introduction of cyber technologies, online access, and electronic messaging galvanised openness in exchanging compassion, passions, and warm dialogue.

The proliferation of social media platforms such as Facebook, LinkedIn, and YouTube presented intimacy podiums to formulate affections and articulate closeness more openly. People in liberal settings feel comfortable expressing intimacies explicitly, but in orthodox and close societies, they conceal intimate relationships to avoid cultural consequences. The desire to share one's innermost with another is a natural human need. Social life is constructed through a sustained sequence of exchange, which is a starting point in interpersonal intimacy. Once two individuals perform social actions repeatedly within the context of social interfaces, their familiarity transforms into intimacy. Homans (1974, p.145) calls it a relationship based on the repeated exchange of rewarding actions.

Enhanced Liberalisation Among University Students

Undergraduate education begins at 18-years of age, and in the first year, strangers become acquaintances, whereas encounters regular or infrequent transform relationships. Their social interactions turn into personal friendships, demonstrating a certain degree of openness for mutual satisfaction and gratification. While maintaining casual relations, they explore common interests, experience feelings, share ideas, and exchange intellectual ideals. As the closeness develops, so do physical and psychological intimacies. Oral communication is the single most vital factor in the 'mechanism through which human relations exist and develop. (Cooley, 1914, p.61). According to Sullivan (1953), Johnson (1952) was primarily responsible for the formulation of the interpersonal relations theory, which recognises the individuals' inescapable interaction and the social order.

The second significant aspect of communication is the 'glance in the eye that conveys the real impulse' to the other person. (Simmel, 1921, p.358). This initial gaze, a few words, and eye contact form the basis of relationship development, says Davis (1973, p.31). Human beings need stimulation to develop just as the plants require sunlight to grow.

Intimacy is meaningful if it entails genuineness, earnestness, and naturalness on the part of both youngsters who may be freshly intimate or deeply emotionally connected and might have taken erratic passionate gambles. Tenderness flashes lead to psychic surgery in which one partner permits others to come into him/her and practice a delightful experience. Intimacy is the exchange of feelings, communication of passions, the transmission of emotions, and declaration of perceptions between two cherished or unfamiliar individuals. From the outset, it must be abundantly clear that emotional intimacy and physical affection are two different phenomena. We have intimate family gatherings at wedding parties, a warm conversation among spiritually enlightened groups, and informal youth meetings at social clubs. When two youth, male and female, have a pleasant conversation in which each one reveals highly personal details and poignant episodes of private life, such a meeting would be considered an intimate experience. If they divulge feelings for each other and share emotional practices and sensitive proficiencies, it would become a meaningful intimacy. It will amount to a profoundly personal attachment if they share delightful moments and experience mutually enriching involvement.

When a university professor delivers a profoundly absorbing lecture that hypnotises students, he/she is praised for academic knowledge and applauded for theoretical foresight and vision. It captivates some students who feel intellectually close to the professor and hold further out of class meetings to expand their rational horizons. Professor-student affinity would be an intellectual intimacy rather than mistakenly treated sentimental familiarity. Rick Garlikov, in his work "The meaning of love," gives an example of medical professionals in hospitals. Many doctors, nurses, and medical assistants, he says, 'Can be intimate on one level while remaining properly professionally detached on another". He cites personal experience as he enters the hospital for an X-rays, where a kind and friendly female staff member welcomes him. She put on her rubber gloves and politely tells him with a twinkle in her eyes as she looks into his eyes; for the next half hour, evolves, becoming his new best friend. She exhibited a sense of humour to establish an emotional intimacy temporarily. It was in no way a physical intimacy but a routine professional assignment that she diligently undertakes each day during her interaction with several patients from different diverse cultural backgrounds. For Rick Garlikove, it was a memorable personalised emotional experience intimate in discernment but extraordinary in nature. We cultivate friendships by helping strangers in difficult times and acclaim admiration through imparting kind words and serving others without material gain or reward. The present writer experienced approbation feelings when an older man in a religious congregation felt grievous chest pain and fell on the floor. No paramedics were insight at the time; my son, a doctor and a G.P., instantly stepped forward, checked his heartbeat and pulse, rendered first-aid, and called for an ambulance to transport the patient to the hospital. May Almighty God reward my son for this act of kindness and enhance his capabilities to serve hundreds of thousands of sick people. My daughter, an Audiologist, and two of my sons, G. Ps, are currently looking after Corona Virus patients under challenging times. May Allah keeps them safe and protected, and they continue to serve for decades to come.

In 1967, Christopher Jencks and David Riesman wrote, 'The academic revolution' described the small size of university faculties and colleges comprising an insignificant student population. The faculty and students had intimate personal contacts on a day-to-day basis. The romantic pedagogical tradition was institutionalised as an ideal of enlightenment. (p.35). Among students and between teaching staff, intimate relationships were encouraged, accepted, and made knowledge sharing invigorating. The female students had complete freedom in choosing courses and interpersonal contacts, both with classmates and the teachers. The student bodies thrived within familiarity and comfort zones and enjoyed intellectual closeness in a liberally modern ambience.

Intimacy has always been considered aspirational, the desire for something shared, and fulfilling a promise of happiness, and it generates an aesthetic of attachment. Lauren Berlant (2000), a Professor at the University of Chicago, states that 'rethinking intimacy calls out not only for re-description but for transformative analysis of the rhetorical and material conditions. The present writer believes that such physical settings provide hegemonism fantasies with an opportunity to thrive in young minds. While attachments consistently develop, redirecting different routes taken by history and biography. We can understand intimacy by appraising our past adventures, current practices, and the future imagining of our lives. Our pragmatic thoughts of sharing our dreams and caring for others will begin to make sense. We rarely address caprices and unrealities of safe zones that are not genuinely safe. According to Brian Massumi (2002, p.28), emotion transforms and affects a conventional consensual form where it extracts meaning mediating into a meaningful intimacy.

On the other hand, Martha Nussbaum (1990) comments that emotions are social constructs expressed for learning purposes through literary tales and social stories. Emotions are subject to disappearance without real awareness. Sara Ahmed (2004) avows that emotion grooms beneath the faculties of thought and reason, exclusively associated with women who are represented close to nature ruled by appetite.

Closeness and Emotional Diffusion

Women's early biological maturation helps develop emotional skills, shape their thoughts and feelings of intimacy, and become capable of influencing situational factors on significant social events and productive life outcomes. Mother-daughter closeness ultimately enables smooth improvement of analytical powers and the judgement of intimate interactions with others.

Jane Austen (Dec.1775-July 1817), an English writer, asserts, 'seven years would be insufficient to make some people acquainted with each other and seven days are more than enough for others' to articulate close relationships. The interesting point is that one can be intimate without emotional correlation. Intimacy is gawking into each other's eyes, conveying a poignant confidential message, expressing sensory feelings that touch the heart, making sexual gestures, and sharing mutually anticipated moments.

Initial eye contact is a fundamental step towards meaningful intimacy because it instinctively has a magnetic power that can unconsciously convey potentially hidden feelings. If a neighbour pass by you but avoids looking into your eyes, you might feel hurt or rejected. But the exchange of pure gaze with another person triggers our brain activity leading to emotional cognition. Looking into the eyes of another person can be a pleasing experience if the response is reciprocal. A shared gaze is a blessing in disguise and the beginning of non-verbal communication. Emotional eye contact transmits our emotions and feeling of adoration and admiration. An unintentional preliminary look can be irresistible and may exert hypnotic influence on the individual who might return a captivating stare with alluring pleasantness. Sensory feedback stemming from lips movements, eye contacts, nods, and bodily metaphors arouses feelings for emotional expression and experimentation.

If a classmate raises her eyebrows and lowers lids, it is similar to expressing pleasure and warmth. A sideways glance over a raised shoulder highlights curves and eye contact indicates kind-heartedness and cordiality. In short, eye contact shapes our perception of the other individual, and those who meet our gaze are considered by psychologists to be gifted, intelligent, and self-conscious. The chemistry of eye contact has mesmeric connotations, and such mutual overtones do share special moments. While profoundly looking into another person's eyes, our pupils dilate; that was an emotional response, causing other's pupils to widen as well. We can read complex emotions based on other individual's eye movements. For example, displeasure causes a person to narrow the eyes, and wide-open eyes transmit niceness and amiability. Dr. Christian Jarrett, a British psychologist, comments that 'eyes are a window to the soul, there is something incredibly powerful about gazing deeply into another person's eyes. Our eyes are the only part of our brain that directly exposes to the world. Concerning intense intimacy, Dr. Jarret says, 'it is little wonder that if you dim the lights and hold the gaze of another person for 10 minutes non-stop, you will find strange things start to happen.

Intimacy involves reliance, approval, empathy, and intimate connection between the two susceptible passions. It is a human emotional contact immersed in trustworthiness and credibility. Powerful personal feelings evolve physical consummation and psychological gratification permitting the youth to indulge in mutually agreeable unexplored adventures. Non-verbal signals play a crucial part in promoting greater intimacy between two people.

Internet and online dating sites facilitate overzealous youth to connect, chat, gossip, and laugh and develop acquaintance with strangers, promote intimacy, and make new friends. Jenni Skyler of The Intimacy Institute of Sex and Relationship Therapy, Colorado, and Julie Spira both suggest a few useful sites for prospective teenagers. They seek intimate relations, good friends, and trusted mates. These websites include Tinder; Bumble; Hinge: Match and Our Times. Preliminary intimacy leads to robust social links overtime and through online connectivity, you can share ideas, exchange thoughts and enjoy similarities. When we establish connections based on mutual trust, it is the beginning of sharing outlooks, affection, secrets, tenderness and hidden feelings. Individuals might use the sixth sense to communicate non-verbally, protecting a sense of privacy that is free from external criticism and scrutiny. Social intimacy prospers between two male and female peers who participate jointly in pleasurable activities such as going out, dating, attending birthday parties, viewing films in cinemas, going to theatres and riding in sports cars for fun and excitement. A connection is a primary social need, compromising and responding to each other's input. Conclusively, intimacy continuously generates a sense of shared pleasure. A young boy or girl experiences powerful feelings of attachment and bonding, which naturally develops from initial passionate perceptions into romance and sensual attraction. On the contrary, spiritual intimacy is concerned with shared values and religious beliefs in your relationships.

According to Aron and Aron (1986), 'intimacy predicts passion' agrees Birnbaum et al. (2016) and Ratelle et al. (2013) rants, 'passion predicts intimacy. Hatfield and Walster (1978) believe that 'passion is a state of profound physiological arousal' since 'intimacy steadily builds up' says Sternberg (1986) and then relationship turns into 'powerful feelings towards one's partner.' (Baumeister and Bratslavsky, 1999). Then physical and emotional closeness inspires feelings of biological needs leading to the intense expression of affection. An infant long for maternal love, and a teenager yearns for peer connection, becoming a significant source of psychosocial satisfaction. Toddlers are touched and hugged by mothers, and they experience emotional closeness, feel delighted, and enthralled. This relational magic remains in their memory as they enter high school and meet other kids. Teenage is a vital stage to initiate social life with peers and classmates.

What boy-girl interactions do we recognise as intimate, was defined by Lippert and Prager (2005), who conducted a study of 113 cohabiting couples in Dallas, USA.? Both female Professors interviewed participants and advised them to maintain diaries of interaction for one week. The majority of respondents revealed pleasant feelings in their private sensual encounters and perceptions of shared pleasure and satisfying social life.

More satisfied couples perceived their interactions as more intimate and showed stronger associations between interaction intimacy and partner disclosure than did less satisfied couples. In 1969, Lori and Gordon devised a 4-month course 'Practical Application of Intimate Relationship Skills adopted by several countries worldwide. It was thoroughly revised and updated in 1995, incorporating practical workshops spanning 120-hours of studies at degree level in universities. The instructors use an integrative approach with cognitive treatment to move couples from non-adaptive relationship patterns to intimacy and pleasure. The students earn social and psychological constituents of real intimacy that entails exclusive responsiveness, consistent reinforcement, caring approach, and unshakable trust in each other. The youth learn through emotional pathways while unconsciously committing human errors during intimate companionships. They obligate erroneous acts in untested connections.

Love is a feeling, but marriage is an indenture- an invisible convention because two different histories acclimatise two individuals, and therefore, their expectations are usually dissimilar. In the beginning few years of connection, they experience displeasures, divergences, and misunderstandings. When intimacy strengthens, all misapprehensions and delusions vanish, whereas empathy and compassion grow. Two intimate teens convey potential social signals more non-verbally rather than in a conversation. Altruistic intentions and motives tend to be at the root of nonverbal expression: moral compass guides youth social interaction and biological connection. Self-disclosure of emotions such as happiness, glee, and pleasure more closely relate to girls who self-express positive feelings. The sparkle in their eyes, gestures of hands and body are signs of goodwill and warmth. Emotional openness is increasingly beneficial because It keeps emotions alive and vibrant, whereas social connectedness vivaciously enlarges intimate relationships.

A stunning smile on a smiley face in a social meet portrays personal and interior feelings. Girls are productive communicators possessing fluent verbal dexterities but do not lag behind boys in non-verbal skills. They discuss private feelings more openly than their male peers. They seek intimacy in relationships, disclose highly personal details, and willingly share intimate feelings. The girls, affirm Moss and Schwebel (1993), are willing to' define and express close positions and ego with a friend and value relationship significantly in their lives'. The girls do not vacillate to discuss personal dilemmas, unpleasant impasses, and socially tricky problems. Their excessive openness infrequently lands them in a susceptible catch22 situation.

In an educational atmosphere, professors observe students' behaviour, attendance pattern, and etiquette. They can predict how many of those would succeed with distinction. Andrew and Rosenblum et al. (1994) carried out a study in a physical health venue. They discovered that researchers could predict academic grades assigned to medical students by their clinical supervisors by rating a sample of students' nonverbal behaviour while interacting with patients in a paediatric setting. In another road crossing observational study, Tova Rosenbloom (2009) discreetly observed 1392 pedestrians (842 female and 550 male) and found more males had the propensity to pass on a red than females. The girls tend to be reticent, self-conscious, and vigilant about themselves and the surrounding environment.

Teens' growth span is the assessment phase gripped with ups and downs, confusions and excitements, commotions and sensations, hullabaloos, and adventures. Youth should act and perform what they believe to be right, irrespective of traditional conventions, and external influences. Intense emotions of wanton desires, emotional, sensual longings, and superfluous sensation-seeking instincts would be detrimental to the moral fabrics of self-esteem, dignity, self-worth, and social modesty.

The most complex task for a teenager is to accurately and correctly describe his/her feelings. How do you feel about yourself? Furthermore, How others think about you? Notwithstanding that, how do you perceive the sense of others? The last bit is enormously cumbersome because some of your peers might be experts in hiding their true feelings, while others could be open in expressing their feelings. Some youngsters are secretive by nature, keep their cards close to their chest, and never clearly reveal themselves. If your friend does not divulge personal details, prefers to be enigmatic and reticent, but pretends to be sincere, how would you build up trust and understanding in a special connection? As such, open-mindedness is necessary for stimulation and receptive companionship is filled with excitement, pleasure, and happiness. Expressive language has a significant sentimental effect on the individual who is unable or reluctant to implicitly express his/her sensitivities. Your communication skills will help untangle hitherto undisclosed mawkish perceptions, which clear the way for serene and trusting relationships.

You can have a morally vibrant, joyful, and exultant rapport filled with empathy, thrill, and excitement without crossing ethical boundaries and decency. Such standards still prevail in contemporary societies where traditional values invite admiration and virtues receive veneration. Youth have a voracious thirst and craving for attention and usually keep a group of peers amused with a longing for illustriousness and popularity. For instance, young authors initially struggle to have their works published by renowned publishing houses. Stephen King's first novel faced thirty times rejection before a less known publisher eventually accepted it. He was so frustrated that he put it in the home garbage bin, albeit his wife incidentally salvaged the manuscript. Similarly, Joanne Kathleen Rowling's first Harry Potter manuscript was rejected by 12 publishers before accepted by Bloomsbury. She commenced writing at the age of six and completed her first novel at eleven, instigating other British kids to begin writing short stories in school days.

We may express our emotions utilising bodily gestures to welcome an adult. An individual may wear a smile to show happiness, laugh aloud to appreciate a joke, and clap hands for a winning team. One can shake hands to say goodbye to a stranger and hug a friend to express feelings. On the contrary, we show negative emotions by feeling sad, upset, deceived, discouraged, disillusioned, and depressed. It is challenging to hide gloom, misery, despair, and unhappiness but not arduous to conceal thrill-seeking emotions and playful sentiments. Within emotions, galvanisation occurs due to explicit motivations that set off specific social configurations and relationships. Exciting adventures trigger emotions and inspire psychosocial experimentation in adolescents. They create a favourable environment for forming connections. The youngsters indulge in enjoyable activities and acclaim intimacies. Emotional suppression is undesirable for adolescents in social settings. If amicably expressed, amounts to sharing feelings with peers is a constructive mode. Openly displayed emotions help to face the challenges bravely. It will ultimately improve curiosity, influence personality, and expand cognition, which is crucial in making judgements, solving social issues, and widening imaginations. It develops thoughtfulness and understanding of others' emotions, motives, and intentions towards oneself. You begin to evaluate people's reactions during interactions that facilitate the identification of emotions.

Emotional suppression in youngsters is not encouraged by sociologists neither condoned by psychiatrists due to unpredictable unpleasant results for healthy social and intellectual growth. Dynamic excessive control is simply the disguising of facial and bodily states, which might wield an overpowering impact on mental well-being. Unhindered consistent expression of personal emotions in a given situation is proved to have comparatively better health outcomes. Gross and Levenson (1993) state that emotional repression has psychological consequences. Whether we express happiness on account of a delightful occasion or demonstrate sadness at a painful encounter, emotions demand free emission to get it off the chest, Conner (1927) and Jones (1935) declare that suppressing a natural emotional response will increase the intensity of the subjective experience. We feel differently at various stages of knowledge, but we should be brave and courageously accept emotional negativity- related to painful episodes, stressful incidents, or unbearable material loss. Acceptance would not deteriorate our feelings; neither would it augment our happiness. In the study of 1000 students from the University of Berkley, Bratt Ford et al. (2018) resolved that 'habitually accepting negative emotions reduces feelings of ill-being and more likely leads to an elevated level of wellbeing'. Peer pressure to conceal unpleasant feelings is tangible but reclaiming peace of mind necessitates the honouring of harmful emotions. We should not superficially hold back our feelings of pleasure, pain, and desire while our facial impression and bodily movement tell different stories.

The emotional actions are the result of our inner states as they affect motivation and self-fulfilment. Many unpleasant situations can be avoided by exercising restraint and applying control over our emotions. In particular, social events sometimes involve exposure to spiteful conversations, unkind comments, and undesirable glares. The psychological impact of unwelcome gazes arouses feelings of antipathy, giving rise to emotional aversion. Under the given circumstances, repugnance can be truncated by dynamic control management, mediating the surrounding with reconciliation and compromise. Series of events create our emotions, which either cause delight, rapture, and jubilation or make us gloomy, low-spirited, and unhappy. Other people's behaviour and dealings impact our feelings in different ways propelling us to respond, appraise, or resent. When urging us to react negatively, our intuition and judgement will prevail if we assess the remarks with insight and emotional control without unleashing irritation to settle the scores. Emotions are unwelcome visitors as much as the unexpected entry of crises and unpredicted arrival of predicaments in our lives. Social relationship breakdowns are emotional upheaval frequently experienced by youngsters. Natural catastrophes differently affect our cognitive health. Our emotions and cognition are integrated into the brain, playing a significant part in the fruition of cognisance. They persistently interrelate while preserving identity.

According to Izard (2009), there are different forms of emotions rooted in evolution and biology. Feelings of love and attachment are fundamental to human growth and effective adaptation. He considers emotion as a phase, and Langer (1967) acclaims that it is not a consequence of bodily expression. Still, the feeling is the central element in emotion reflected in the spontaneous expression'. Reflections about human feelings are somewhat thought-provoking but not particularly commend by other psychologists.

Similarly, a physiologist, Professor William James (1884) gives a detailed description of emotion utterly rejected by renowned sociologists, psychologists, and brain specialists. Our natural way of thinking about feeling is that the mental discernment of some fact electrifies the emotion's mental fondness. This latter state of intellect gives rise to physical manifestation. James, however, proclaims that the bodily changes follow the perception of the exciting fact directly and that our feelings of the same changes as they occur is the emotion. Common sense says we lose our fortune, are sorry and weep, meet a bear, and are frightened and run; we are insulted by a rival and angry and strike. James further states that the hypothesis here to be defended is that this order of sequence is incorrect, that the one mental state is not immediately induced by the other. Hence, the bodily manifestations need to be construed and understood first and foremost. A realistic, rational statement is that we feel sorry because we cry, angry because we strike, afraid because we are ashamed, angry, or fearful. We might see the bear and judge it best to run, but we could not feel scared.

James believed that the sensation of bodily changes is an essential condition for the experience of emotion, and it played a central role in every aspect of mental reflexes. Ellsworth (1994, p.223), a century later, professed that bodily sensations are not the whole experience but are the part that makes the entire experience emotional. Schachter and Singer (1962) indicated that emotion is a combination of cognitive and physiological responses. James had argued that every minor change in bodily sensation creates a change in emotional experience. Tomkins (1962) and McCarter (1964) considered facial expression to be the primary source of emotion, a viewpoint reaffirmed by Professor Carroll Izard (1971). James erroneously declared that there were 'no special brain-centres for feeling. Other scholars, physiologists overwhelmingly disputed this theory.

We should have a firm belief in our emotions, and these are subject to modification and alteration depending on the nature of the encounter or surroundings in which we happen to be present. We might have mixed feelings about some issues and cannot instantaneously express our emotions without souls searching and using intuition. Whether pain or pleasure, both elements have close links with our brain cells and nervous system. Feelings of agony and gratification relate to cognitive functioning, and one can manage to cope with the resultant outcome better.

Religious beliefs make us stronger in the expression of feelings, offer moral awareness, and self-consciousness. Sufi Saints obscure their emotions and spiritual experiences from the public eye, but some gladly disclose through singing, dancing, writings, and poetry. Western scholars hesitate to delve into the emotional side of faith and religious beliefs out of concern that can serve as acknowledged markers of the Islamic faith, giving rise to the enquiring young university students to investigate. This unbiased research for the truth behind Divine revelation would highlight the integrity and authenticity of the glorious Qur'an. Many Western scholars of Arabic literature have translated Qur'an into several major languages of the world.

If we tearfully pledge our heart to a Deity, we could feel spiritual enlightenment and emotional attachment to the Lord, The Creator of the Globe. Academic curiosity leads to a fresh understanding of how people, through religious practices, create relationships and express emotions such as love, ecstasy, hope, and contentment. Emotion intertwines into the fabric and composition of spiritual life.

As Emile Durkheim (1912) succinctly put it, 'Religion is a kind of social glue, a shared experience that unifies individuals into cooperative social groups'. The actual value of faith lies in its healing power, predominantly its supremacy to regulate our emotions. It trains feelings of responsiveness and benevolence for others and offers sustenance to the sufferers. Many Sufi Saints in Tunis, Morocco, Turkey, and Tashkent created social bonding by consoling melodies, joint worship practices, sharing feasts, observing fasting, conducting prayers in congregation, and mutual care. Also, Sufi poets have, through poetry, transmitted emotions based on reminiscence in serenity. Dr Annmarie Schimmel (1922-2003), a German-born Orientalist and a Professor at Harvard University from 1967 to 1992, and a Professor of Religion at Ankara University, Faculty of Theology 1954-

1959, illuminated Maulana Rumi's (1207-1373) allegory and remained engrossed for 40 years. She believed Rumi introduced the whirling dance in Konya to his disciples and utilised powerful poetic means to express the vision and conveyed emotional experiences. She also composed beautiful poems that are frequently quoted by scholars of comparative religion. Poetry is the instinctively natural tide of formidable thoughts and feelings since it takes its origin from emotions.

Emotions vary from culture to culture as new feelings come to light. There is a degree of flexibility in how these emotions are expressed, experienced, and declared or professed. Dr James Cowles Prichard invented the term moral insanity in 1835, which initially means emotional nonsense. Patients who behaved unsteadily without mental illness were not necessarily morally insane because they could not control their emotions. The Queen Mary University of London's Centre for the History of the Emotions has set up an Emotional Lab to conduct scientific and physiological research on the subject. It would be useful to follow up on their research findings consistently. In our living memories, Innumerable perpetual occasions in our buzzing minds reflect complex relationships with unanticipated emotional outcomes. Consequently, our feelings expose through the tangible impact of these occurrences. However, the cognitive role of passion, craving, perception, and imagination, diverse individual experience, and commotion cannot be underestimated, which frequently leads to emotional reactions and physical sensations.

Couple's Fondness and Intimacy

Childbirth is a blessing for both parents that brings into their marital matters tremendous excitement and then, nestling and hugging enhance feelings of intimate closeness. Snuggling with a new-born gives rise to a tender form of physical intimacy and a compassionate kind of affectionate touch. The breastfeeding process is an indescribable type of pleasant experience for the mother, testing her patience and dismantling former time schedules. With increased caregiving responsibilities, the expectations are high for her to please both the husband and the infant equally. Understanding partners always cooperate in making the house a charming place for the new arrival. Touching, picking up, and bathing the little angel are joyful acts. They empathise with the wife, who initially struggles to balance a partner's love and child affection. When the father holds the baby in his arms, he experiences renewed gratifying feelings that promote a couple's emotional intimacy. The husband recalls the process of pregnancy, surgery visits, health worker meetings, and intimate conversations about the intended birth of their biological child with great satisfaction. If a child is born through caesarean, he remembers the post and pre-surgery procedure with his wife's human feelings accompanied by reassurances. The couple's new openness strengthens marital bonds, increases respect, and regenerates intimacy. The innocent cries and beautiful smiles of toddlers reinforce a sense of passionate attachment bringing them closer. The simple pleasure of parental attention and affectionate devotion create pleasantness resulting in enhanced emotional intimacy.

Parenthood proliferates intimacy, flourishes couple's love, and strengthens their relations. They participate more in activities related to looking after the infant and augmenting personal interactions and reflections. Transition to fatherhood is a fascinating surprise inventing opportunity for warmness and enriched affection for the soulmate. The acts of physical touch between mum and kid and openings of emotional togetherness between partners get nourished and nurtured. Marital intimacy gathers bountiful sustainability and a welcome boost for a combined perception and a collective future. Child-rearing tasks demand time commitment from both parents who might have other dedicated job obligations.

Reduced time together and condensed social life are challenging aspects of human aspirations. Naturally, some disagreements over childminding and division of duties may arise. (Belsky & Pensky, 1988), but some couples experiencing odd patches in relationships feel revitalised after the childbirth. (Wright et al., 1986). It opens an avenue to discovering common grounds and collective interests with increased interaction visible in their wellbeing. (Katariina Salmela-Aro, 2006). Such feelings give rise to joint nursing, harmony, and reciprocity. (Dignan, 1995). They may go out for a short walk in the evening when the child is sleeping or arrange to babysit for a night out dinner and laughter.

The process of realising and preserving psychological intimacy soothes the soul as the couple learns better to understand each other (Levine, 1991). With a child as part of the discussion, the couple profoundly communicates and divulge unsaid secrets. Such conversation fosters emotional intimacy, and it is an essential source of marital happiness. (Dew and Wilcox, 2011). In short, a shared experience of parenthood is wonderful for dedicated couples who do not get seduced by other captivations. Contented husbands gleefully share all the inherent excitements to achieve gratification and satisfaction. Professor Paula Nicolson (2011) of Royal Holloway University of London upholds that ladies experience a sense of psychological fulfilment, which is candidly linked to motherhood and offers them an extra edge of confidence. Refreshing child focus shapes an understanding of intimacy that empowers them to develop a coherent sense of distinctiveness without losing their unique identity. (Erikson, 1968). It is a fusion of the two individuals having a real concern for each other (Erikson, 1993) and a genuine need for healthy emotional growth (Maslow, 1954). Individual behaviour reflects the desire for intimacy in couple relations (Schaefer & Olson, 1981), achievable through self-disclosure and validation (Perlman & Fehr, 1987). Intimacy is overwhelmingly a relational construct, and self-esteem exhibiting the interplay between togetherness and individuality (Bowen, 1978). Individual aspires to establish self-identity and experience real intimacy (Cassidy, 2001). Couples have an instinctive craving for marital fulfilment (Greef and Malherbe, 2001) as a mother of an infant struggles to maintain a fair balance between maternal duties and meeting the husband's emotional needs. Life changes happen when partners become parents, delineating the need for the buffer against declining marital happiness. They have to balance closeness and individuality.

Maintaining Rapport and Energising Passion

A couple's Emotional Intimacy is critical to relationship satisfaction as it is the "proverbial elephant". (Acitelli & Duke, 1987). It may require significant sacrifices and compromises to promote moral strength. (Erikson, 1950/1963). Emotional intimacy is related to spiritual, psychic, conscious, and unconscious feelings simultaneously shared by a couple. Two people have similar feelings at the same time (Coutts, 1973, p. 16). They begin to share steep knowledge of one another, divulging hitherto withheld secrets and feats. Robinson and Blanton's (1993) studies indicate that lasting marriage's significant feature resulted from emotional, physical, and spiritual intimacy developed through sharing thoughts, feeling, joys, and pains.

Several studies involving married and cohabiting couples have produced data using a Personal Assessment of Intimacy in Relationship Inventory (PAIR) comprising a

36 item instrument to access types of intimacy in relationships. A couple can share a perception of lovingness in different ways with the earnest hope of maintaining devotedness over a lifetime. An acceptance of each other relates to natural nonverbal gestures or exciting intimate conversation. Affectionate partners openly discuss hilarious episodes and adventurous fantasies, whims, and dreams. Almost every couple aspires to enhance and enrich intimacy and make relationships colourful and connection exhilarating. Affection grows, breadth and openness increases, and understanding intensifies in intimate togetherness. Even incompatible couples become exceedingly compatible through the discovery of mutual feelings of adoration and reverence. When an increase in dynamism and sparkle accompanies the emotion of intimacy, it is an encouraging sign of improved confidence and self-assurance. Intimacy gets nourished with truthfulness, honesty, and spiritual belief. Drawing on faith reveals the purpose that carries us forward, making us capable of absorbing pain and suffering from silence and suppleness.

Thomas Moore (1994) observes intimacy in people who are soul mates as they share feelings of comfort and wellbeing (Coutts, 1973, p. 14) and demonstrate intense bonding while respecting autonomy (Augsburger, 1988). Libby and Whitehurst (1977, p.283) emphasise intense physical and emotional communion with another human being. It is a subjective relational experience in which the core components are trusting self-disclosure to which the response is communicated (Wynne and Wynne, 1986, p.384). Mental and physical wellness takes the lead in positive relationships (Dandeneau and Johnson, 1994). Intimate interaction involves self-revealing and positive involvement with the partner since it is the feelings of closeness and fondness in a loving relationship (Sternberg, 1986, p.119). Intimacy is an enduring romantic relationship associated with the level of commitment, affective, cognitive, and physical closeness one experiences with a partner. Moss and Schwebel (1993, p.33), studied sixty-one definitions of intimacy and concluded that seven themes are significant, namely: Exchange or Mutual Interaction; In-depth affective awareness-expressiveness; Shared commitment; Feelings of cohesion; In-depth cognitive awareness-expressiveness; In-depth physical awareness-expressiveness; Communication or Self-disclosure, Generalised sense of closeness to another. Olson (1977) asserts that intimate experience is a feeling of attachment, possibly with a variety of persons that do not significantly involve a personal relationship because, in such intimate relationships, intimate expression occurs. Likewise, Gala postulates emotional intimacy as experienced in a close relationship versus a past emotional experience with an acquaintance" has different dimensions. Crowe (1997, p.235) quite rightly opines that men and women have predictable differences in their wishes for intimacy. Sometimes, it is not easy to achieve a comfortable compromise in this sensitive social area.

Intimacy is a beautiful seed that always needs nourishment (Lewis, 1989, p.77); otherwise, it might die without blooming. It's mainly thriving depends on both partners' willingness to energise passions, endorse diverse opinions, and galvanise unity without sacrificing distinctiveness. Intimacy gives rise to mutual feelings of tenderness and openness, pleasantness, and kindness. We cannot ignore barriers in intimacy, such as suspicion, mistrust, and excessive curiosity. We have the urge to know about the past adventures of our soulmate. In some instances, the notion of superiority complex causes unpleasantness within intimate relationships. If one partner recalls what used to happen in her family of origin in other relationships? Her behaviour pattern might originate from the family she grew up in and how she perceived parents' relations as a couple. Unpleasantness will likely prevail if one of the partners replicates past roles and interaction patterns in the current environment. This superiority complex is prevalent in female partners from developing countries who derive strength from past links creating obnoxiousness in nuptial affairs.

Intimacy is a relational construct, mutual validation, and care (Mitchell, 2008) and affection and cohesiveness(Prager, 1995). According to Reis and Shaver (1988), intimacy is an interpersonal process, a slow but consistent journey to garner perfect emotional association and mental satisfaction. Well, differentiated partners usually enjoy good relationships safeguarding their individuality without losing a sense of self, which

Bowen calls "differentiation of self" (1978). The couple may express concerns and thoughts freely but stay connected, albeit some might display symptoms of uneasiness due to mild tussles and disagreements. There may be an interplay between togetherness and individuality, and that chemistry demands attention and amicable solution. Deficient intimate feelings become an issue that might have arisen due to a reduced level of relationship satisfaction. When two individuals think, feel deeply in love, and interact socially, intense emotions are profoundly present.

However, emotionally charged situations are unhelpful in satisfying relationships. Keeping open communication lines helps solve complex scenarios when both partners show a willingness to negotiate and unravel vulnerabilities. The desire to address concerns infuses a renewed spirit of commonality and compassion. They preserve mutual respectfulness, acknowledge individual dignity, and admit the causes of social estrangement. The Couples must maintain pleasantness at the personal level and pay particular attention to fulfilling each other's needs. It would strengthen intimacy and infuse loveable feelings in their kids (Cassidy, 2001) who are watchful and observant of their parental behaviour. It is reassuring to help each other and depend on each other to become emotionally connected and passionately attached. Although men avoid discussing emotional issues (Merves-Okin et al. 1991), the female partner should initiate conversation showing consideration and thoughtfulness for harmonious solutions.

Women tend to be more emotional than men because they are more open in discussing matters and seek happiness in intimate relationships. They express feelings to promote attachment level and reduce social concerns facilitating intimate closeness, psychological nearness, and emotional affection. Two people may claim to be close but still lack the intimacy that indicates the formation of close relationships. Real intimacy removes both the emotional and physical boundaries that might exist between two individuals. Women portray mutual feelings of tenderness and display dynamic connectivity to achieve social intimacy.

Women equally enjoy a giggle and chat with their female friends and share intimate matters, but it is different from their relations with the opposite sex. Robin (1985, p. 33) declares that women are more capable of emotional intimacy because they allow themselves to be more intimate and cultivate a more profound level of intimacy. Female links with friends and college-fellows are pursuits for social belonging, acceptance, and identification. Women express, recognise, and uniquely experience intimacy on account of their affectionate and emotionally open perceptions, physiological discernments, and psychological sensitivities. Female relationship satisfaction is directly correlated with emotional attachment rather than merely physical togetherness with the partner.

CHAPTER V - FEMALE PHYSICAL FEATURES

Female adolescents are predominantly sensitive about their features, complexions, and body images. Physical metaphors stem from the overwhelming desire to look gorgeous and stunningly beautiful compared to peers and friends. Profound competition exists in the circle of pretty girls, their facial features, and visible appearances. Mostly in high schools and colleges, lassies astoundingly compete with each other in terms of who draws more attention from boys and who looks fabulously more gorgeous than fellow teenagers. For instance, blue eyes, curvaceous nose, symmetrical eyebrows, and blonde hair are considered exceptionally terrific topographies of adolescents. Girls as young as 15-years of age, either like hair's waved or bleached, eyebrows plucked or pencilled, lashes curled or coiled, and eyes mascaraed. Some girls have their teeth clenched or glazed and use lipstick to brighten lips. While others aged 18 to 19 have their breasts silicone, hand nails shaped or manicured, toenails coloured, and use facials, creams and makeovers to look attractive, pretty, and cute to invite attention. Young girls watch movie stars on the television, see fashion shows, modelling, and catwalk competitions. They wish to imitate role models by spending a massive sum of money and time to appear beautiful and acceptable in contemporary society. Their primary focus is on visible appearance rather than on enhancing inner beauty, self-esteem, and self-confidence. The present writer has no intention to approve or disapprove, analyse, or criticise any culture's fundamentals since the world has turned into a global village due to rapidly developing cyber technologies. However, fashion trends have revolutionised young boys' and girls' thinking patterns and girls belonging to diverse cultural backgrounds. The author agrees with Virginia Woolf (1929), who records in her 'A Room of one's own' that as long as "you write what you wish to write is all matters; and whether it matters for ages or only for hours, nobody can say." For myself, I admit that any book or research article is a humble contribution to the body of social, psychological, and communal literature. It could be enlightening for some seekers of knowledge while little or limited value for many people who dislike reading but have an overwhelming desire for watching television programmes, movies, dramas, and serials.

On the contrary, boys need to possess a pleasant attitude, friendly outlook, tall and handsome, muscular body, and above all, socially amicable, cheerful, and harmonious etiquette. For instance, during the Elizabethan era, young English girls used saffron and sulphur to dye their hair red for the sole purpose of emulating the hair colour of Elizabeth 1. Presently, girls dye their hair blonde or auburn to imitate Hollywood film actresses and fashion models. Marilyn Monroe in the 1950s and Jean Harlow in 1the 1930s had platinum blonde hair well-liked and admired by hundreds of thousands of girls in the West. Beauty ideals differ considerably in various cultures and continents. In

African countries, flabbiness is a sign of beauty and fertility for a happy wife, but slimness in Europe epitomises social accomplishment, pleasure, and acceptability. Many young girls struggle to adapt to media standards of a perfect body and impeccable features.

Andrea Dworkin, a U.S. philosopher, categorically stated in 1974 (p.6) that women's beauty is a cultural practice that is undoubtedly time-wasting, expensive, and painful to one's self-esteem. However, ladies use make-up to appear ideal, attractive, and beautiful. For decades, affluent girls have used plastic surgery for boosting various private body parts and uplifting cheeks, nose, and forehead. Self-conscious female strives to enhance attractiveness through surgical procedures that guarantee optimum revamping and embellishment of oneself. Lennon et al. (1999) underlined that the 'stereotyped representation of women in media, culture, and societal level increases the pressure to conform to the ideal body or beauty type. These are authentic, harmful cultural practices for young girls who waste their natural energies, talents, and money to embellish their skin and bodies superficially. Prettiness is a natural gift that cannot be acquired by unnatural and peculiar means. Cuteness cannot be borrowed, imitated, or seemingly attained, but self-belief can make the young girls morally strong and socially resilient. Ingrained Western white beauty standards have adversely affected the girls across the globe since the cosmetic surgery business continues to prosper in non-European countries. Even some surgical procedures are utterly painful for girls who go through excoriating discomfort for the sake of altering physical features.

In East Asian states, double eyelid surgery is ubiquitous among young female well-off girls who spend an astonishing amount of money for this luxury to appear intensely appealing. Asian girls use cosmetic products to whiten and lighten their pale and dark skin, making them attractive and beautiful.

The fusion of beauty obsession makes young girls waste their emotional resources, changing and frequently damaging skin and facial features. Female body image is not just a vehicle of pleasure and desire but says Frost (2001, p.42.) is believed to have a higher exchange value when it approximates to the romantic image. When the subject of gorgeousness becomes a sharp focus for girls, their figures are cast-off as gadgets to abuse them where their bodies' values are encroaching those who are unable to accomplish the beauty ideal. As such, the beauty ideal drives the vacillation of girls' self-respect and self-confidence. Media and showbiz industry unwittingly represent unrealistic ideas unsuitable for imitation, albeit, young girls amazingly aspire to achieve superficially created beauty norms.

Attention and Upkeep

Fashion magazines such as Elle Fashion Forecast, particularly in Europe and the U.S.A., promote the latest brands and designs meant for girls enticing them to look more appealing, attractive, and inviting. The photographs of slim smart teens make them look exceedingly beautiful and remarkably pretty, mainly appearing desirable for men. Phelan (2002) quite rightly comments that modern-day fashion makes a statement of what society wants women to be (p.2) and expresses the dominance of a social class. Romanticised beauty in the West determines men's relations to women and women's connections to themselves, asserts Wolf (1990, p.59). Fashionable appearance is the sole aim of young girls, says Phelan (2005, p.138), and meets the standards of beauty glamorised by the media.

Consequently, stringent societal demands induce girls to be beautiful, immaculate, natural, and striking. Self-consciousness is in-built in girls' freshly developed position as the entity of stare; ladies are to be eyed at and sumptuously eroticised. Teenage culture underpins the impulse that the girl's power is connected to sexual desirability, and those a bit flabby without white and bright skin may feel ashamed.

The high heels augment women's' beauty had been in and out of fashion for decades, albeit initially invented in Venice in the 16th century. (Benamou, 2006). High spiked-heel increases pressure on the ball of the foot (Phelan, 2005, p.183), causing discomfort due to deformed toenails. Some prosperous ladies undergo toe tuck surgery to fit into fancy footwear, although all surgical procedures result in adverse impediments producing soreness and triggering inconvenience in walking. Innocent girls with moderate family background go through embellishing and cosmetic procedures for achieving a perfect body adored by wealthy men that might eventually mobilise ambitious girls to move upwards into a sophisticated social class. Mothers in various cultures induce daughters to undergo specific painful processes for enhanced physical features. For instance, the forceful piecing of ears, walking in high heeled shoes, and plucking natural hairs are standard practices. Girls have absolutely no leverage but to accept the enforced cultural standards. However, girls retain family values and are supposed to be kind and respectful. The last few decades have seen a massive change in their perception of obedience to parents or husbands. They elatedly emulate modern girls' discernment of independence and making an endeavour to acquire equality and fighting for women's rights. They still need to learn how to keep their cool while expressing emotions with gestures and the ability to restraint impulses.

Light skin colour has long been a passion for the girls who use cosmetics to brighten their skin. In Roman times, ladies secured face whiteners made of ceruse- a lead compound that is applied to the faces and necks to attain a pale appearance. However, skin lightening cosmetics do more harm than good and carry numerous health-related complications. These creams contain hydroquinone and mercury that cause neurological damage to the skin. We can minimise neural impairment to the tender physical membrane by rendering health warnings to naïve teenage girls. Brown skin colour is traditionally associated with the labour and agricultural communities who consciously toil in the penetrating heat of the sun for an infinite number of hours every day. In the last century, tanning bodies of European ladies became a sign of stunning beauty and good health. Girls have been using lotions, sprays, and creams on their faces and bodies for the acquisition of artificial tan. Frequenting tanning salons or spending time under the sun at popular beach resorts makes young girls vulnerable to suffering medical conditions such as body dysmorphic disorder. Among girls, tanning has become an addiction as well as fashion emulating film actresses and celebrities

The use of products and creams to enhance appearance and complexion are considered revitalisation and euphoria for appearing exceedingly prettier, profoundly attractive, and intensely acceptable in a glamorous and fashionable world. The female desire to use beautifying products is one of the dominant reasons that enables multinational giants to accrue huge profits through the development and production of mascaras, blushes, lipsticks, and eagerly sought cosmetics. The annual female beauty contests in countless countries worldwide are publicity campaigns for commercial gains and trendy promotions.

Likewise, facial hair growth is a visible sign of uneasiness for any woman. Habitually, most girls resort to actively removing the unwanted hair by any practically sustainable procedures, whether such techniques could be waxing or threading. The entwining is common in many cultures, which involves the hair removal expert delicately holding one end of the cotton thread in her mouth and keeps the facial hair between the cord, which wounds around the beautician's fingers like a loop. The yarn is looped around a few hair chutes, and then the strands are instantly removed with abrupt actions. Beauty parlour staff also apply electrolysis method to electronically obliterate unsolicited hair on any part of the ladies' bodies. Young girls seek maximum attractiveness either by dying hair blond, golden or purple and styling them into curls. Physical grooming has been the main focus of the female ideal. In the Middle East, women had long been using walnut extract, henna, and camomile to give a brighter look and mesmerising shine.

In the showbiz, blonde hair of Brigette Bardot, Jean Harlow was trendy among girls of that generation, and it had become a beauty trend worldwide. However, medical experts and beauty clinicians have questioned the safety of hair dyes. Patlak (1993) has raised serious health concerns since most peroxides are derived from petroleum sources, says Sherrow (2001). The female body is heavily mediated by culture and expresses the social pressure brought on to bear on it. The female body is a biological fact. (Keywood, 2000, p.320) and a signifier of volatility and fluidity but also inextricably associated with the bodily secretions of female reproduction. Beautification and power of appearance enable girls to invent themselves and their bodies wearing designer branded dresses and tantalising outfits. Female attractiveness has four dimensions: adherence to cultural fashion and beauty, the satisfaction of others' needs, acquisition of male attraction, and performance of family skills. Her inner beauty lies in upholding beliefs and values, showing wisdom and becoming self-confident, remaining elegant and graceful in a multicultural world. Females should defy the beauty myth traditionally promoted by the media and society, which is unrealistic and difficult to emulate.

The girls should believe in themselves rather than attempting to imitate other girls. Utopian beauty ideals create bitterness and antipathy among adolescents who must stop feeling dissatisfied about their biological, physical structure and visible complexion and need not be trapped by the beauty backlash, which repudiates the diversity of natural attractiveness and desirability. There is a common consensus among researchers that no definition can capture the beauty in wholeness based on its variation within various cultures and societies across the globe. The real beauty dwells deep inside your heart and soul rather than apparent countenance and manifestations.

Facial Descriptions and Images (POEM)

Restrain your smile, do not throw
Live and learn as you grow

Horizontal wrinkles on your forehead
As your eyes open wide instead

Jaws drop and show your lips
Here are suggested beauty tips

When upper teeth become revealed
Hidden smiles are no longer concealed

Sign of familiarity, the person one knows
A Frisky nod that purposefully shows

Emotions exhibit indications on the face
A rational eye can perceive the grace

Facial Expressions are constrained
When the feelings are restrained

Some find it difficult to conceal
You can imagine how they feel

Emotional features give it away
Facial cues have plenty to say

Eyebrows motion, raising and dropping
Quick movement in flashing and floating

Affection, fondness, and infatuation
Emotions vary in every situation

Facial expressions do tell the tale
Positive or negative; however, they prevail

[Composed by Dr Nazir Ahmad,
May 17, 2021/ Shawwal 5, 1442 Hijra, Monday]

CHAPTER VI - EMOTIONAL AFFECTION AND COMPASSION

In social relations, we frequently are much concerned about the physical comfort of the individual. If the person feels grievously painful, we demonstrate a sympathetic attitude, offer support, and, if injured in an accident, call the ambulance to arrange for the hospital. As Hume (1742) describes, 'natural sympathy produces a corresponding feeling in human beings, confirmed by Adam Smith (1790: 10, 12) 'our fellow feeling with passion' on account of the incident. Naturally, emotion reflects the innate quality of human sympathy that enables us to recognise the persons' vulnerability and suffering. The interface's emotional power fluctuates depending on the touching chumminess with the individual involved in the accident. We have no kinship or lineage with friends, colleagues, or peers, but our emotional nearness and lovingness bring us closer as they often give our lives direction and a gratifying sense of purpose. Feelings play a vital part in an emotional response to a tragic situation or an unpleasant experience. If a person is accused of wrongdoing and then cleared, that makes the individual angry, frustrated, and unforgiving. Instead of vindictiveness, one should review the feelings of resentment, increase self-awareness, and show the calmness and move forward. Hidden emotions in certain situations remain unknown because we do not always smile due to exhilaration but owing to intense grief. We can watch people laughing aloud in distress and trepidation. Obvious observation of undisclosed smiles and laughter would do little to sense how the person is feeling. The mental powers, thoughtfulness, and profound inspection of facial expression would present a vivid picture of other's emotions. Once we comprehend the emotional state of an individual based on foresight and sagacity, we may exhibit compassion with sympathetic facial gestures and kind words. Feelings are an integral part of self-consciousness. Any unexpected incident evokes our emotions; sharing them with chums instigates a moving reaction. Cracking a funny joke in a social gathering is highly likely to exhibit positive feedback invoking amusement and entertainment.

On the contrary, the situation would be reversed at the display of an intimidating anecdote or whopper, causing awkwardness and displeasure. In both instances, facial expressions convey the emotional response, i.e., exhilaration at the first joke but annoyance at the nerve-racking fabricated tale. We learn to read faces and facial expressions through experiences, social involvements, and social interactions. Salovey and Mayer (1990, p.189) state that "the ability to monitor one's own and others' feelings and emotions to discriminate among them, and to use this information to guide one's thinking and actions" would promote and strengthen emotional control.

Emotional Management

Self-awareness is a substance and a foundation for kids to simultaneously ascertain their feelings and establish endurance-led strategies to deal with moods and thoughts. The new-born infants' uncontainable crying grows into the 3-year-old's aptitudes and seeks comfort from parents. Growth of emotion parameter is multidimensional, building on embryonic dimensions for self-control arising from brain mellowing, intangible progression, and communal contacts. Teachers and parents have an indelible psychosocial influence on children's emotional management. When a teacher begins a formal lesson and usually asks pupils to keep quiet and concentrate on learning, they pay heed and stop talking. It has an impact on their personality development and temperament.

Pre-school infants rely entirely on mothers to learn self-control, whereas school-going children have increased exposure with peers and teachers. When toddlers get upset for being denied a favourite toy or ice-cream, they are unable to control emotions and may cry or grumble. Mums explain the reasons for denial at a particular time of the day, and they begin to understand that desire is not always instantly fulfilled. It teaches them self-restraint, emotional control, and patience. The school-going kids learn to get up early in the morning, brush teeth, wash hands and face, change clothes, wear socks and shoes, prepare the school bag, put the books in it which might be overdue to avoid the library fine, and leave in time to mark attendance. Likewise, children at the weekends, some learn to ride a bicycle, bake cookies, help mum in the kitchen for washing pots and pans, and then read books, make drawings, and paint. Both self-control and emotional management begin between 3 to 4 years of age when they learn to manage impulses and control their desires and yearnings for toys, video games, and food. Managing emotions need parental help so that the kids slowly develop their self-control capabilities. Most of all, mothers must not feel frustrated, angry, and impatient. Of course, kids' demands are not justified and sometimes unreasonable to be accepted or supported. The children slowly begin to feel and think about the non-fulfilment of their needs. The mother should give her kid the words to describe his/her feelings, which is a preliminary step towards helping and assisting in the management of emotions.

There are a large number of activity-oriented games that necessitate impulse control for children who might feel irritated while playing. They have to stop or continue playing to make them think about why to end the activity that caused annoyance and infuriation abruptly. Emotional control is guidance to overcome frustration and prevent displeasure for innocent adolescents. Children should repel highly personal responses to upsetting provocations and calm down whenever they feel upset. Scientific evidence suggests that ill-treatment of infants have an insightful effect on the development of rational power, affecting the progression of neuroendocrine, cognitive, and interactive systems. In early childhood, any unpleasant, distressing episode leaves a lasting impact on neuro-biological systems giving rise to stress and nervousness symptoms. It mainly impacts the hypothalamic-pituitary-adrenal axis, which is one of the body's central strain response systems.

Infant neglect occurs in complicated social and interpersonal settings such as social deprivation, a derelict locality with high unemployment, lowly community, lack of social support setup, modest lodging conditions, and meagre access to social welfare. Benoit et al. (2008, p.2) proclaim that increasingly little girls sustain emotional mistreatment and physical abuse, whereas little boys encounter neglect and inattention. Physical abuse evolves hitting, pushing, shaking, slapping, and spanking and harsh treatment relates to striking infants with a belt and stick. All such painful procedures are stressful experiences for kids to remember the agony of emotional scars. Emotional negligence is the failure to supervise exposure to non-intimate violence, inadequate nutrition, scant clothing, and unhygienic living conditions. An infant might have witnessed a violent father shouting at his/her mum, heard the hitting sound from the adjacent room in the house, seen mum's blue eyes, broken bones, and bruises on her neck and face. Such emotional innocent observation leaves negative dynamic marks on the innocuous mind of a child who has not developed personal awareness of unpleasant incidents. The infants' victimised mum has impressed upon the naïve mind an impression of her helplessness and insecurity. As the child grows with improved emotional self-awareness and begins to recall the episodes of distress witnessed at home, he/she fathom how disturbing the past has been?

183

In later life, the children sometimes react to stressful events according to past experiences. They have difficulty with focusing on and completing academic tasks, planning, and processing information. They lack curiosity, thrust for knowledge, and have flawed moral reasoning. They find it difficult to attune to others' emotional conditions, leaving them sequestered and socially isolated.

Infants need a safe environment because exposure to unsafe situations and stressful settings causes emotional distress. Lieberman and Van Horn (2000, p.11) have worked on child-parent psychotherapy for young children. These kids faced exposure to family violence in a relationship-based treatment model, which includes the premise that 'child-caregiver attachment relationship is of paramount importance as the main planner of children's response to danger and safety within the first five years of life. Emotional and interactive problems in young children need proper attention within the context of the child's primary attachment relationships. During the five years of life, risk factors operate within the context of transactions between the child and the child's ecological environment, e.g., family, surroundings, and community. Interpersonal violence is a traumatic stressor that has specific adverse effects on those who witness or experience it.'

Dr Matthew Rouse, a Clinical Psychologist, comments that some kids are instantaneous- have a vast, healthy reaction, and they cannot inhibit that comportment. Dr Rouse observes emotional control concerns as a permutation of temperament and learned conduct because kids' self-control is temper and personality-based. When parents give in to their demands and outbursts, they take longer to develop self-control. Self-restraint is a skill that children can practice through observation and interaction with family members. The parents should either confront or completely circumvent delicate mischievous situations but handle each incident with a supportive framework and understanding. Let the kids relax, take a break, and divert attention from an activity that frustrates and disturbs them. If they do well, shower praise, encourage and acknowledge good work with a treat or reward. Mother may take her child for a walk in the park, listen attentively, and respond positively to build a trusting relationship. Such an outdoor activity will make them reflect and be thoughtful, enabling them to control impulses and become capable of regulating their emotions in different settings. They can set goals and have the motivation to achieve them without distraction. They learn to pause before reacting and think before answering any questions. They ascertain to track their progress, meeting deadlines for homework, projects, and school assignments. Self-emotion management builds the habit of prioritising expectancies, accomplishing targets, and organizing time obligations.

Parents should try to avoid situations in which children might experience negative emotions such as walking in the dark alleyways or the deep narrow tunnels and swimming in the shallow waters on the sea resorts. Instead, participate in jubilant and hilarious activities that make them feel thrilled and seek an experience that will make them feel relaxed, comfortable, and calm. Inspire youth to think before saying a word or reacting with tranquillity, calmness, and serenity. A thoughtful child is emotionally stable, which shows their focused concentration on subjects studied or tasks performed and goals accomplished. Feelings stem from touching mother with affection, a friend with excitement, peer with joy, and listening to soothing music that enlightens the soul and touches the heart. Concerning feelings, I have recently browsed the book' Way to the peaceful warrior' by Dan Millman (special edition, September 2000), who has beautifully described emotions as the weather patterns of the mind. These configurations can be manipulated through our thoughts, through the practice of observation, and by persistently scrutinising our feelings. It is a simple mental exercise by questioning yourself what are you feeling, and more importantly, why are you feeling that Way?

The direction of our thoughts can be modified to feel differently about a specific event or derive different outcomes of the same game. Our thoughts instigate enjoyment beyond our expectations as we experience an emotional delight. Our emotions and perceptions are interconnected. If a youth shows self-importance and behaves in a certain way that indicates a feeling of superiority and ego talking, he/she is more likely to hurt others. In such settings, ego stands in the form of demonstrating self-control. It is a clear indication of the lack of emotional self-control due to the habit of insolence and bold attitude towards others. Such audacity and defiance within social circles are not appreciated. Some youngsters complain and blame others for almost everything but hardly accept fault or concede personal mistakes. The best prescription is silence and meditation for 10 to 15 minutes every day, sitting quietly in a remote corner of the house and reflecting upon one's actions, retorts, and reactions that caused obnoxiousness and unpleasantness during interaction with others. This exercise will promote self-control leading to restraint in emotional expression. Inevitably cognitive self-awareness focuses on our thoughts and ideas, but emotional self-awareness affects our feelings. Emotional competencies relate to managing our emotions and managing our relations with others. We use our instinct and common sense to guess other's emotions and act accordingly.

Smiles Go Extra Miles (POEM)

Smile and laughter day and night
Nothing to ever cause you a fright

Dampens anxiety, improves your mood
Young and old, infant or brood

Do not ever feel depressed
Unhappy, miserable, joy suppressed

It is a precious asset, like your knowledge
You earnestly learnt at school and college

Wisdom and smile, nobody can steal
Keep it safe, comfortable you will feel

Dispense it more, and more it shall grow
Your real self profusely it will shows

A Smile is our unique treasure
Costs nothing but gives pleasure

In times of stress and indeed gloom
Offers us solace like a fresh bloom

If you are upset or considerably sad
Enlightens feelings, makes you glad

A Smile is a wonderful timely infection
Spread it widely without inspection

Display your emotions and reflection
Distribute it lavishly without selection

Transmit it justly and explore connections
Acts as a mirror of your real perception

Confidence shines through; each smile
An Irresistible grin with the expected style

It comprises of natural magnet power
Broadcasting radiance, thriving like a flower

Cheeks raised, beaming from ear to ear
Dimples do become profoundly clear

The cheerful pretence for a lovely face
Glimmering eyes with fabulous grace

Glorious are those who wear it every day
A Smile is a response to whatever they say

Beaming smile glows and shines
Touches emotions beyond the spine

You can see through many fake smiles
Having Looked deep into the eyes

Peeking eyes might hide, human sensations
Arch maws, caring smiles reveal venerations

Distribute plentifully this distinctive treasure
Disseminate this vibrant asset with great pleasure

[Composed by Dr Nazir Ahmad
August 13, 2021/ Muharram 4, 1443, Friday]

Smile originates in our sensual strips when a gaze meets a welcoming look. It transmits an affable memo to our brain, ear gathers an assumed word electrifying the left frontal, temporal region, and then blushing to the exterior of the face stirring both muscles into a movement of the lips. Five facial muscles generate upward move of the lip corners, "e.g., zygomatic major, zygomatic minor, levator anguli, oris, buccinator, and risorius." The significant zygomatic heave our lips upward whereas the orbicularis oculi cuddle the outside curves into the form of a crow's foot, revealing a smile, commonly known as 'Duchenne Smile. A famous Anatomist proclaimed in 1862, in his work 'Mechanism de la Physionomie Humaine' that zygomatic major can be transformed into action. Still, incredibly sweet emotions of the soul influence the orbicularis oculi to contract. The unpretentious smiles fall into the sphere of a gentle soul. Smile mimicry is a form of facial expression, a propensity to imitate and harmonise the movements and attitudes with the other individual. Resultantly, emotional convergence mimics the perceived feedback. If you meet a person who habitually smiles relentlessly, it can make you smile as well. It is not unusual to imitate the smile of a close friend, partner, or a college fellow on account of frequent interactions and personal interfaces that occur regularly.

Feedback smiles are considered social indicators and often demonstrate approachability, openness, and social frankness. Such a smile is a touchstone for two individuals to continue conversation and exchange of communication.

It acts as a relational incentive for giving and receiving pleasure without crossing the ethical boundaries. Researchers provide scientific proof that smiles duration is between 2.785 to 3.682 seconds. Dutch smiles are commonly called low variance brief smiles lasting 3,32 seconds and even as short as 2,36 seconds. Also, feedback smiles are produced by the Zygomatic major. The play smiles that occur at schools during playtime activities are relatively much longer, exceeding four seconds.

In 1979, Frances held a 5-minute assembly for guests where they were interconnected face-to-face with one another. The dimension disclosed that the participants smiled for 35.20 seconds, which was the total mean time per person. Frances noticed that, on average, each person laughed 3.77 times during the complete session. Smile is an expression of emotion experienced and felt, whether happiness or friendliness, declares Kraut and Johnson (1979).

Smiles are a perfect fit for many occasions ranging from meeting a former schoolmate or a college friend. (Landis, 1924). Although most smiles are enjoyable and make you feel beautiful, some laughs, say Keltner (1995) is embarrassing and excruciating that can cause disappointment and unease.

Whenever an individual experienced positive emotion, a smile naturally followed, albeit smile falls into several types depending on the situation that prompted it. For instance, affiliative smiles accelerate social bonding through politeness and affability, pleasantness, and amiability. Dominant smiles elicit the impression of a superiority complex in people of wealth and power. Reward smiles are exposed during sensual and social relationships and then amplified by gratifying ambiences. Magdalena Rychlowska, Cardiff University, Jack, Garrod, and Schyns of University of Glasgow, Martin, and Niedenthal from the University of Wisconsin, Madison co-jointly conducted various studies in their respective field of psychology to uncover different smile types, functions, and effects. One of the U.S-based tasks involved 107 white Caucasian students, out of which 71 were female. They were shown many animated facial expressions and then asked to select one particular type of smile out of three displaced. Most students selected smiles with high accuracy but lower detection sensitivity for an affiliative smile. In a second experiment, 62 students, 41 females, took part in observing how smiles convey different social messages, e.g., positive feelings and social connectedness. For example, a reward smile involves eyebrow flashes, sharp Lip puller, affiliative smile entailed Lip Pressor, and dominance smiles comprised unilateral Lip Corner Puller from right to left. However, the reward smiles increase sensory input and feelings of pleasure. Smile physiognomies include strength, proportion, and duration. Whether a person truly feels happy depends on the observer and how he/she perceives it. If we ask a friend to drink a fresh and sweet orange juice and concurrently watch the facial expression to detect the smile's nature, it is followed by offering a grapefruit juice to another friend and observing the face. We can notice that the one who drank sweet juice would simply display a pleasant smile, but the one who sipped sour and bitter grapefruit juice is unlikely to smile.

Smiles Meanings and Functions

Smile in standard interfaces is ubiquitous as it begins from infancy, says Washburn (1929) and Wolff (1963). The clear difference between two distinct smiles is the opening of the mouth and muscle movements of eyes. (Brannigan and Humphries, 1972). Marc Mehu and Dunbar (2008b, p.337) highlight the smile-oriented social interaction and the resultant bonding formation, leading to specific relationships. Argyle (1988, p.214) states that repeated and extensive body contacts during relaxed conversations replicate closeness between two persons. One can observe such socially cherished connections from a distance as both individuals exchange smiles and grins, giggles, and sneers. Their faces would naturally display laughs and cheers.

Symmetrical smiles tend to epitomise enjoyment signals genuinely and incarnate pleasurable patterns. It shows in your discernments and real emotions because the smile of gratification involves the intuitive movement of the muscles, which orbit the eyes. A smile is contagious since we can comprehend the inherent emotional condition of the person flaunting a smile. Its quality of communicability makes the smile readable for the eyewitness to extricate the meaning behind the smile validly. In some cases, detection of the connotation of a particular smile appears cumbersome partly due to deception scenarios that may warrant analytical evaluation to uncover the impending intention of the smiler. Scientifically, Dr Niedenthal studied a sizeable number of brain scans to explore the intrinsic source of many smiles and accentuated methodically conceived observations. Smiles are the' visible part of an intimate melding between two minds. Sometimes the lips open to reveal teeth and other times stay closed'. In certain instances, eyes crinkle, and the cheeks rise with a smile. Also, the dimple in the cheeks becomes more visible with a refreshing smile experienced personally by the present writer who bears a deep dimple in his chin. As muscles of the face pose a specific gesture or gesticulation and the smiling individual locks eyes with another person, the recipient unconsciously mimics a smile. In turn, this gracious smile produces a brain activity called the orbitofrontal cortex. This activity principally occurs if we have already established an intimate relationship with another person. Parents frequently experience it in every household with newly born babies. The orbitofrontal cortex becomes active when the mother watches her baby smile. Any family with two or more small kids finds that their children exhibit unprompted natural smiles, which correspond to parental affection, fondness, and warmth. It is not surprising that the infants can bestow facial expressions with great exactness and always respond to a parental smile with an innocent smile.

Infants unimpeded and unrestrained by common rubrics engage in face-to-face interfaces with their mothers. In the first six months, toddlers express more standard smiling when staring directly at their mother's face. They recognise generic smiling when their mothers are smiling, although they may not be looking straight at their mothers. When kids smile, the muscles around the eyes contract, raising the cheeks high, thereby depicting a pleasant smile. Ten months old, infants produce smiles that lift their cheeks when the smiling mothers affectionately pick them up for a cuddle. Their smiles become open-mouthed at the age of 12 to 18 months. According to Dickson et al. (1997), the cheek-raise open-mouth smiling predominates during physical play. Infant gazing at mothers is an archetypal social action, and mother smiling is a striking social signal for the innocent babies. As the children grow up, so are the smiling patterns and social conduct visible in their communication with school peers and classmates. Young girls' smiling faces make them appealing and attractive in social circles, boost mood, and even the immune system. Smile is an indispensable treasure similar to knowledge and wisdom that cannot be imitated, replicated, or borrowed.

Ron Guttman, a Professor of Psychology at the University of California, Berkeley, claims in his book "The Untapped Power of smile" that smiling inspired him tremendously. It took him on a journey that introduced him neuroscience, anthropology, sociology, and psychology. Through research and investigation, he discovered the untapped power of smile by live experiments related to university students' wellbeing and academic success. He declared that over 30 per cent of us smile more than five to twenty times a day, but children dish out smile around 400 times per day. Ding and Jersild (1931), while engaged with the Teachers College of Columbia University, New York, made an interesting observational study of infants to discover their smiling and laughing patterns. It was an observational record of 59 children aged two to five years of Chinese origin at the kindergarten and nurseries in Chinatown, New York City. They carried on observing the kids for several months and made notes. Each child was kept for no less than four hours as they noted the occasions which gave rise to smiling and laughing among male and female children. Interestingly, the little girls smiled more than the boys, whereas the boys laughed more than the girls.

Smiles and Laughter Learning Tools

Smiley faces spread smiles, and laughing lecturers draw laughter into the class to dissipate boredom, squandering tediousness, and untangling complex topics. Academic learning precipitates seriousness for the achievement of set goals in the light of student learning capacities, cultural cues, and linguistic hues. Knowledge diffusion without a certain degree of hilarity and professor-student interaction without some form of social bonding and intellectual openness would not accomplish desired sequels. Different cultures have different standards of student-teacher relations in educational settings. Online remote knowledge delivery mechanism has a colossal impact on traditional face-to-face classroom chalk and talks about teaching practices. As yet, formal school, college, and university classroom environment will not vanish overnight. Just as printed books, literary fiction and non-fiction, popular saucy magazines, and children's literature in published form have not receded. Instantaneous disappearance of the classroom and the obliteration of the printed word would not transpire in the foreseeable future. How do we continue to make formal education, pleasant experience for the youth, enabling them to build a better future for future generations?

Ethnographic Studies

The present writer conducted an observational study of Arab university students' laughing and smiling habits during and after formal lectures at King Abdul Aziz University, Jeddah, Saudi Arabia. In fifteen years of teaching assignment, I availed the opportunity of regularly observing my five different classes of 25 to thirty students over a long period and continued to make notes in the diary. I was interested in recording their laughing intensity (medium, loud, or very loud), duration of chuckling, occasions of giggling, incidents of tittering, and jolliness, especially at the end of lectures. I had experienced the British cultural environment in which I studied and worked closely for 12 years with English, Scottish, Welsh, and Irish colleagues and friends. The Saudi culture varied considerably in many aspects from European settings. Their habits, traditions, lifestyles, and conventions differed substantially from the English people's openness, candidness, social freedom, and autonomy. Informal teacher-learner exposure, friendly communication, and open dialogue were regular in British institutes of higher education. While teaching the

User Education course to students at Southwark London, I had reservations about cracking jokes, lest it might hurt one of my students who belonged to multicultural and multi-ethnic upbringings. Over ninety per cent were white British pupils who could better understand and enjoy light retorts.

I was certainly aware that laughter improves the brain's dopamine system, stimulating students' incentive and recollection, particularly enlivening educational attentiveness. This concentration results in better absorption of the subject matter. My task of bringing joy into the lecture hall was less challenging in an all Arabic speaking Arabian culture. I had developed bonding and a sense of belonging within each new cohort at the beginning of each semester. Before joining King Abdul Aziz University, Jeddah, Saudi Arabia, I had a couple of years' experience at King Faisal University Dammam, in my stride. I knew the language and cultural compassions and harnessed laughter's constructive impact to augment pleasantness in my classroom. Reading aloud from a pre-typed lecture was utterly dull and speaking harshly unacceptable. The students did not feel comfortable with some professors displaying rudeness and showing impoliteness. The well-prepared lecture notes were a prerequisite to maintaining pleasantness and gaining student confidence.

In contrast, short episodes generating smiles or laughter made the talks amusing for the learner, eliminating chances of wearisomeness. I have intermittently overcome in-class distractions through light social puns, rejuvenating their devotion to the topic under discussion. Knowledge co-construction was one of the captivating strategies repeatedly applied in the postgraduate classes, making them an integral part of the learning process.

While observing engineering students at King Faisal University Dammam in 1978, I discovered the causes of laughter through an experiment. John Sweitzer and I, in cooperation with the media laboratory, showed students clips of Jack Lemon's movies "It Should Happen To You" (1954), and "Some Like It Hot" (1959). A group of students from the Faculty of Architecture and Planning viewed funny clips with considerable interest. John and I sat beside them to record their emotions and incidents of laughter during the viewing of two rib-tickling films. The classical sound was emitted, triggering students' emotions of thrill and enchantment with the witty facial expressions of Jack Lemon, making the whole experience delightful. I heard the tittering sound of laughter, three of them giggled hysterically; others chortled with a relatively low volume of sound. Their knowledge of understanding and speaking the English language was excellent. Sometimes the laughter was a kind of crackle rather than a chuckle, displaying a sense of hilarity, relaxation, and leisure. After viewing, they remained seated in the library, still laughing and joking, exchanging personal views about the clips. Their loud voice was a mere reflection of cultural upbringing and freestyle communication behaviours.

I have opted for observational research to gain qualitative insight based on my classroom presence during formal lectures and face-to-face interaction in my departmental office. However, such findings are difficult to measure by statistical evidence. I gathered information about students during my attachment with Southwark College, London, and teaching at King Abdul Aziz University, Jeddah, Saudi Arabia. I closely watched their behaviour, social interactions, and emotions. I observed the moods, tempers, and anger in a natural environment. It is evident that almost all youngsters at college or university share the universal perception of freedom, independence, and autonomy, but despise restraints, intimacy ceilings, and ideological chains.

My tenure as Professor at King Abdul Aziz University Jeddah, Saudi Arabia, enabled me to build viable strategies for imparting knowledge to both Master's degrees (male and female) and Bachelor's degree students. The Faculty of Arts and Humanities comprised Departments of Psychology, Sociology, English Literature, History, Geography, Media Studies, and Information Management as well as Arabic Literature and Islamic Studies. Mostly the students of psychology, sociology, and media studies enrolled in my elective courses, English terminologies, audio-visual resources, and information retrieval. In the process of knowledge co-construction, I developed my comprehension of human psychology and adolescents' social relations, Arab culture, and family affairs.

Cashin (1985) once asserted that a certain amount of 'humour or personal anecdotes enhances a lecture. Equally confirmed Zhang (2005, 113), in her remarkable research results that humour might enhance students' affective learning, create an enjoyable classroom atmosphere, lessen students' anxiety, increase the usefulness and liking for the instructor and the course and facilitate students' willingness to participate in the classroom. Sigmund Freud (1905) presented the relief theory in which he stated that laughter acts as a safety valve to release pent-up tensions and a means of releasing suppressed thoughts. According to his theory, laughter is a homeostatic mechanism that reduces psychological pressure. All laugh-producing situations are pleasurable because they save psychic energy.

Most of the students aged 18 to 26 were native Saudis, but a few came from Yemen, Syria, Jordan, and Palestine but none from non-Arab countries. In general, Arab youngsters are open-minded, easy-going, pleasant, and amiable in their outlook, attitudes, and perceptions. They smile frequently, laugh profusely, giggle copiously, cackle abundantly, and converse recurrently, particularly after the end of their lectures. In the formal lecture halls, they behave differently, show manners, appear sober, and respond positively and respectfully to the professors. All are not entirely attentive and focused on their studies; some represent frustration and dispiritedness for several reasons. This apathy is due to family matters and social norms imposed by inflexible tribal parents who allow little freedom for their adolescents to socialise and form relationships. In the course of lessons, at least fifty per cent of Saudi boys actively ask questions and engage in meaningful conversation. Still, a small minority tends to remain disengaged, and an odd few remain partly detached. The Yemeni and Palestinian students habitually possess unpretentious temperament and display natural smiles. Jordanian boys exhibit self-effacing smiles and inadvertently stay focused during seminars with an active academic contribution that stems from their desire to learn and enhance knowledge. Although many of my students hailed from prosperous backgrounds enjoying affluence and abundance, the smile of dominance is rarely detected, but affiliative smiles are widespread. Boys coming from less well-off families appear to stretch their lips and do not make teeth visible to friends and acquaintances. I have personally watched suppressed smiles in Palestinian students who repeatedly demonstrate tight-lipped smiles, rarely opening their mouths.

On the contrary, middle-class Saudi university students intermingle with each other pretty freely, show real humour and happiness, sometimes without baring teeth. In some instances, their cheeks are enlightened, eyes glowing, and deep dimples showing. Perceptible is their smiling and laughing habits at the university canteens and dining halls where they spontaneously crack jokes and display cheerfulness and rigorous smile euphoria. Rapture is the result of a block clapping another mate on the back with sparkling eyes and pumping arms giving rise to laughter. While having dinner, I have heard a loud sound of laughter when one student is telling hilarious cultural jokes that makes others slapping thighs, clapping hands, and moving heads. This thigh spanking continues for a few moments escalating into the realms of guffaw and horselaugh. The same practices prevail at canteens and cafeterias within the university premises in-between lesson breaks and lunch intervals.

I have also noticed students teasing each other, physically nudging with shoulders and elbows. Arms swinging while walking, talking, and smiling are not uncommon cultural rehearses in the Arab world. Academically high-achieving students tend to smile more than engaging in sudden bouts of laughter, and customarily, do not involve in sexual touching, cognitive mocking, and mischievous taunting. Their laughter sounds exhibit excitement and pleasure, sometimes like roars, thunders, and psycho screams, loud and high pitched. Once outside the faculty building, they would feel the emotion of happiness and delight by grabbing one of their classmates and enquiring about the car episode that occurred the night before when he was accidentally spotted by a friend in an awkward position. He would be grouped the next morning and faced teasing and taunting until he admitted the manifestation and told them the truth. This kind of confession would inspire the emotion of embarrassment but warning others around him. The students would laugh and joke in and out of the class, accompanied by a high-pitched voice. The volume of laughter in Arab youth is customarily high-pitched and sporadic. When they laugh, the scientifically measured laugh range 60-65 dB is not followed because their laughter sound is far higher, probably 75dB. Moreover, they scream or give grunting roar like a lion, baritone pitch like a leopard, and produce waterfall burble sounds. On the whole, they are sincere in their outlooks, joyful in their attitudes, pleasant in etiquettes, and hospitable in welcoming foreigners.

A certain amount of quality satire is necessary to generate students' interest in acute studies. Monotonous creeps into the classroom unannounced, and wearisomeness appear on the faces after attending three or four consecutive lectures. Sequential lessons without a break are trying, taxing, and tiresome for all students. If I was delivering the last lecture of the day, the task of retaining their attention became challenging. My primary objective of bringing some hilarity into lessons was to a) Improve student focus, b) Keep them on their toes, c) Rejuvenate attention, d) Invigorate learning, e) Minimise sameness., f) Sustain social cohesion. Students in the morning lectures appeared fresh, dynamic, and full of energy, but dreariness was apparent in the mid-day and afternoon lessons. My self-prepared handouts delivered at the end of each lecture acted as backup learning aids profoundly admired by the students who could not always absorb and memorise all components of the tedious topic. Once I was teaching a theme based on chapter five of my book, which was published in London by Routledge & Kegan Paul in 1985. I asked my students whether anyone had already read it.

One student nodded and said, "but I found it unexciting because it did not include any comic." Dear young man, I replied, "I do not write side-splitting books, "which you might have seen in the book store. He confessed, Sir! I hate book shops. Then What are you doing here in the classroom, young man? My fiancé would refuse to marry me if I failed, said the boy. This brief altercation was amusing for other students who laughed as I watched with a soft smile.

The use of audio-visual resources in education was an exciting subject involving the preparation of slides and transparencies in our Multi-Media Laboratory. Every student in a class of twenty-five could not grasp the stuff discussed in a one hour lecture. I supplemented my talks with transparencies and slides to illustrate the notable arguments. One student seemed apathetic, yawning, and twitching his fingers. Why are you so tired and dreamy? I questioned ! Sir, I feel peckish, got up late, had no time for breakfast, and rushed to the university to evade absence. I accessed my bag, retrieved a homemade fresh sandwich, and passed on to him. Suddenly, another student asked for a soft drink, which I had, and I gave him as well. The third student pulled a packet of crisp out of his pocket and begun to eat. Unspoken permission for them to relax, laugh, and enjoy for a few minutes, warmed the atmosphere for purposeful instructions and training. These emotionally pleasing simple acts brought smiles on their faces, eradicating mental diversion, and increasing perceptual attentiveness in my class. For effective delivery of subject contents, student alertness and concentration were my top priority. I warmly welcomed their diverse amusing reactions to my light puns that helped built rapport and enhanced intellectual engagement, especially with Master's degree students. Naturally, I stayed connected, academically supportive, and commonly available in the department throughout the working day. Approachability without restraint had a promising impact on my students who felt reassured to see me and seek guidance. If I were still in the classroom, I would amusingly hear their colourful stories, laughter, sounds of enormous variety such as the cracking sound of a boiling electric kettle, babbles and chatters arising from gossips. They felt bonded through humour and playful activities.

Most importantly, the last lecture of the day was always testing, visibly fatigue displayed on students' faces. A few remains seated, cracked puns and jests, talked about intimate relationships, discussed movies, football competitions, and forthcoming wedding functions and family or friends' gatherings at sea resort.

Once I was the superintending end of the semester final exam when a student asked for a pen, borrowed mine, but broke the tip and laughed, stating, Sir! I would buy you a new one, but it was a Parker young man; oh! I cannot afford that; giggles and laughs in the hall, show some dignity, and get on with your examination; please, I exclaimed. They listened, calmness restored, and the exam ended well.

Seminars permit cordial interconnection with a limited number of postgraduate students who bring in their completed projects, make presentations, raise issues, ask questions, and intermingle to share knowledge and develop social connections. There is more calmness, frankness, and forthrightness in small study groups and graduate seminars but virtually no formality. I deplore stiffness and correctness and prefer directness and honesty, particularly in educational settings. Both the students and professors have ample chances to discuss, smile, laugh, and learn conjointly.

Seminar rooms were the perfect location for relaxation, slackening, conducting open-dialogue, and even discussing non-academic adventures. My students also talked about their overseas voyages and escapades with simultaneous bursts of laughter. Although I had devised my vital teaching strategies, learned the art of breaking the ice, and presenting lecture contents with powerful voice and hilarity, I was immersed in their jesting exploits, encouraging them to share experiences. Sometimes my classroom momentarily erupted into laughter when I uttered a light-hearted joke for promoting a spirit of casualness to diminish the typical remoteness that had been prevalent in Arab culture.

Light-hearted cheekiness frequently paid off to create intimate learning situations. Entertaining events transmitted either by myself or the students invoked laughter without emotionally hearting anyone. Upbeat witticisms meticulously brought fun into on-going lessons making the learning experience impressively inspirational. Sometimes, I would change the pitch of my voice to awaken a few weary and sighing students sitting right at the back of the class to avoid contact and to remain unnoticed. The beginning of every week unfolded pleasant episodes during professor-student dialogue leading to smiles and laughs. The students exchanged comical words and fabricated all sorts of excuses. I found contrived justifications for not turning in assignments at the appointed date that was grippingly mirthful. After lectures, some like-minded students always stayed, talked, and professed previous weekend experiences to each other in their native tongue, which I completely understood. One would say that he was at Sharm al-Sheikh in Egypt, enjoyed every moment of seaside view, others would talk about meeting his finance at the International shopping mall. At the same time, another would moan about his father's disapproval for his chosen lassie.

Time and again, I continued to test the impact of my gleeful but trivial frolics on the retention and engagement of students. Unambiguous and Concept-specific humour reinforced my notion to activate student pathways and facilitate learning, engross instructions, and expand knowledge. 'Rule of Thumb' was that Upon entering the classroom for every lecture, I greeted students with a generous smile, revealing my dimpled chin and emitting "Sabah al-Khair" Good Morning Boys before commencing roll call and formal conversation. I firmly believed that I was on a sacred mission to impart knowledge and serve the community. The response was vigorously warm and enthusiastically amicable. However, the senior Master's degree students sometimes took advantage of my pleasant and frank manner. In 1996, teaching resumed at the university after the Winter holidays and, also some wealthy students had returned from Europe and the U.S.A. with great exciting stories, fibs, and jokes. A group of three Master's degree students had been spending a couple of weeks in London every year since the 1990s. This friendly trio first watched John Barrowman, a British actor, singer, and comedian performing in Matador at the Queen's Theatre, London in 1991; then as Raoul in The Phantom of the Opera at Her Majestic's Theatre in 1992; as Claudia In Hair at the Old Vic Theatre in 1993; and as Chris in Miss Saigon at the Theatre Royal, Drury Lane, in 1993. The three of them were fascinated by his mesmerising and spellbinding theatrical performances. Yet again in 1996, they visited London, roamed around Piccadilly Circus, Marble Arch, Oxford Street, Tower Bridge, and the Royal Albert Hall, where they watched John Barrowman showed stunning performance "Who Would Ask for Anything More." One of them in my class asked for permission to describe their recent enjoyable London trip. I nodded in affirmative, and he started telling me about their incredible and lovely time in London, which was full of excitement and amusement. While talking about theatrical episodes, he abruptly said, "You look like British celebrity John Barrowman because you have "Ghamazat fi aldhiqn," i.e., a dimple in the chin and "Shaer Bunny Kathif," i.e., dark brown hair. As usual, I simply smiled and reminded them that I was a Professor, unlike John Barrowman, who was indeed a trendy British celebrity. I further researched and noticed that his sister Caole Emily Barrowman was a Professor of English at Alverno College, Milwaukee, Wisconsin. John certainly possessed dimpled chin, a most noticeable defining characteristic. Throughout their studies, the students used to stare at my chin and smile.

It was my usual practice to say funny and silly things to generate laughter and smiles in the classroom. I would elaborate on their numerous cheating practices in the examinations, explaining how foolishly students get caught, but how some of you manage to get away without being detected? A student would probe, if I was aware of all the cheating avenues employed by the students, why did I not catch them? My response was that I was supposed to prevent blatant cheating but ignore devilish, iniquitous eluders, and artful dodgers. However, I had modified exam pattern to eliminate any chance of deceitful practices.

In a frank and open dialogue, I asked them who was your favourite professor and why you did not like some of the faculty members (excluding myself)? They named a few professors perceived as funny, kind-hearted and engaging and making lectures more exciting with anecdotes and real-life examples. Boring professors were considered authoritarian and disciplinarian who hardly smiled or laughed, but crammed too much stuff in a single lecture. The students preferred the teachers who articulated funny jokes and did not jam-packed excessive reading material in one discourse. One of the subjects allocated to me in the syllabus was 'Classification and Cataloguing,' which necessitated innovative teaching of Anglo-American Cataloguing Rules and also, Library of Congress and Dewey Decimal Classification Systems. Both subjects were somewhat tedious, mind-numbing, and weary. It was, therefore, exceedingly pertinent to keep the students attentive and intent while unravelling the concepts and describing intricate cataloguing rules for foreign names and non-print ephemeral materials. I was conscious about dry courses without content-related humour significantly reduced student learning power and retaining command. I had mastered the art of provoking laughter on numerous occasions in the past when my students had felt distracted, tired, and sleepy. The uninteresting topic habitually made them inattentive and unmindful.

In my lecture on various classification systems, I asked the students who devised the Decimal Classification Scheme. A student stood up and said, Sir, I would never invent such an annoying thing, another student spoke, how do we suppose to know about it, Sir if you don't even know yourself. There was a burst of collective laughter as I smiled and felt relieved for the pleasant classroom climate. Likewise, I was pleased to know that some of my students had returned from London after eighteen days of winter break. I enquired about their visit to London and sightseeing activities since I had lived in London for eleven years before joining the university in Jeddah. They told me how much they had enjoyed visiting Madame Tussaud, Art Gallery, Piccadilly Circus, and particularly theatres. I again asked, did you see the British Museum in Russell Square, London, which is not far from Euston Train station. One humorous student said, Sir, we had gone to London to enjoy a live performance of famous comedians and humourists, why should we go to a place giving little pleasure and no excitement except thousands of shelves full of books.

The present writer, while serving Southwark College London for several years, equally observed the personal characteristics, smiling protocols, and laughing manners of English and ethnic minority pupils in the college. Uninterested in learning and gaining formal qualifications, some ethnic minority boys habitually crackled, causing a disturbance in the college library. Thus, serious and sober learners lost focus and complained about the inappropriate persistent loud laughter. Lunch one-hour break was precious for some to study and work on their projects in the library while others walked in the library to enjoy, loudly talk, giggle, and peal without due regard to genuine readers. It was and still would be debatable whether the library should be a knowledge hub to produce scholars, inventors, and professionals, or it should be a playing arena for jolliness and merriness. In those days, I (the present writer) wrote an article entitled. "Problem of Discipline in College Libraries," especially in the cosmopolitan city of London, published in a professional journal, "New Library World," London (October 1975). I highlighted significant factors, family backgrounds, and parental training in terms of disciplining children in domestic settings. I also noticed with considerable satisfaction that the English boys and girls were far less disruptive, more orderly and, better behaved on the college premises. They seldom disturbed other pupils while remained seated in the library, albeit talked, smiled but distracting laughter was hardly the trait of local English, Welsh, Irish or Scottish youngsters. Observation of girls' movements in the same college indicated good behaviour and deep regard for others. I would gladly term it as a voluntary suppressed laughter inferring concern for the academic library atmosphere. Girls talk to each other a lot, smile abundantly, and laugh without raising the voice. In the college dining hall, the girls usually play with their hair, lift the chin to expose their necks, sometimes bite nails and lips. Some of the girls fidget with their earrings, twiddle with neck chains, fiddle with eyelashes, and flutter their eyebrows. Conclusively, English girls are pleasant, well-mannered, refined, and courteous. These girls seldom offend boys but do compete with other girls in looking more attractive, acceptable, and accessible.

Mehu (2011) conducted an observational study of White Caucasians in the U.S.A. in which he selected eighty-four subjects, forty-one male and forty-three female, and categorised them into three age groups. The first group aged 15-25, the second group aged 25 to 35-year-olds and the third group 35-45-year-olds. He secretly observed the subjects in four bars and cafes during regular social interactions. Mehu looked at them at some distance to record firstly, natural smiles, and then deliberate smiles, including false or miserable smiles during social communication. He noticed asymmetric laughs and sudden smiles, focusing on whether the subjects smiled with a closed mouth or open mouth. The other objective was an assessment of the intensity of laughter. The exercise revealed deliberate smiles' positive connection with head nods of boys and girls. Physical intimacy was observed at a distance of up to 20 meters to ensure that men and women do not become conscious of being watched. It was chronicled .that the girls having bodily contact with their male friends exhibited a higher rate of laughter and demonstrated open mouth smiles than the girls who had no physical contact. Another significant observation was that young boys and girls are more inclined to form close social relationships, and they smiled and laughed more frequently during interpersonal communication in social settings. Youngsters naturally feel emotionally close to each other, talk freely, enjoy, and laugh instinctively.

LeeAnne Harker and Dacher Keltner (2001) Psychology professors at the University of California, Berkeley believed that genuine smiles are not sparks of emotion. Landis (1924) had much earlier reported that not all smiles are natural expressions of happiness. Interestingly, William Shakespeare's drama "Hamlet" exhibits a scene in which the actor speaks 'One may smile, and smile, and be a villain' because people display smiles when telling lies.

Predictable perception informs us that even a simple smile or grin can make us feel better in times of despair, misery, and desolation. This acuity reaffirms psychologists' findings in which Professor Coles and his colleagues (2019) from the University of Tennessee at Knoxville combined data from 138 research studies. They tested 11000 participants discovering that facial expressions have a small impact on our feelings and that 'smiling can make people feel happier,' although effects are small and heterogeneous. (Science Daily Online, April 12, 2019).

On the contrary, mesmerising smilers do not always experience pleasing emotions since people do smile for a variety of reasons, sometimes to camouflage sadness, disguise sorrows, normalise information exchange, and at other times merely to influence the delicate situation. Stroked and replicated smiles classically fluctuate in numerous modes such as equilibrium, pace, timing, and harmonisation of muscle instigation. We must have experienced a warm welcome by air hostesses and cabin attendants on aeroplanes, especially in the business class. They greet all passengers with a whole-hearted and caring smile and throughout the journey, several times while handing in warm/cold towels, newspapers, night sleeping suit, or serving drinks, food and dispensing with small gifts. They keep smiling until the plane lands and eventually at the exit a big smile good buy.

Similarly, Stewarts in ships and waitresses in restaurants greet you with a huge smile. In 1978, Tidd and Lochard carried out a study of an affiliative smile and reported in the Bulletin of Psychonomic Sociology. They declared that smiles are not merely for show, but exert an impact on others' behaviour. They observed waitresses in restaurants happily welcoming customers and proclaimed that men gave more extensive tips than females to a smiling waitress. Also, smiling creates leniency and smiling facial expressions are a signal inducing a cooperative move. Moreover, men are highly likely to trust female faces and women to imagine male faces. (Scharlemann et al. 1999, p. 11-12.).People minimise their worries, reduce anxieties, dispel fears, and boost moods with pleasant reflections. It is an admirable feature to keep smiling for emotional wellness, social pleasure, academic engagement, and caring commitments. In an unpredictable world of complex challenges, we raise our spirits through social connections, spiritual beliefs and cheerful dispositions.

CHAPTER VII - LAUGHING MATTERS IN SOCIETY

If laughing is the foundation of joy and relaxation, it matters a lot in routine substances. On the contrary, if a person is emotionally heart, the pain lingers on. It is pertinent to admit that laughing matters, but emotional damage tatters, shattering the physical and psychological peace of mind.

Laughing matters as long as it does not humiliate, despise and demean others. Laughter is a blessing, especially if it brings reprieve and smile on the lips of sisters and brothers. It should not rot, damage, and tatter the feeling of our fathers and mothers. Before discussing why people laugh and the degree, categories, and intensity of laughter, it is quite relevant to describe the nature of laughter based on cultural diversities, geographical location, and environments. How did conquerors ranging from Hannibal, Napoleon Bonaparte, Cyrus the Great, Julius Caesar, Alexander the Great, and then Romans or Byzantines treated their subjects are full of excruciating and tumultuous episodes in the history of the world? Ostensibly, the entertainers always consider the audience's feeling and avoid causing emotional hurt. Their downright light jokes do not target minorities and disabled communities.

Expressive Laughter

The comic kings conspicuously practiced it, such as 'Fabulous Furry Freak Brothers' in the 1960's. An underground comic depicts the procurement and pleasure of frivolous drugs by American youngsters. Gilbert Shelton, the creator, ridicules counterculture, printed in The Rag newspaper, Austin, Texas. He portrayed three fictional characters, Freewheeling Franklin, with waterfall moustache and ponytail; then, Phineas Phreak, a chemistry genius to prepare drugs such as marijuana, and the third funny character were Fat Freddy Freekowtski, an ignorant compulsive eater who takes care of drug dealings and often loses the substance. The comics became so popular that the exhilarating cartoons regularly appeared in journals such as 'High Time,' Rip Off Comix' and 'Playboy' in addition to a well-sought book 'Fred 'n' Heads. The public relished lampooning of upper-class personalities as a grand act of caricature prodigiously. The choice of costumes like cowboy boots and the cowboy hat makes the comic strips enlivening and elating. These stunningly designed images show the social activities of the society in a fun-loving way. The founder of Comics, Gilbert Shelton, had invented catchphrases that are extraordinarily popular today. He once said, "Dope will get you through times of no money better than money will get you through times of no Dope." Literate societies that emphasise literacy and ensure everyone should be capable of reading and writing make use of the knowledge created by satirists, comedians, and wags. Anne Herbert of the Los Angeles Public Library slightly modified this phrase and displayed it inside the library. It reads, 'Books will get you through times of no money better than money will get you through times of no books" Another phrase of Shelton is

218

that "While you are out there smashing the state, don't forget to keep a smile on your lips and a song in your heart." Interestingly, most of their comic stories begin with a sense of openness and genuineness but precipitously incline into rib-tickling and funny pantomime.

Spectacular are the cartoons in the British magazine 'The Private Eye' and 'The Punch.' The Private Eye has amused the public with exquisite depictions and diligently coined phrases for imminent individuals. For instance, the cartoon and the relevant terms make it more exciting. For example, Lord Goodman becomes 'Lord Badman,' and 'The Dinners' Goodman,' On March 12, 2013, the Sultan of Brunei was visiting USA when President Obama jokingly mentioned that 'we are going to encourage him to do some shopping because we want to continue to strengthen the US economy'. The Britishers tend to read a lot, watch entertaining shows on television, and are mostly fun and thrill-seekers. An Englishman at the University of London in the 1970s and 1980s found of visiting pubs used to describe how the blokes got drunk and laughed hysterically. It was the usual practice at the weekend nightlife in pubs and clubs where natives forgot the apprehensions, anxieties, and worries of daily life. They laughed for no particular reasons, but the enjoyment and hilarity always filled exceedingly the social atmosphere in a social setting. Their merriment got enhanced by the sound of romantic music and passionate songs. While some of them in the tavern would play darts, sing, and dance, tell jokes, exchange fibs and untruths. Anyone of them uttering a freshly concocted hoax would make others laugh frenziedly. One of my former postgraduate classmates at Manchester Metropolitan University was working in the British Library London. He told me that his friends in the pubs never talked down, insulted, offended, and intimidated strangers. I was pleased to hear his positive comments because I personally found my English colleagues and classmates in London and Manchester profoundly respectful, kind, and helpful.

Intimidating Laughter

Another tardiest example of relentless laughter comes to light in the remarkable photograph of four highly intelligent, superbly successful three former Prime Ministers and another super former world-renowned diplomate gathered at New Delhi in October 2019. (The Times, English Daily London October 22,2019). These four dignitaries included Tony Blair (former British Prime Minister), John Howard (former Australian Prime Minister), Modi (Indian Prime Minister), and Henry Kissinger (former U.S. Secretary of State for Foreign Affairs). These four distinguished luminaries were profusely laughing to show the world the power of their laughter. They appeared relaxed, delighted, happy, and united in their symmetrical laugh that indicated success, achievement, accomplishment, and thoughtfully conceived future direction. However, they seemed to be enjoying every moment of togetherness, and a joint loud laugh is the affirmation of their diplomatic attachment and intellectual commitment to shaping the world. Who knows, in the prevailing unpredictable climate of Corona Virus-19, the Nobel Peace Prize winners still might succeed in transforming some designated parts of the globe per their aspirations, objectives, and expectations. The Divine intervention might reverse their diplomatically contrived plans . The real Superpower is the Power of All Mighty- the One God, the Creator of Universe, and the Planner of planners.

Intimidating laughter is caused by a specific political and dogmatic situation. Through laughter, we can strengthen social and diplomatic bonds, understand the sufferings of the world, show intellectual superiority, and outline mutual coordination of future actions. The laughter is an expression of emotion, sending a signal to the world, indicating a new grouping of powerful elites. Some psychologists assert that the laughter is antisocial and belligerent since it beguiles some people but intimidates others. Laughter can be a mixture of evil and hypocrisy, just as we may witness state-approved merriment during the reign of Stalin. In the 1930s, nearly 200,000 natives were imprisoned for telling subversive jokes. Unsurprisingly, Bolshevik Nikolai Bukharin saved his skin by producing jokes about the mass-murder of peasants. George Bernard Shaw (1934) noted that Stalin possessed a keen sense of comedy. Stalin laughed at Grigory Zinoviev's begging for life before execution. He often laughed to coerce others, including his entourage. According to Lord Shaftsbury (1711), laughter and humour allow us to polish one another and rub off our Corners and rough Sides by a sort of amicable Collision.

The funniness and jokes cause laughter that might be harmless or intimidating. George Orwell (1945) proclaims you might define humour that causes laughter as 'dignity sitting on a tintack, whatever destroys dignity and brings down the mighty from their seats, preferably with a bump, is funny. And the bigger the fall, the bigger the joke'. It is not uncommon for dictators to suppress laughter and imprison jesters. The Bolsheviks lampooning started in 1918 that rounded up Bim and Bom clowns. (Thurston, 1991)

Aristotle (1941, p.1459) remarked centuries earlier that something that excites laughter is something ugly. Andy Medhurst (2007, p.25) claim that laughter depends on the conflict because laughter always involves change; the change can be both destructive and constructive. Even gallows have experienced laughter at certain occasions when a convicted person was about to face capital punishment. At moments before execution, William Palmer looked at the trapdoor on the gallows and innocently asked the hangman, "Are you sure it's safe." Palmer was called "Rugeley Poisner" for killing his friends and some family members. Charles Dickens calls him the greatest villain due to his crimes and criminalities.

Mass hysterical laughter engulfed a small town called Kashasha in Tanganyika (now Tanzania) on January 30, 1962, when three boarding school girls giggled and continued perpetually until more girls joined them, becoming a large group of ninety-five girls. It is unclear whether the laughing girls paused to have dinner, sleep, or go to the bath. It is unclear whether it was a teenage hysteria that had gripped the young girls. The female teaching staff was not affected by the laughter epidemic, although the school had to be closed on March 18, 1962. A Ugandan born psychiatrist Dr Benjamin Kagwa visited Kashasha to study the fundamentals of the epidemic. He termed it a mental conflict due to the Western colonisation of African people. Focusing on mental illnesses in East Africa, Professor Gordon published research results in 1936 in the East African Medical Journal. He underlined "pressure of thought, emotion, behaviour, of intellect, imagination, foresight, all formed an unprecedented experience for the native brain involving inevitable adjustment or inevitable catastrophe" (xxviii). He mentioned nothing about mass hysteria or colonial rule. Carothers disagreed with Gordon and linked East African mental illness with colonial rule and blamed Christianisation and secular education. The epidemic had affected other people, as reported by Dr. Kagwa, who talked to his people claiming, ancestral spirits caused the madness. He believed the epidemic ran along ethnic lines.

In Greek culture, the unconstrained laughter was a manifestation of superiority, a type of scorn, ridicule, and derision.

Laughter is a universal phenomenon in individual behaviour across all cultures and civilisations. Human interactions trigger spontaneous laughter on certain unusual occasions when a large number of people gather to view exceptionally significant international contests and competitions. For instance, stimulating events held annually around the world provoke bursts of enormous laughter. Oscar Academic Awards held yearly in the U.S.A., best-performing actors, actresses, producers, and directors are granted tumultuous welcome with hand-clapping and ruptures of laughter at the presentation ceremony. Similarly, we witness Eurovision Song Contest, Cesar Film Awards, French Cannes Film Festival, and Roman River Music. We observe London Gigs, Live London Music Show, and Festival of German Films held every year are an act of entertainment for the masses. These events exhibit spurts of enormous laughter among thousands of audiences who made an effort to ensure attendance. Most of all, International Beauty Contests such as Miss World and Miss Universe widely create implausible and farfetched excitement, exhilarating and delight for the audience and the worldwide viewers. People in attendance not only give a massive round of applause but laugh hysterically for the winner. The girls winning the Miss Universe and Miss World Beauty Pageant, in the process of crowning, cover their faces with their own hands to control the jubilation and excitement. Immediately, their smiles transform into laughter and euphoria. In 2019, upon the crowning ceremony of the Thai King, the public lined the roads of Bangkok to watch the glittering procession, clapping, singing, and laughing to accord warm welcome and a sense of acknowledgement of authority.

An uninhibited sniggering accompanies a variety of sounds that people produce in the torrent of giggle and snicker. Spontaneous cackle is unsolicited as it is a voluntary form of human conduct. Initially, laugh commences with vowel-like sounds, vocalised clicks, and noise rupture. Chuckle articulates high spirits and cheerfulness. Discrete emotions exist in laughter, such as joy, anger, fear, contempt, surprise, and embarrassment.

Edmonson (1987) initially provided a phonetically based analysis of laughter and perceived a few unique vowel sounds in these trials. He found out that hardly any consonant sounds were delectable whether the mouth was open, closed, or in a partially opened shape. He observed the laughter was mostly transpired with outward airflow. Deliberate laughter seems to initiate in frontal cortical areas with allied neural gesticulates touching the brainstem.

The voiced laughter usually unveils discrete vowel qualities such as hah-hah, he-he, hoo-hoo, or hoe-hoe-hoe. The variations in the style of laughter occur if the jaws are lowered. Spontaneous laughter entails subcortical pathways, paralleling the noncordial production mechanism that mediates emotion-triggered vocalisation. Laughter is inevitably a global human possession, a typical means of communication that occurs primarily in social situations rather than individual cases. When we feel superior in skill, features, and cleverness, we inadvertently offend others due to a disrespectful lack of respect. We might laugh at a fat person with a huge belly and ridicule the individual for personal happiness. This type of euphoria at the cost of other's scornfulness is utterly disgraceful and overwhelmingly unjustified.

Laughter is an incredibly powerful tool for non-verbal vocal expression. It is a hilarious tool to compromise social rapports, augment social relations, and conceive emotional happiness. Some of the phrases displayed on various items, banners, and walls are fascinating and interesting. The present writer has noticed some slogans at doctor's surgeries, community centres, theatres, and observed household items for sale at jumbo branded multinational stores. For example, "Keep Calm and Carry On," "Live, Laugh, Love," taken from Bessie Anderson Stanley's 1904 Poem "Success." He experienced the trust of women. At House of Fraser and Marks and Spencer or John Lewis, pillows for sale bear the phrases; "Live Simply, Dream Big, Be Grateful; Give Love, Laugh Lots: on bed covers, you can see embroidered or embossed words such as "Live Like there is no Tomorrow, Laugh Until Your Sides Hurt, Love...Like You Have Never Loved Before".

Intimidating Laughter (POEM)

We live in a wonderful world
You must have already heard

Superiors have always prevailed
The opulent have never failed

Wealthy have displayed greed
Want more to fulfil their need
Hypocrisy sows the unjust seed
Profiteering is their only creed

They laugh at others to seek pleasure
Intimidating those to attain leisure

Such a pearl of laughter wisdom deplores
Unfairness, arrogance, not anymore

Superiority laughter is a fact, describes Hobbes
Bain agrees; such laugh is a culture of nobs

Bigwigs seek exhilaration and ecstasy
Grandees relish and experience supremacy

Laughing with someone is a genuine laughter
Laughing at someone is a recipe for disaster
[Composed by Dr Nazir Ahmad, September 2, 2020/
Muharram 14, 1442 Hijra, Wednesday]

Health Benefits of Laughter

Laughter is authentically a therapeutic agent as it alleviates strain and wields remedial impact in stress and distress. Its potential healing power in depression is universally acknowledged. The scientific evidence suggests that laughter can reduce the adverse effects of rheumatism and autoimmune systems in the human body. In deliberate laughter, muscular movements

227

around the mouth are spontaneous. The robust connection between laughter and numerous health conditions necessitates dynamic synchronised muscular flexing in the diaphragm, gut, and ribs. Laughter tends to intensify the heartbeat, increases oxygen intake, and amplifies respiration. It communicates the verbal, emotional state to others. It is said to be a "diffused signal, reflecting feelings of tension release, satisfaction, or safety." (Rothbart, 1973.). Laughter considerably enhances aerobic metabolism and builds resilience for pain endurance and tenacity. One of the studies reported in the Journal of American Medical Association affirms that patients suffering from atopic dermatitis react significantly less to allergen skin tests after watching 90 minutes of Charlie Chaplin's Modern Times. Laughter incites T-Cells production; it releases positive neurotransmitters and hormones while levitation the level of endorphins. It lessens stress hormones such as cortisol and adrenaline, which can impair the function of the immune system.

Laughter offers a panacea to minimise pain threshold and develop pain tolerance convention drastically. Laughter sounds alone can evoke positive emotions presenting innumerable health benefits. It provides a means of sharing favour with others, such as lower-status individuals laughing more at jokes told by higher-status people (Fry and Rader, 1977). Province's (1993) study noted that in a small girls sample of 1200 illustrations of laughter, the females laughed more than their male equivalents, but both laughed less when the speaker was a woman. Equally beneficial is the availability of intermingling opportunities, personal connections, and according to Glenn (2010), "laughter exists to create social bonding," and youth can strengthen social relationships. It is a medium of emotive rejoinder that can magnify the optimistic feelings on both sides, and a familiar interface would reinforce more laughter and inspire sensual feelings. Laughter is an emotional cure, a key to health therapeutic creative vitalities, and an astoundingly invaluable tool for floorshows, nightspots, burlesques, and lounges. The pranksters, buffoons, and tricksters augment their performance through busts of laughs and chuckles. It was for this reason that "Laugh Box" with a pre-recorded laughter which quickly became very popular for prompting laughter among the television viewers.

In the 1960s, Fry conducted a thoughtful study of cabarets, clowns and comedians, produced scholarly articles, also devised a well-conceived educational programme for training hospital nurses, paediatricians, and social workers as clowns. It is a part of the national health programme, and the science of laughter is termed gelotology. Bateson Group (1956) has formulated a double-bind theory to explain the psychogenesis of schizophrenia in families and focused on the role of humour in cementing feelings of family or in alleviating inhibitions. (Watzlawick, 1977).

Irvin Zola was a Professor of Human Relations at Brandeis University, Massachusetts, who believed emotional, social, and intellectual support of other people was necessary for comfortable living. While in hospital, he recalled, "My physiotherapist Ms. Elizabeth Ernst helped me question authority and opened my eyes in quite a different way. In retrospect, I think she was encouraging me to look beyond myself to see how I was part of a larger world. One day she gave me two books to read. One was a textbook in psychology, and the other was Gunnar Myrdal's American Dilemma". He interviewed out-door patients before meeting the physician (in the U.S.A.) or General Practitioner in the U.K. He quizzed several sick people discovering that the Italians habitually grumbled about their symptoms, minor ailments, and affected body areas more than Irish people. The Italian shows dramatise and exaggerate health issues to seek medical help when it interferes with their social life. English, Scots, and Welsh people usually go to their G.P.'s when health issues affect their job performance.

Zola (1983, p.120) observes health and illness as a social phenomenon. Gareth Williams (1996) studied Irvin Kenneth Zola and his philosophical writings and posited that Zola was a serious man with a sense of funniness. The present writer's two sons are medical doctors serving as G.P.'s who educate me about their patient interaction and the manners with which they conduct surgeries. They possess compassionate, patient-oriented feelings of concern and wellbeing and exercise a caring and empathic approach that alleviates suffering and dampens mental and bodily pains. Sometimes, they use light humour and playful banter in amicable conversation during consultations. Exercise of simple wittiness puts the patient at ease, and he/she feels engaged, responsive, and better understands the treatment options. Some patients do not swallow puns or dislike even modest retorts. They feel valued, with a chance to speak and openly raise health issues. Then, my son Dr. Adeel says, 'I use the comforting word and uplifting language by making a sound meaningful suggestion, supporting his/her concerns and either prescribing medication or referring to the hospital for necessary tests. My son Dr. Nabeel asserts that 'kind chat of a kind-hearted G.P. is an invaluable tonic than paracetamol or any other pain killer.' With his natural sense of wittiness, he can put all his patients at ease during the first few moments of consultation. My son believes cultural background and family values positively impact patient behaviour, firmness, and conduct. Some individuals are more persistent in demanding medication, asking for sick note based on personal social issues and relationship problems.

As early as 1989, Berk took blood samples of his patients consecutively after every ten minutes and divided all the subjects into two groups. One group was presented with funny videos to watch, while the other group viewed no such tapes. Noticeably, the cortisol levels of funny video-views considerably dropped compared to those who did not observe any videos. In the health sector, wit and laughter assists in the healing procedure. A burst of well-prolonged laughter is beneficial since it activates the hypothalamus, pituitary, and adrenal glands and brings extra oxygen. The true moving story of Professor Norman Cousins, who taught psychiatry at the University of California, Los Angles, is an inspiration for health professionals and especially doctors handling patients with serious health ailments. Cousins (1979) proclaimed that he was suffering from ankylosing and spondylitis, and no cure was in sight. Cousins had previously researched the biochemistry of human emotions for fighting an illness that confirmed the injection of jesting and laughter to combat disease and lessen pain. He left the hospital, moved into a hotel accompanied by a nurse to look after and administer medication. He regularly watched hilarious videos, funny episodes and read comic books. He practised belly laughter for ten minutes with an anaesthetic effect followed by two-hour pain-free sleep, which he dearly relished. When the laughter effect wore off, he switched to funny television shows such as "Candid Camera" along with massive intravenous doses of vitamin C and then repeating bouts of laughter to enjoy further two-hour pain-free sleep. One day, his nurse left a vase for him for a urine sample, but he put apple juice in it for the sake of fun and hilarity. When the nurse returned to collect the urine specimen, she was surprised to notice the colour of the sample and said, "It looks a bit cloudy today." Cousins replied, "Oh, perhaps I should put it through again," and drank the apple juice. The act was unbelievable for the nurse since she had never experienced such a situation. When Cousins explained the mystery, there was loud laughter. Cousins passionately believed in the integrity of words, the power of hope, and the practicality of optimism.

In the U.S.A., the substance addicts customarily enjoy group laughter in their digs, nightclubs, and discos. The youngster mainly enjoys pathological and drug-induced laugh (Bechterew, 1894). Renowned psychologists (Lipps, 1898; Martin, 1905; Heymans, 1896) have researched comics and hilarity, focusing on emotional health. Its positive effect on social health is observed by Weisfeld (1993), who considers it as a means of social stimulation or as a status manipulation (Alexander, 1986). On the other hand, Wilson et al. (1977) reported environmental factors that play a significant part in hilarity appreciation and incitement.

Canned Laughter & Carnival Laughter

In huge social gatherings at national, local, and community festivals, people in a happy mood display joy, delight, and excitement. Carnival laughter reveals and discharges the audience's genuine emotions, irrespective of status, power, wealth, and class. The participants from diverse hues, cultures, and races consider themselves equal in such an ambience and unhesitatingly unleash truly free emotions in the form of laughter.

Canned laughter makes jokes seem exceedingly funnier and overwhelmingly wittier. Adding laughter to a fun increases the humour value no matter how least funny the trick might be, says Professor Sophie Scott, University College London, Institute of Cognitive

Neuroscience. She believes that we respond much better to spontaneous, genuine laugh, somewhat canned laugh. Most television programmes in the past were recorded in the presence of a live audience, and therefore they felt amused and laughed profoundly at funny incidents. Canned laughter was added to make less entertaining episodes more accessible and to increase public viewing. The profound use of laughter to induce laughter was a significant ingredient of television Sitcoms. On September 9, 1950, the laugh track was utilised for the first time to test the public response to Sitcom viewing. It had an overpowering impact on the viewers' perceptions of humour because the dubbed-in-sounds of laughter had the persuasive power of encouraging and inspiring the public to join in the laughter. We also noticed in the 1920s when music recording companies identified the incredible power of laughter with the circulation of "The Okeh Laughing Record," evolving coherent trumpet playing that spasmodically intersected titanic laughter. In the following decades, several music tycoons such as Woody Herman, Louis Armstrong, and Spike Jones postulated their records for the same purpose that brought them abundant wealth, fame, and notoriety. The uniqueness of canned laughter tempted many psychologists in the U.S.A. and Europe to conduct qualitative research and publish their findings. Their research outcomes proclaimed that the canned laughter did momentously augment the viewers' laughter.

Contagious laughter appeared in Tanzania in the 1960s where groups of 12-18-year-old school girls commenced laughter without reason, and then, it rose to epidemic proportions. No such episode has come to our attention in any European country where titter in offices and giggle in bars have customarily been widespread. But belly laugh is associated with young girls at schools, colleges, and universities in social conversations and emotional interactions between opposite genders. The teenage girls often make funny faces to inspire laugh, splish-splash water on each other for amusement, and toss snowballs in winter for excitement and laughter. While playing together, the boys habitually shake heads, fling pebbles at each other, and use their legs to hit and even sometimes cause hurt.

Herbert Spencer conjectured in his 'Physiology of laughter' (1860) biologically about a person's natural trait as it originates within the human body. He states that there is no distinction between liberation and ideology because laughter is the condition of philosophy. It offers us with the gap, the very space in which dogma can take its complete swing. It is merely through laughter that we convert into ideological subjects. As such, we laugh and breathe freely; then, the ideology truly has a hold on us. Modern humour could not have developed fully without antecedents. Since fried chicken postulates an egg, the snags of fun and waggishness are relatively chronological and evolutionary. While discussing the biological aspect of laughter, Ludovici (1933 draws our attention to the fact that laughter reveals the teeth; instead of using the word laughter, we should use the words "shoe teeth." Professor Mary Russo discusses carnival laughter and asserts that 'It is the laughter we have now: other laughter for other times, carnival laughter remains on the horizon with a new social subjectivity. (1994, p.73) Albert Rapp (1948), who developed the theory of laughter and comedy, says laughter is related to love unless related to hate as it resembles the Homeric 'Old Man of the Sea.' George Bataille, a French scholar and philosopher who researched at the British Museum in 1920, and after that postulated his thinking about laughter, says, 'In fact. I can say that, insofar as I am doing philosophical work,

Bataille comments, that "In my philosophy is a philosophy of laughter. It is a philosophy founded on the experience of laughter, and it does not even claim to go further. It is a philosophy that doesn't concern itself with problems, but only the issues confronting him. He enunciates laughter as nonknowledge escapes insight, motive, and understanding. Laughing is the forming of a community of empathy and helping others in times of need. If I observe an older man with perhaps low vision, hitting a roadside tree, and tipping over and falling on the footpath, I have a choice to make, continue walking to catch the bus to reach home in time, or help the older man sympathising with him. If I am insensitive to others' distress, I might laugh at him. If we take a few moments to ponder the situation, the matter would appear to be serious that did not command laughter. The burst of laughter would be degrading to the poor man lying on the footpath. Indeed, comedians perform all sorts of unusual acts to stimulate laughter for the amusement of the audience. Still, in real-life scenarios, such a peal of laughter would be intimidating and morally inappropriate. Habitually,

Youth tend to laugh at numerous incidents at school or college. For example, if a boy gets locked in the toilet and cannot come out due to the absence of a school keeper, his /her classmates would stand beside the toilet door and jointly explode in laughter. Instead of pitying and uttering consoling words, they are highly likely to tootle, shout and laugh, causing embarrassment for the One trapped inside the toilet. The jesters usually crack such jokes that impel the crowd into downcast giggles and laughs. In real-life settings, we should not move past the moments of distress and incidents of suffering but pause and empathise.

For the enrichment of public euphoria, Canned Laughter established a foothold in Comedy Shows, first in the United States. Canned laughter is applause on television programmes that have been pre-recorded and added to each episode of the television programme series to make it sound as if there is a live audience. In reality, this laughter does not make jokes any funnier. Pre-recorded laughter entices and encourages the viewers to laugh as well. The television studios either begin tampering up or tampering down laughter recordings to suit the desired impact. Douglass's Laugh-Track appeared in 1950 at the Hank McCune Show that boosted great success and approbation from all segments of the society. When Dr. Robert Provine (1992) presented canned laughter to an audience of students, his scientific investigation found that it could elicit visible smiling and audible laughter. He discovered that it was the inherent humour of the situation that triggered students' positive emotions. Moreover, emotion-based reactions do occur to hearing laugh sounds.

Magnetic Power of Laughter (POEM)

Due to the mesmeric and hypnotic qualities of laughter, the present composer says:

Physical wounds get healed
And Captivating lips unsealed

Laugh begins with opening jaws
Rhythmic sounds without flaws

Laugh instigates with a tempting sound
Such happiness is scarcely found

It is a medication for blues prevention
Don't ruminate this, a new invention

A remedy for the dry atmosphere
Amusing message loud and clear

Brings blood pressure under control
Belittles arthritis on the whole
Fascinating drug for the noble soul
Seldom makes you out of control

Relieves the sick, from grievous pain
Mitigates anger, and enlightens brain

When stinging hurt puts you down

It acts as a jewel in the queen's crown

Often, we conduct a serious talk
Find no time for a morning walk
Maybe not a laughing matter
Makes you feel somehow better

Laughter is a signal for a social connection
Presents an opportunity for positive interaction
Guides the recipient for sound direction
A proper deterrent for fictional detection

Dispels worries, qualms, and fears
In intense laughs, you wipe the tears

Inflammation is greatly reduced
When relief and respite produced
Young hearts naturally seduced
Strangers get innately introduced

Laughter has, charismatic charm
Absorbing power, does no harm

Lonely hearts, look mesmerised
Pretty faces seem hypnotised

Glittering venues, glamorous crowd
Ensnared, enticed but all feel proud

Gatherings are for Pull and Excitement
Attracts masses for sole merriment

Downtrodden souls copiously cured
Pleasant emotions effusively restored

Even introvert feel enthralled
An extrovert is not appalled

Socialisers customarily socialise
Deceivers consistently disguise

Sometimes you laugh, although feeling sad
Sadness will dissipate, don't feel bad

[Composed by Dr Nazir Ahmad
September 20, 2021/ Safar 12, 1443 Hijra, Monday]

Laughing With someone is a Panacea for emotional wellbeing, but laughing at someone is not permissible in a just society. It undermines and emasculates the sensitivities of people facing deprivation, starvation, and horrendous health problems. In 2018, Bryant and his associates examined a set of thirty-six recorded laughs produced by 884 English speaking girls belonging to twenty-one diverse societies and cultures across six regions of the world. They were anxious to discover whether each such laugh was real or simulated. The girls taking part in the research identified two types of smiles with an accuracy of 56 per cent to 69 per cent. The results indicated very high consistency across cultures in laughter judgements. Ruch and Proyer (2008b) have delineated and premeditated the fear of being laughed at as a non-pathological measurement. Titze (2009) noticed many of his patients showed stiff posture and a 'wooden appearance' whenever faced with a humorous scenario. Humour research led to the investigation of Gelotophobia in the field of psychology. The research articles then started appearing in the International Journal of Humour Research, followed by the establishment of the International Society for Humour Studies.

Initially, Ruch, Proyer, and Weber (2010) introduced a theoretical framework for studying humour, whereas Proyer and Ruch (2010) researched temperaments towards ridicule and mockery. They believed there were several explanations 'why people might get laughed at in their daily routines' and mentioned the mean-spirited side, which could count as bullying. They have discussed three essential concepts in this field, namely, Gelotophobia (the fear of being laughed at), Gelotophilia (the joy of being laughed at), and Katagelasticism (the pleasure of laughing at others). There is nothing in which people more betray their character than in what they find to "laugh at." (Goethe, p.45). Thomas Carlyle comments, 'how much lies in a laugh: the cypher-key, wherewith we decipher the whole man' (p.44). We learn of Mr. Tupman in Pickwick Papers that his laughter was forced, his merriment feigned. (p.113)

A German scholar believes that gelotophobes incorrectly sense huge laughter of an affirmative value, contemplating it as negatively inspired. Sometimes, it is tough to characterise and differentiate cheerful bantering from mockery. Some individuals with obvious Gelotophobia retort to classical derision setups with disgrace and fear, but they show these emotions in reaction to affable mocking.

Laughing matters if it heals the sick and consoles the oppressed, but it matters more when destroys the dreams of desolate and shatters the hopes of subjugated societies. The subdued people do laugh at themselves about their misfortunes and also laugh in tribulations. Some even laugh off their worries when frustrations reach new heights, and their sufferings are endless. Iraqi people are still wondering and sometimes laughing why their country faced indiscriminate bombardment that annihilated millions and destroyed the economy under the pretext of weapons of mass destruction.

In satire and parody, people find meditative amplification of disdain emotion and a sense of kindness. Comic laughter involves insight and understanding because we laugh at various things in different laughable settings to attain relaxation and tranquillity.

Comedy is embedded in the social order as it deals with individuals' relationship to society and society to the individual, says Elizabeth Drew (1937, p. 169). but it also anchors itself in this world with its faulty and more comfortable emotional and ethical judgment. (p.170). Laughter emotion transpires with a specific frame of mind and a particular type of gadget. Comedy is the simulation of meaningless action, and a hollow feat and laughter offer respite from human troubles, weaknesses, and temporary relief from hitches, imperfections, and snags.

Conversely, untimely laughter at the wrong place can be a nuisance for others around us. Superfluous and lousy laughter causes distractions to students in libraries, disturbance to patients in hospitals, and unpleasantness to individuals in old people homes, care homes, and even in cafes and restaurants. Laughter would be considered equally distasteful in places of worship and meditation, reverence and spiritual awe. Delightful laughter is emotionally beneficial at wedding rituals, birthday parties, family celebrations, religious and cultural festivals, music contests, film award ceremonies, football grounds, and youth amusement parks.

Funny jokes naturally arouse laughter and hilarity, and some tricks are preposterous taunts that make the listeners look foolish and stupid. Banters are bitter and awful and revive pain. Dan Crompton's 'A funny thing happened on the way to the forum' 'A Collection of Wits and Wisdom' and 'The Laughter Lover' are an excellent read for those looking for home entertainment with hilarious jokes to make you laugh. For example, a patient attends the G.P. surgery at the appointed time and tells the doctor that "whenever I get up from my slumber, and for half an hour, I feel dizzy, and then I am fine. The doctor says, O.K., I suggest you should get up half an hour later, then'. It is natural for barbers to talk to every customer and exchange gossips copiously, fibs, and blathers. In the early 1970s, a famous British Parliamentarian, Enock Powel, once went for a haircut to the hairdresser. The barber asked him, 'how should I cut your hair, Sir? Right Honourable Enock Powel just uttered two words, IN SILENCE.

In Europe, satirical magazines are a pleasurable and humorous source of entertainment for people with and without any formal education. French sarcastic, fun-loving punishers are famous for producing comic materials of a very high standard. French journal "La Caricature" since the first issue in 1830, contains coloured drawings and graphic images inviting public laughter and humour. They sting the monarchy, ridicule the politicians, and appraise sportsmen and women. On November 14, 1831, just over 12-months after the first issue, the publisher Charles Philipon was brought before the French Court in Paris on treason charges but luckily escaped prison. However, his colleague Honore Daumier got a six-month prison sentence. The cartoons had illustrated King Louis Philippe and the bourgeoisie attacking the ruling elite. Beginning in 1848, "Kladderadatsch' (Unholy Mess) was published in Berlin, Nebelspalter" (Fog Splitter) from Switzerland, and "Kikeriki" from Austria were some of the satirical serial publications deriding big names such as King Luis Philippe, Wilhelm II. Satire journals have credibly entertained the readers and viewers, amused the general public, but angered the ruling classes, including Royal Monarchy, politicians, and bureaucrats. In the U.K., Private Eye uncovered many vital scandals such as Profumo that engulfed Harold Macmillan's government in 1963 and nine years later in 1972, compelled Reginald Maudling to resign. Some magazines have faced libels and paid hefty fines for unneeded ridicule. French magazine Charlie Hebdo goes against human values by causing intimidation and humiliation to individuals and communities worldwide. This magazine was sued 13 times by Catholics for deriding the Pope and once by the Grand Mosque of Paris authorities. Intimidating others is not freedom of expression but a reflection of a cheap mentality, causing emotional hurt to ordinary people. They believe in the `Prophets, saints' and Pops' integrity and spiritual power. These magazines disseminating productive humour are a lifeline, hope, and powerful tools of resistance in dictatorial societies where opinion is suppressed, fundamental freedom curtailed, spiritual sentiments overlooked, and human values ignored.

Tickling laughter is another form of stimulating giggle and cackle caused by another person's action. Armpit tickling triggered laughter, especially in small children. Soles of the bare feet itching by another individual generated laughter too. Quite often, mothers perform this amusing act on their infants to make them laugh and create hilarity for fun and joy. Laugh is sublimely intrinsic in the infants' nature. When they innocently see their mother laughing, they also begin to laugh without understanding the reason for such laughter.

On the contrary, the elderly laugh quietly and inaudibly but depict a cheerful posture since laughter remains in the stomach. It is a potential source of gratification, fulfilment, and pleasure for young and old, men and women from all backgrounds and settings. Laughter does not always happen as a reaction to anecdotes, but even negligible comments, modulations, and nods instigate laughter. We only laugh while hearing a joke and consider it a funny gag, and more comic situations are expected to cause more laughter and more positive judgment. (Calvert, 1949). In 1905, Evelyn Martin questioned some people about their capacity to suppress laughter while watching funny cartoons. She postulated that the quelling laughter dwindled the funniness of the jokes, albeit expression of laughter immensely increased the jolliness. Consequently, she admits that "laughter and a feeling of satire go hand in hand. (p.104). Calvert supports this assumption and states that if we consider a joke funny, we laugh since more amusing situations simply cause more laughter. If we suppress our natural desire to laugh, in effect, we are inhibiting the experience of pleasant emotion.

CHAPTER VIII - **HUMOUR HEALS** COMEDY CURES

Humour Prevails (POEM)

Many styles of humour prevail
Timely limericks hit the nail
Spares no one in joking trail
Ronald Reagan or Dan Quayle

Witty banter amuses and absorbs
Sorrows, stings and leaves none bored

Tension eases, and esteem restores
Humour heals, and comedy cures

It generates and sparks hilarity
Stimulates intellectual prosperity

It promotes social interaction
Presents a chance for reflection

Humour nurtures emotional health
Reviles inequality and immense wealth

The Humour performers are orators
Instruct audience and act as inspirator
They sometimes imitate perpetrators
Stir jolliness and witty debaters

Brilliant scholar Thomas Carlyle
Sartor Resartus makes you smile

Heroes & hero worship in great style
Prophetic reflection of genius Carlyle

Hilarious clowns cheer you up
As though you have won the world cup

Impersonators, though improve the mood
Whether young and old, child or brood

Humour, irony happen side-by-side
Life in itself can be a bumpy ride
Irony represents a descending slide
Jester simulates an emerging tide

[Composed by Dr Nazir Ahmad,
August 10, 2021/ Muharram 1,1443 Hijra Tuesday]

Humour Rectifies

Although emotional wounds are beyond sadness, humour offers temporary respite and recovery from trauma and leaves us comparably more resilient when we summon compassion and move through feelings of discomfort. In adversity, tears stream down our cheeks in the absence of anyone to console, soothe or support; the humour comes to our rescue for joyous reprieve and exuberant mood. An additional recipe for overcoming anxiety is to surround oneself with like-minded people who happily share positive thoughts and indulge in creative activities. We cannot afford to block emotions, albeit feelings might aggravate magnifying gloominess.

We should halt pondering over past cold experiences and spiteful events, avoid disconnectedness but focus on minor accomplishments, positive deeds, and remarkable triumphs. Emotional pain describes Bolges (1999) as 'broken feelings that involved the experience of being wounded, loss of self, disconnection.' It correlates with direct and latent tissue damage, and it is a hollowness due to loss of connotation in life.

Affection, compassion, and closeness develops through laughter and humour into significant lifelong affiliations. Echoes of German, French, Dutch, Turkish, and British spirit rectify blues, and comedy cures despair, bringing back gladness and excitement on the faces of lonely and isolated individuals. Social psychology is interweaved in human emotions portraying belonging and revealing flaws of youth perceptions, affecting thoughts and behaviour. Particular morphology exhibits the intensity of youth experience and the quality of emotional expressiveness in interpersonal relations.

Humour has various overtones for different people at distinctive, unpredictable moments in life. Humour can be a natural extension of one's feelings, mischief, and impishness, or it might have developed as a means of managing an individual's unpleasant environments. Purposeful humour unveils the real character of public figures and ruling dignitaries, including politicians and power brokers. It is precisely humour that obliterates the epic and narrows any ranked remoteness. It helps the public to view and perceive the real charisma of politicians. Thoughtful mood strips away illusion and awe, and we can judge them critically, appraise their words and actions in a better way. Politicians do possess a sense of humour and occasionally crack jokes subsequently and frequently repeated at various platforms. Sir Winston Churchill, British War-time Prime Minister, was sitting beside a lady who did not like his politics and unnecessary chatter, and she told him, "If you were my husband, I would put poison in your coffee". Churchill replied,"If I were your husband, I would drink it".

Our culture and our allusions have an unavoidable impact on the formation of our sense of humour.

In the present century, wittiness is universally present in comedy shows, films, musical concerts, theatrical performances, stage dramas, comical books, magazines, and paintings. Plenty of fun is accessible on the internet, Facebook, Twitter, YouTube, Snapchat, and many similar emerging technologies. Entertainers diligently generate laughter tickling public emotions with merry jests, and comic threads. Episodes such as "Perfect Strangers." "Seinfeld" and "Three's Company" generate tremendous amusement and fun for the audience. Rightminded comedians discourage deadpan and derisory jesting, although, sometimes specific anecdotes do cause hurt to one sector of the community by bemusing others. An offensive joke is deplorable, especially which ridicules and derides any particular race, faith, or civilisation. Ruling elites, exclusively politicians, are the prime target of comedians and joke crackers as they communicate truth to the general public. Some cultures typically treat humour very differently, as it is evident from Zhang's research findings (2005), who studied Chinese perception about fun and its acceptance in society. She determined that fun did not make Chinese students feel comfortable because funniness tinted their attentiveness and aberration. People may accept comics to manage tension and apprehension. In 1998, Flowerdew interviewed lecturers from Hong Kong. They used their native language rather than English to narrow the distance between their students and themselves by employing jokes and quips in their native Cantonese language.

Comedians' Productiveness

Comedians of the 18th and 19th centuries cracked jokes to entertain others. In contrast, literary writers such as Thackrey and Dickens wrote down humorous, literary plays, anecdotes, and tales that hardly caused infraction or humiliation. The readers relished the wit; the theatre visitors enjoyed playful acts portraying the time that impacted their lives. All types of jokes create fun, although some performances cause unpleasantness among humourists instigating public controversies. Some entertainers did not write down anything but uttered fibs and titbits on the spot without regard for the viewers assuming that they were in attendance purely for the fun and thrill. From 1820 up to the 1950s, ladies' minorities, and the disabled were the prime target in comedy shows, and rarely any act was treated undesirable. The comedians competed to produce stunningly laughable

251

jokes to attract more and more audience and fans. As the values changed and societies became more diverse since the Second World War, cultural standards, political correctness, and social norms transformed.

Minorities and female campaigners lobbied the politicians to pass laws for equitable opportunities in the job market, education, and welfare. On the contrary, these laws helped considerably improve deprived communities' conditions, and women managed to acquire professional and supervisory positions in numerous institutes and companies. They became financially secure and more empowered to make decisions about their life.

Consequently, power parity consistently reduced tolerance and increased feelings of independence, freedom, and liberation. Psychologically, it had a lasting effect on social relationships, behaviours, and moral standards. For instance, comedians decreased mentioning girls, immigrants, unemployed, and underachievers in the society who might feel emotionally hurt if they get mocked in the creation of anecdotes. As such, in offices, institutes, and multinational stores, no man could say a word to a female colleague that might amount to harassment, transforming into embarrassment and even dismissal. Not only clowns and humourists have become more sensitive and careful; the strangers no longer exchange views at cafes and weekend markets with the opposite sex for fear of being rebuked. Since the turn of the century, social values have drastically changed, sensitivities have increased, and face-to-face laughter occasions have almost vanished. However, the internet, online contacts, social media outlets, and smartphones have opened new avenues for developing meaningful relationships within the jurisdiction of personal safe zones. Youngsters and adults tend to be comparatively more reserved, less humorous, and self-conscious who treasure privacy, exercise discretion, and safeguard their own space.

German-Turkish Comedians

The comedians' appearance based on fair complexion, liberal perception, and mixed-marriage connections crack jokes on the German stage for the amusement of all sectors of the society. The longevity of mutual relations, historical war alliances, and overwhelming economic cooperation offer plenty of amicable ammunition to jokers to enact and create reciprocal puns. German jesters of Turkish origin tracing generational roots have played an indispensable role in intercultural mediation, curtailing misunderstandings through light-hearted banters. Over three million Turks, the vast majority born and brought up in Germany, make up the largest non-German population. Comedian stand-up shows, newspaper articles, and T.V. political debates brought to the surface the concept of national identity. President Christian Wulff, in 2010 supported the integration of Turkish people declaring that Islam was a part of Germany and acknowledged centuries-old connections. In 2012, German President Joachim Gauck disagreed with Chancellor Angela Merkel and buttressed Wulff's stance on the touchy matter. He agreed with

Wulff's intentions, which meant, 'Guys, take a breather and open up to reality. And the reality is that many Muslims live in this country'. Gauck elaborated 'I would have said that the Muslims living here belong to Germany' (Federal President's Office, ed. Der Bundesprasident, Web. January 16, 2014.)

Following year again on June 15, 2015, a German Exhibition displayed collective emotions of the society "Immer Bunter - Einwanderungsland Deutschland" (Evermore colourful - Immigration nation Germany").

German-Turkish comedians currently embody the educated voice of the general public, exhibiting comedian hand and body gestures for amusing the audience. Germans press their thumbs into the palm and wrap all other figures around it during a conversation. In the U.S.A., raising a middle finger at the other person can cause insult, and hands in the pocket while talking to another person is considered relaxed manners. However, it is insulting to keep hands in pockets in Germany. Usually, people pull down their eyelids to show cynicisms. Comedian makes these gestures to depict scepticism and mockery. They also portray traditional Turkish habits that generated laughter among the audience. Cultural quirks and Turkish traits can make you laugh, such as chaotic driving in Istanbul could be an adventure for a holidaymaker from England. Abruptly cutting in front of another car is usually without any regard for mutual safety. Honouring an appointment and turning up on time is not part of the culture.

Turkish comedians on the stage would perform for a few minutes and then disappear promising the crowd,

"I shall be back in a minute", but they keep waiting for three minutes, then he would appear and say, "well, I am not late like the plumber who once promised to come right away, and arrived after three hours. We are a relaxed bunch guys."

Listen, we are warm, welcoming, and kind-hearted, and more compassionate than others.

We, the Turks, are the Jack of all trades If you meet a man in Bursa and asks whether he can fix a broken pipe, mend the wrest watch, check an electric socket. He would say, don't worry, I can fix everything, that is normal.

The soap operas are hugely popular not only within Turkey and in many other parts of the world. Most operas magnify rich Turkish heritage even long before the advent of the Ottoman Empire. Multicultural harmony and tolerance are essential facets of diversity depicted in the media, stage shows, and festivals. Women had enjoyed the increasing presence in German comedy as Anke Engelke performed in her award-winning 2004 sketch show "Ladykracher." Martina Hill in "Knallerfrauen" 2011 amused the spectators through satire, parody, and caricature touching on numerous social issues.

Among the most famous German-Comedians are Kaya Yanar, born in Germany to Turkish parents, Bulent

Ceylan, a Kabarett artist, Serdar Somunch, a well-known comedian accentuating a reciprocal process of integration. For example, Ethno-Sitcom, called "Turkish Delight" by Karin Yesilada (2008), presented Turkish-German characters firmly entrenched in German culture. It portrayed Turkish-German friendship groups and ethnically blended families. In "Everyone Loves Jimmy," cheery Ben refers to Arkadas as "my family" He is the son of a wealthy father Metin, owner of a construction company and mother Gul with tight trousers and no headscarf, but high heels. Turkish family warmly welcomes Ben in their household. As the father's business collapses and decides to move back to Turkey, Ben intervenes, "I am not going to let my family move back to Turkey." Jimmy's parents become fully immersed in German culture, albeit having a first generational accent. Mother Gul professes that "we are modern parents." It is just one example of how the film industry and television dramas have positively impacted ethnic Turkish-German relations. As such, an optimistic multicultural depiction of communities encourages a positive social, psychological, and emotional climate for peaceful coexistence and serene cohabitation.

French Jesters

French comics have unquestionably produced some legendary jesters entertaining the crowds with their remarkably amusing anecdotes, charmingly mirthful expressions, and poetic metaphors. Comics gleefully tackle complex scenarios with beautiful utterances and jovial lingos representing the cultural, social, political, and economic conditions of the globe. They transmute the confession, the ambiguity, and inconsistency in the power structure. Colloquial exclamations predictably contain multiple connotations, sometimes causing trouble and annoying specific segments of the society. Their witty remarks are often well-adjusted, purposefully intended to generate joy, transmit hilarity, and produce laughter.

French Comedian Pierre Pechin (La Cigale et la fourmi, 1975) and Michel Leeb (L africain, 1980) disseminated ethnic typecasts and indigenous pigeonholes, navigation dissension, discord, and uneasiness among the people. In the 1990's Russell Simon gained popularity as a stand-up comedian who made the French laugh and giggle throughout his shows. The other three notables have been Gad Elmaleh, Elie Semoun, and Jamel Debbouze, performing across a diversity of cultures, presenting values and beliefs without targeting particular groups. Amelle Chahbi, Claudia Tagbo, Saint Laurent, Malik Bentalha, and Thomas N Gijol have left their imprints on the French comic world.

Infrequently, targeted derisive humour and hurtful idiomatic expressions have caused embarrassment and anxiety due to its capacity to undermine non-indigenous factions. Implications for such comics are undesirable, resulting in a social division and divergence of a society.

Oliver Barlet rightfully admitted that the French cinema reflected 'a permanent misunderstanding in their relationship with Arab immigrants, a desire of both assimilation and dissimulation.' Ethnic-based comedy limits itself to target the other, to set boundaries to distance itself from it, says Oliver Mongin. On the other hand, the present writer believes that the multicultural and multi-ethnic comedy of assimilation permits an optimistic viewpoint for the future and recapping audiences and spectators of the prototype of social concerns with a firm depth behind the character. Jamel Debbouge courageously took an unusual step in establishing Jamel Comedy Club in Paris in 2006. Its schedule comprised an innovative comedy format, a T.V. Café-theatre, a talk show. This club opened the door to the general French public. French nationals of Arab descent actively performed, changing native French people's fundamental perceptions about Arab culture.

Interestingly, they entertained the crowds through pun, fun, wittiness, and comedy. Jamel Club interprets urban youth culture in social media, theatrical venues, and French television. The rhetorical spirit of race-based slapstick shows through emotive cheery lexes and amusing terminologies. They accentuate the structure of unfairness through the expression of subjective anecdotes and personal narratives. Multilingual jargon, e.g., "himar" (in Arabic), meaning donkey and "pathos" for Catholic, form part of amusing lingos. Christie-Davies correctly states that 'Jokes are the thermometers that help us understand social reality; they are not thermostats controlling that reality.' However, comedy can help heal the emotional wounds of divisiveness, reduce anger, and minimise animosity. It can help reconstruct and transform hybrid identities, facilitate fusion, and expedite cultural acceptance, assimilation, and unification. Comedians act as a friendly bridge between the divisive communities, bringing joy and happiness, dissipating fears and frustrations. Humour should not insult people based on colour, creed, and faith, and also, specificities of minorities need no highlighting to promote the harmonised society. Lately, French film has been much admired for the positive depiction of ethnic people and bringing together diverse groups through comedy. Laughter is essentially an integral part of human body movements and unique expressions.

Yassine Belattar, a French-Moroccan renowned comedian, is a son of a cleaning lady. A taxi driver, who was born in Paris, has been a resounding voice of diversity in France. His decisive phrase "We are French Together" had made him "Clown of the Republic" though occasionally criticised by far left. So, he sent a message to President Macron raising concern about being slated by some sectors of French society. Emanuel Macron, the President, texted back, advising Belattar, "Just keep going, ignore It: criticism follows talent." What a wonderful compliment by the President of the French Republic succinctly encouraging him to carry on with visible and comically emotional exclamations. Belattar modestly professes that five family members, including grandfather, fought for France in the Second World War. He possessed a natural sense of humour and defied the calamity with comedy. Comic allegories in French movies and the comedian dictums on stage have a profound positive impact on society.

In the presence of Arabic speaking audience, the dialectal lexicon has recurrently generated laughter and merriment. French stand-up comedy sometimes appears to be less superficial and more politicised than other European states. Another French-Moroccan comedian is Gad Elmaleh, familiarly known as "the Jerry Seinfeld of France" who has starred in Woody Allen's "Midnight in Paris." He has performed great acts full of funny descriptions of all sorts, jovial statements, and ridiculous puns. He is the best-known Francophone comedian in the world. Now, Fary, the new Black French comedian, is entertaining the masses with his funny looks, facial gestures, and bodily movements. Notwithstanding that, his appearance, with loose glasses and the style of pants and "Who has got swagger like me," is a pleasant entrance in the comical French world. He lures public attention and abundantly distributes smiles and laughter to his audience.

Interestingly, for centuries the French and Belgium society have been competing in poking fun at each other, albeit the Belgians have long been the butt of French jokes. The Belgians have migrated to France to seek employment in the mining industry and worked along with natives, customarily laughing and joking for delight and relaxation. Once, the trade unions announced the strike that every minor would go on strike from a specific date. French natives observed the rule and did not turn up for work, but Belgians went to work there as usual. The French mocked the Belgians as "Strike Breakers."

Making fun of other folks comes intrinsically to most of us because we always want maximum pleasure to relish at the cost of perpetuating pain and put someone down verbally. Nerve-racking words and impudent jargon can hit another person tough even harder than a blatant blow to the chin. Insolent and brazen talk and presumptuous words can cause emotional damage to a well-educated young person.

Emotions are entrenched within prose, poetry, sketches, and drawings produced by intellectuals, literary humourists, and cartoonists. Before the invention of printing, manuscript medium included waffles, phrases, comic paintings, and pictures to communicate literary allegories, personal experiences, and imagination. Voltaire, the renowned French satirist, was arrested in 1716, exiled from Paris, and in 1717, he endured imprisonment in the Bastille. Juvenal, the Roman poet, was expelled from Rome on account of slating a companion of Emperor Domitian but permitted to come back after the next ruler Hadrian, ascended to the throne. The political insinuations of satire are so frightening that autocratic and oppressive regimes around the globe have systematically tortured, censored, slain, and deported satirists, comical writers, and lampooners.

Multi-ethnic European Comedians

Traditionally, Arab culture stems from original tribal conventions and conservative overtones in which women cannot cross conformist boundaries. In humour and comedy, women have faced barriers and hesitated to touch on socially sensitive matters about morality and ethical values. The cartoonists' drawings show dimensions of reality, albeit despised by the rulers; Arab women have taken risks, displayed courage, and challenged the power nuclei through caricatures and artistic wonders. Their imaginative drawings and innovative cartoons have contributed towards the fall of tyrants. Zaki Shafaqa, a Jordanian cartoonist, admits that the world of cartooning is frightening and threatening to women who deliberately sidestep this field to avoid adverse reactions of society. In the Arab world, comedy is a masculine field and a no go area, especially for the educated, conscientious ladies who are supposed to remain submissive, compliant, and docile. University graduate Arab girls are dutiful and amenable but dislike inferior treatment and unjustified disparity. Some of them have boldly entered the comedian sphere through caricature, gleeful drawings, and meaningful sketches of notable individuals. Rawson Hallak, a Jordanian girl, is a respected comedian representing hijab-wearing women in the Western world's comedian territory. Zvi Bar' el (2007) draws attention to women's perils in producing cartoons of dominant personalities.

Moreover, Arab women feel embarrassed to touch the mode of male-female relationships. A laugh is considered suspicious, says Judith Stora-Sandor (2000), because it is linked with pleasure and belligerence since we habitually laugh at the expense of someone. Cartoons devised by Arab girls depict an accurate picture of Arab culture and society.

Owing to comedy popularity, an association of the 'Cartooning for Peace' was established in 2008 under the French 1901 Law. The office bearers of this association compiled a comprehensive collection of all cartoons published in the Le Monde newspaper for the exclusive purpose of promoting human rights and the freedom of expression. James Scott (2005, pp.8-12) sheds light on Horace's books on satire ethics, discussing mild disdain and playful wit. The first ten poems appeared in 35 B.C. in which he deals with the challenges of reinstating traditional integrity, resisting debt and moneylending with high interest, and encouraging new men to replace exploiters and take their position next to the aristocracy. Self-reliance is the foundation for his objective for a quiet life rather than political craving and uncontrolled determination. Horace asserts that satire is a defensive weapon to protect the poet from angry confrontations. His full name in Latin is Quintus Horatius Floccus, born in Venusia, Italy. The history of satire for confronting the autocratic and greedy but raising concern for the oppressed emotional and social well-being has been ancient. Arab women deserve acclamation for their daring cartoons inspiring the masses to overthrow the tyrants and despots.

It all commenced with the notorious "Arab Spring 2011" when in the rampant face of strict censorship, suppression, and control of all forms of free expression, the Arab ladies made cartoons for gaining freedom through intellect and emotion. Humorous sketches helped in the social protest movement, providing tools for ridiculing prime ministers and presidents of various Arab countries.

Hana Hajjar has been a female Saudi cartoonist who has been designing cartoons for the Arab News; an English Daily published from Jeddah, Saudi Arabia. She knows her boundaries and never draws anything related to sex or religion. The aim is to uncover the reality behind the mask of deception, and Arab lady cartoonists like Doae El Adl (October 2012) of Egypt transmit her message through metaphors. For instance, one of her cartoons entitled "The Second Republic of Abscission" illustrates a group of men and women with hair and moustaches getting trimmed with a giant pair of scissors. A cartoon is the hidden portrayal of the realistic expression of oppression and press censorship. Arab Spring 2011 witnessed the fall of dictators, such as:

President Abdulaziz Bouteflika, (Algeria, 29 December 2010)

President Zaine El Abidine Ben Ali, (Tunisia, January 14, 2011);

President Hosni Mubarak, (Egypt, February 11, 2011);

President Muammar Gaddafi, (Libya, August 23, 2011);

President Ali Abdullah Saleh, (Yemen, February 27, 2012)

Also, unrest, protest, and political disenchantments were widespread across other Arab countries, including Iraq, Syria, Sudan, and Bahrain.

Post Arab revolution offered hope to female Arab Cartoonists to use their comic abilities and convey an emotional message to the new rulers for the betterment of deprived Arab communities. Riham El Hour, a Moroccan caricaturist, Dalal Ezzi, a Lebanese cartoonist, and Nadia Khiari, a Tunisian satirist, vigorously expressed their thoughts defying gender stereotypes and exposing flaws in political power and continuation of unjust policies in Arab lands. Among these female comics, Doae El Adl of Egypt stands out since she worked for an Egyptian newspaper "Al-Masry Al-Youm," producing political cartoons depicting Hosni Mubarak and supporting the 2011 revolution. His comics were printed and widely distributed at the 18-day Tahrir Square uprising in Cairo. Good caricatures were sketched and published at the right place at the right time, stimulating public emotions, and producing desirable results. The stirring of emotions by female Arab cartoonists resulted in an emotional response to fuel the uprisings and rebellions. Unfortunately, the cartoons, funny portraits, invective sketches, and parody portraying royalties and rulers, politicians, and aristocrats cannot realistically change the mentality of power and greed and yet, might conceivably break the ice in the predominant calamity of Coronavirus-19.

Twenty-first-century comedians from different ethnic roots regularly perform at the Royal Albert Hall in London for the sole purpose of making people laugh, enjoy, and relax. Among the humourists are Wary Nichen, Sezar Al-Kassab, Mamoun Elagab, Leila Ladhari, and Elgar Room. The comedian background makes spectators laugh as we observe that Leila Ladhari is half Austrian, half Swiss, with one of the grandparents having Tunisian roots. Wary Nichen has Algerian heritage, Sezar's Scottish mother and Iraqi father, and Elagab is from Sudan. They co-jointly bring cultural variety in their puns, Arab social witticism in their gags, tribal riposte in their jokes, political gibes in their utterances, and traditional facial expressions enthuse and galvanise laughter. Their funny anecdotes and silly narratives provoke humour and stimulate profound laughter.

Humorous events, slapstick shows, and stand-up comedies are amusing platforms of youth gatherings, allowing interactions, frank conversations, intimate banters, and socialisation occurrences. Individuals co-jointly enjoy puns and jokes and exchange funny stories. The psychology of laughter has a pleasant impact on teenage social aspirations. Purposeful attachments, resolute intimacies, tenacious fondness, and emotional management shape our lives, making them meaningful, delightful, evocative, and exhilarating. Laughter and humour frame relationships as emotions invoke thoughts, causing expression of our amicable feelings towards friends and college mates, chums, and professional colleagues.

Comedians Reign (POEM)

Comic heroes peacefully reign
Give us respite, reduce our pain

Comedians strike with a funny joke
Whack audience with a hilarious stroke
Public emotions are rarely fraught
Entertainers are earnestly sought

Comedians are above the law
Johnny Carson without a flaw

Patricia Paulson and Allen Steve
Profusely witty, poignant heave

Waggish on stage Dick Van Dyke
Carol Burnette's comic strike

Comedy is an anticipated trait
Everybody loves no one hates

Happiness and sorrow co-exist
Jennifer and Jane Saunders do persist
Actress Josephine Brand always insists
The temptation of fun you can't resist

We live, enjoy, with love, exist
Intensely, joke, turn and twist
The parish boy, or Oliver Twist
Born in a workhouse, lost in mist

Incredibly humorous Miranda Hart

Sarah Millican, a comedian smart
Bridget Christie has learned the art
Dawn French, inimitably plays her part

Charming audience, an incredible skill
Responsive joviality without any frill

Male English comedians, Evans and Carr
Atkinson, and Peter John Kay, are superstar

Stunningly hilarious Benny Hill
Watch and laugh but sit still

Do not forget Michael Yarwood
Comical imitation well understood

Jokes of Jim Davidson taunts and jeers
Merriment triggers blushes and tears

Davidson snores fast and plain
Resonances of a speeding train

Cognitive sickness, comedy cures
President Adams loudly snores
Tragedy diminishes, comedy endures
George Washington sporadically snores

Lord Melbourne snores, like whistles
Roosevelt wheezes amusing chisels
On rostrum always fall and dance
Satirists lampoon with a hazy glance

[Composed by Dr Nazir Ahmad,
January 4, 2020/Jamada Al-Awwal 20, 1442 Hijra,
Monday]

Talk Shows Literature

Objective talk shows are mostly unbiased presented for harmless pleasure and undamaging humour. Modern comedy makes your stomach clench and reveals your teeth irrespective of what is beneath. The witty British characters David Mitchell and Robert Webb reigned for twelve years in a sitcom serial "Peep Show" full of tongue in cheek and funniness, so did Jennifer Saunders and Joanna Lumley in "Absolutely Fabulous" from 1992 to 2012. The sensual loose character of six friends in "Coupling" aroused interest in the excitement-seeking young generation of college kids. Their dating lives are filled with intense jokes. Nobody can ignore the colourful insults of Peter Capaldi and then the two on-going episodes of Fleabag and Catastrophe on British television.

An impartial show has either a problem-solving or therapeutic perspective, but socially inspired displays evolve violation of societal norms focusing on youth relationship conflicts. The Jerry Springer show was an appropriate example exhibiting scandalous intimate revelations. We may remember it as an escapist live U.S. television programme where couples unleash anger in an intensely harsh and vulgar manner. Jerry allowed sufficient freedom and time for those on screen to present their case without any interruption. The spontaneity and richness of interaction between two partners enabled audiences and viewers to take sides in each conflict. Some believe this programme was too violent and unpleasant, while others supported the learning aspect of solving personal disputes after hearing detailed arguments from both sides. Jerry Springer generated academic and social interest by making commendable brilliant concluding remarks depicting his thoughts and emotions. The young men and women openly discussed all aspects of social and moral issues and manifestations involving cheating on the partners to compulsive dishonesty and lying. Real-life negative emotions took many forms during each programme ranging from intense anger to physical violence that had to be controlled by Jerry's security guards. It was a real-time presentation, but certainly not real-life entertainment. As a programme host, Jerry appeared to remain neutral and did not necessarily take sides. He attempted to solve and settle many relational disputes among the participators.

The young age is a delicate period of life in which youth explore their emotions, supposed to be a knotty wiggle of tangled impressions. The comedians make us laugh while acting in funny movies. Johnny Carson used to lift the right-hand index figure, glance at the roof, then thumb touches his lips while telling a joke to amuse the spectators. Jack Lemon films "It should happen to you" (1954), Some Like it Hot (1949), The Apartment (1960), Missing (1982), The Player (1992), Short Cuts (1993), and his navy comedy-drama Mister Roberts (1955) entertain millions around the globe. Then we can view Matt Richard's "Just for Laugh-Montreal (2013), and Jocelyn Chia's "Comedy for Attractive People" (2015) enthral the audience with comical anecdotes and side-splitting narratives. Chia was from Singapore, qualifying as a lawyer but practising utterance of most hilarious jokes and claiming to be the winner of Funniest Lawyers competition. Europe and the U.S. have many distinguished comedians as one can find Jack Lemmon in his "The Front Page" (1974) as he causes longing through the delivery of multipurpose and skilfully timed jokes.

Conclusively, humour has proved to be the tested social antiseptic psychological medicine and physically relaxing biological solution for mental, emotional, and spiritual nourishment.

CHAPTER IX - LITERARY HUMOUR

Literary Humour appears in scholarly works of renowned poets, playwriters, song composers, novelists, dramas, prose, and movie scriptwriters. Dramatists and screenwriters have produced humorous episodes of lasting entrainment for the masses across all cultures and civilisations. Literary Humour appears in abundance in the literary creations of Charles Dickens, Herbert Spencer, William Makepeace Thackeray, and many French, German, Italian and Dutch intellectuals. For instance, upon the occasion of 200th birthday commemorations, Dickens was awarded the final designation of "Comic Crusader." More appropriately, I believe, "Emperor of Literary Comedy" would be predominantly a distinguished accolade for Charles Dickens. On his 200th anniversary, The London-based Daily Telegraph (December 21, 2011) published a report praising his humorous contributions to the body of English literature, including Dickens's quote that "Comedy turns the world upside down.". Charles Dickens dexterously entertained millions of people around the world.With his pen and quick-wittedness, conquered multi-million human hearts without causing intimidation, hurt or shedding a single drop of blood. It was a literary victory without physical slaughter and mental torture. To reinforce this point, the present writer studied the works of Dickens, Eliot, Carlyle, Kipling, Spencer, Thackeray, Bernard Shaw, Bertrand Russell, John Milton, Jonathan Swift, and Shakespeare in the Bachelor's Degree in

English Literature courses. Charles Dickens ruled and still rules the English speaking world of literate souls and sparks humour, delight, and thrill in the minds of ordinary people who endeavour to watch plays and dramas. I would personally call Charles Dickens the King of Comedy and the Prince of Parody.

Dickens's earlier novels are much funnier, but the works produced later in life are inevitably less humorous and satirical. Virginia Woof called Charles Dickens (1874-1936) the most delightful of all caricaturists, but Chesterton in his work entitled 'Chesterton on Dickens' says the spirit of Dickens's genius was an exaggeration. This book of Dickens prodigy came into print in 1906 in New York, followed by numerous scholarly favourable commentaries, critical appraisals, and complimentary reviews.

T.S. Elliot said Gilbert Keith Chesterton's book on Dickens was "the best on that author that has ever been written," as Chesterton adds that 'its merit is precisely that none of us could have conceived such a thing...it is the best of all impossible worlds.' In 1942, the new edition of this book was published under the subtitle "The Last of the Great Men." In the introduction of this book, Alexander Woolcott says that it is readable, and he has read it more than a dozen times and relishes its conclusion. Romantic poets such as Coleridge, Wordsworth, Keats, Byron, and Shelly mesmerise the young readers, whereas Tennyson, Geoffrey Chaucer, Virginia Wolf, and Keats captivate the individuals with their imaginative, poetic works generating emotions and engendering feelings of pleasure and desire.

Henry James accused this celebrated satirist's 'caricature of assigning sentiments to a troop of hunchbacks. Although Woolf profoundly disagreed with such conjecture. Dickens's far-reaching usage of caricature openly contested normative insolences of the nineteenth century. Thackeray unhesitatingly conceded the label of caricaturist and subsequently proclaimed his works as caricatural. In his novels, he too incorporated caricatural sketches and graphics. Through caricature, Dickens conspicuously transmits actuality, diffuses veracity, and spreads sanity. His indispensable ascension to fame materialised with the publication of "Pickwick Papers" (1837-1838) that earned him the designation of 'Comic Genius.' Mildred Newcombe (1993, p.230) made a remarkable assertion on his novel as a 'Spontaneous creation of a young genius' yet learning to control his ability. He was the founder of British mobile circus, the best substitute for modernity, says Professor Michael Hollington of the University of New South Wales.

Moreover, Dickens himself described that "In the clown, I perceived two persons; one a fascinating unaccountable creature of hectic complexion, joyous in spirits though feeble in intellect with flashes of brilliancy; the other, a pupil for Mr Barlow. I thought how Mr Barlow would secretly rise in the morning, and butter the pavement for him, and when he had brought him down, would look severely out of his study window, and ask him how he enjoyed the fun" Mr Barlow would certainly view clown as his pupil. Although his characters are excellent performers but somehow lack emotions and therefore, Dickens's comedy lacks the portrayal of factual distresses and vindictiveness. John Carey (1973, p.68) points out that Dickens himself sometimes experiences the real-life viciousness which he depicts in comedy for others to understand. Also, Robert Patten (1967, p.358) looks at Jingle's comedy as misery and sadness of Pickwick's empathy, whereas Anny Sadrin (1993) believes Dickens is bidding a simple joke with Jingle's dialogue. In 'Memoirs of Joseph Grimaldi (2008), it is stated that the characters in the novels of Dickens are radiantly exposed as comic or wicked that permit selfish cravings, instigate sentiments, and evade fretfulness. In 1936, when Dickens was reviewing Grimaldi's biography, he composed a poem related to a funny incident involving the grandfather of Joseph Grimaldi, who was a famous clown. Once, he knocked a chandelier off the ceiling while performing, directly injuring Turkey's ambassador in the front row. Charles Dickens humorous poem is as follows:

Hail Iron Legs! Immortal pair

Agile, firm knit, and peerless

That skin the earth, or a vault in Air

Aspiring high and fearless

The glory of Paris! Outgoing compeers,

Brave pair! May nothing hurt ye;

Scatter at will over chandeliers,

And Tweak the Nose of Turkey,

And should a too presumptuous foe,

But dare these shores to land on,

His well-kicked men shall quickly know

We have Iron legs to stand on.

(CHARLES DICKENS)

Dickens played Captain Bobadil of Ben Jonson's 'Everyman in His Humour' in a commendable production enacted in 1845. His performances in amateur theatricals during his career invited approbation from many intellectuals and the general public. He was much praised for his enactment in 'The Merry Wives of Windsor.' John Stonehouse (1935) skilfully compiled a comprehensive 'Catalogue of the Library of Charles Dickens.' For a while, Dickens was engaged with Italian street and professional theatres, and in France, he attended several theatrical performances. His comic passion took him to the United States for a closer look at the enactment of side-splitting presentations in theatres. Dickens's literary Humour is evident in the 'Great Expectations' in which events are admirably hilarious.

In Germany and Austria, where the German language is the primary communication source, Comic writers and comedians have entertained the public with amusing literature and theatrical presentations. Every year they have "Karneval" period in which carnival fools and stand-up comedians perform live, cracking jokes, singing, and executing sensual dance to amuse the audience. For example, "The Schwank," initially published in 1515, has been an exciting, funny story in German literature sprouting crude humour. Andreas Gryphius was a renowned German comic tale writer; his earliest work "Herr Peter Squentz" was published in 1658, followed by "Horribilicribrifax Teutsch" in 1663. Both of these witty publications imbued a new spirit in the German culture and showbiz industry. Other well-known comedy writers who left a rib-tickling effect on stage performance were Heinrich von Kleist (1777-1811), who produced "Der zerbrochene Krug" in 1808, and a year earlier, "Amphitryon" in 1807 became outstanding contributions to the comedian literature. Albert Lortzing (1801-1851) and Johann Strauss II (1825-1899) diligently composed opera. All of these plays were repetitive performances in German theatres across the country. In the mid-1930s, "Vater und Sohn" (father and son) cartoons brought joy to the general public. Since the beginning of the present century, German entertainers as stand-up comedians have been giving stunningly funny performances on television and theatres. German ladies have enthusiastically captured a significant chunk of stand-up and television comedian market. Among the popular shows include "Die Wochenshow performed by Anke Engelke, appearing in series from 1996 to 2000. Martina Hill appeared in the "Heute" show as well as her sketch show "Knallerfrauen" (2011). Also, Hella Kemper has presented "Genial daneben.". Other German women comedians are Gaby Koster, Nadja Sieger, Ursula Schaeppi, and Mirja Boes. From the 1950s, a renowned German humourist Bernhard Viktor Christoph-Carl Van Bulow (1923-2011) was an excellent cartoonist as he started publishing his sketches in the Stern Magazine. He was the mastermind of well-known television series called "Loriot," featuring another comic actress Evelyn Hamann (1942-2007). Literary Humour is associated with Heinz Erhardt, who composed ironic poems such as "Die Schnupftabaksdose" in 1912. A German cabaret musician often included jolly rhymes and puns in his songs while playing a musical instrument and entertaining the audience. In the 1980s, Harald Schmidt used to appear on late-night satirical talk shows as his live Kabarett show "The Thistle," "The Pepper Mill' and "The Laugh and Shoot Society" were profoundly funny, pulling millions of viewers across the country. One of the standard jokes was that 'How many Frisians does it take to screw in a light bulb? Five! One to hold the bulb and four to turn the table he is standing on'.

Concealed Humour was conveyed through paintings depicting touches of comedy and a range of human feelings. For instance, Titian's ingenuity is visible in his scientifically executed colourful paintings for Philip II of Spain. Titian's incredible brushwork, farfetched use of oils on canvas reflect the richness of his artistic capability. He produced erotic pictures between 1552 and 1562, and the opulent nudeness in photographs is the result of fulfilling the royal's desire for such images. The paintings are currently in control of the British National Gallery, Trafalgar Square, London.

The sense of Humour has always been linked with either heartfelt or insensible absurdity, which is also rampant in socially appropriate behaviour. Craik et al. have designated ten styles of Humour out of which five categories are evident: e.g., Socially Warm Humour; Reflective Humour; Competent Humour; Earthy Humour and Benign Humour. They also mentioned aggressive Humour involving teasing, sarcasm, ridicule, and mockery. Earthy denote indulgence in rude and vulgar humour, whereas good mood relates to limericks and witticism. Socially warm is admirably a positive and optimistic sense of humour that promotes and facilitates social interaction.

Humour in the Classroom

Pranks and humour are universal across all cultures, successfully practised in college and university classrooms as viable learning tools. The creation of a social environment mitigates tensions and enhances student engagement, self-confidence, and retention power. Light jokes keep the students alert, active, and on their toes, enabling them to be willing participants in contributing ideas during seminars and topic-oriented discussions. The lively atmosphere creates excitement, invigorates thought, and rouses curiosity that permeates learning. Humour wakes up the sleepy, galvanises the tired, and electrifies the inactive college scholars. Cheery professors narrate funny stories to develop self-motivation, boost confidence, and generate fun in the knowledge co-construction process in the classroom, thus making the lessons more inviting and conducive to learning. Humour strengthens psychological bonds between student and lecturer, improving rapport, enjoyment, and happiness. A more promising and encouraging atmosphere would uplift the mood of learners making the learning enjoyable, informal, and pleasurable. A light touch of cheerfulness causing hilarity and thrill would elevate the spirit of student commitment. Humour induced education significantly strengthens the young memory and concept retention powers. Candidness and frankness bring shy and outspoken students together in building social bridges and fashioning new friendships.

Provine (2002) proclaims that humour improves classroom climate, minimises tension, and makes learning a real-life experience. Humour not only promotes understanding but endorses student attention. (Fisher, 1997). Timely humour in the classroom settings can foster mutual openness and respect and contribute to effective teaching. (Kher et al., 1999). The fun-driven broadness invites active participation in collaborative learning that benefits all students. Powell (1985) asserts that humour promotes confidence, enlivens classroom settings, and creates a positive attitude towards learning new material. Bryant and Zillmann (1988) researched the practicalities of fun and reaffirmed that it indeed promoted learning in the classroom. Ziv (1988) carried out experiments to prove this point in which enhanced learning occurred.

In-Prison Reflections & Echoes

Literary works emphasise the cultivation of inward morality as opposed to outward forms of social behaviour. The academic writers have encountered captivity owing to their contradictory reports, articles, and prose in newspapers, magazines, and books. While facing confinement, their eye-opening emotional reflections have enriched English literature. Susan Willis Fletcher, in her book, "Twelve Months in an English Prison' (1884), recounts her experiences "as if I had been sitting in a theatre, and seeing a play enacted on the stage." She ingeniously ventures beyond immediate confines. In her imagination, Susan feels outside the prison boundary walls enjoying a theatrical performance. She writes, 'In the summer of 1880, while visiting my mother in the United States, I went to jail on a charge of obtaining jewels and clothing of great value. Having spent some time in custody, I was released, but on returning to England, in April 1881, faced the same charge again. I appeared at the Central Criminal Court, Old Bailey, London, and sentenced to 12-months incarceration. She describes how her grandfather came to her and said, 'don't you think you were born to preach. He took me into His loving arms and said, Oh. God, make her strong to do her work'. (1884, pp.3-5). However, at the trial proceedings, Susan Fletcher could not tell her own story to the presiding jury.

Similarly, Xavier de Maistre, in his book, "A Voyage Around My Room," (1794) asserts, he was placed under house arrest in Turin for 42 days, and he kept his spirit up by envisaging his triangulations between the walls and around the furniture as an expedition. Confinement memories and creativities are depicted in an Egyptian lady scholar and writer's "Memoirs from the Women's Prison" (1981). There was a strict restriction for prisoners to possess books, blank papers, and essential notepads in Egyptian prisons; Miss Nawal El Saadawi was kept in isolation and seclusion for long durations in the prison cell. She used toilet paper and eyeliner instead of pencil for her creative writing and life in prison. The eyeliner somehow was brought to her by a friend of another inmate. Nawal says, 'since childhood, a dream has inhabited my imagination, I write my words and people read them…those are the people who make a homeland, and my homeland has become those people.' An Iranian prose writer `Mohammad Dowlat Abadi, was apprehended by Raza Shah Pahlavi's brutal secret police for his published novels.' These books were repossessed from the house of another Iranian dissident chased by the regime. The police confiscated his books and brought to the attention of higher authorities who had ordered the immediate arrest of Dowlat Abadi. He has been a strong advocate for freedom of thought. He retained in his memory, a sketch of his life and treatment in prison. After his release, he wrote a book "Missing Slouch: (1979) within seventy days of his cherished freedom. His most iconic multivolume work is "Kelidar" In his novel

Slouch, he describes the tale of the mysterious disappearance of a villager during the 1979 revolution in Iran. The family gets scattered, facing economic hardships, deprivation, and social collapse. In this unambiguously readable novel, he vividly portrays the trials of Soluch's wife and three children.

In "To Althea, from Prison" (1642), Richard Lovelace wrote a poem from his prison cell in Westminster Abbey, London. Lovelace narrates,

'Stone walls do not a prison make,

Nor Iron bars a Cage:

Minds innocent and quiet take

That for a Hermitage.

If I have freedom in my Love,

And in my soul am free,

Angels alone that soar above,

Enjoy such Liberty

Comedy confronts the epitome and eliminates any objective and composed rationality of the model concerning eternalness. Some humour is conservative and serves to emphasise social harmony, says Simon Critchley (2002, p.11). Comedy is perceived as a by-product of communal dialogue, and it sometimes brings arrogant to their knees. When Humour makes sense, it twigs from what does not make any sense; therefore, the audience uses common sense to understand the excitement of comedian acts of joy. Humour in comedy is best described by George Speight (1955) as competing fluids in the body since humour decrees conduct and form physiognomies.

Literary intellectuals have portrayed humour both in constructive and destructive manners. If used in good ways, humour can articulate and nurture social bonds, bolster moralities, and act as a shared emollient for people from diverse cultures and communities. Some of the past movies such as 'O Brother, Where Art Thou' 2000; 'About a Boy' 2002; 'Old School' 2003; 'Borat' 2006; and 'Train Wreck' 2015, are rated top comedian films in the Western world. Just to name the few, a large number of British, German, and French movies evoke awesome humour, instigate comedy and wittiness. Mel Brooks, a mesmerising comedian, feels that "The tragedy is when I cut my figure. Comedy is when you walk into an open sewer and die" An ordinary person cannot be subtle to the shock which the rib-tickling frequently covers. Some comedians hardly exercise self-restraint in humorous utterances as long as they can make the spectators laugh. In a comical situation, evil always happens to someone else, and imitation of inferior people has become a hobby. We often derive decadence in the depiction of less fortunate members of society and amuse ourselves by mocking them in a caricatured form. We do not require a sense of humour to laugh at them because we quickly yield to inducement and willingly accept what is being prodded upon us. Despite comprehending frivolity, vulgarity, and rudeness in the comic, we enjoy without making a judgement of the intensity of offensiveness.

Pure pleasure seldom contains funniness, but funniness (is more often none other, but fun is terrible) is more active and vital. (F. Schlegel, 1794/1979. P.20). Anthony Ludovic, in 'The secret of laughter' presents an evolutionary version of a person's feelings of superior adaptation to some specific situation or his environment in general. He mentions Hobbes's theory of "sudden glory. Thomas Hobbes (1651/1957, p.36), the author of 'Superior theory' opined that grimaces express not the triumph of a socially beneficial victory over evil and imperfection. Still, our selfish and sudden vain glory arises from the fact that we consider ourselves nobler, smarter, and the difference is only in the scorn's function. It is a belief of perfection and importance in ourselves, by comparison with the susceptibility of other people. For Kant (1790), affection arises from the 'sudden transformation of a strained expectation into nothing.' Comedy is a representation of inferior people, and Hobbes believes that there is something wrong with the person who can feel good about himself only by looking down on others. Many centuries ago, Romans were accustomed to deriving extreme pleasure and humour in brutally ridiculing underprivileged humanities. In great numbers, Romans used to be present at the Colosseum to enjoy watching the Christians clawed and battered by the lions. They guffawed and smirked at the unbearable inhuman torture and brutalised death of innocent victims in the arena. In those Roman times, public persecution and executions were a popular fashion and a well-liked source of downright entertainment. For Byzantine Romans, it was just a pure comedy to display barbarism, savagery, and cruelty, on the one hand, to exert the power of the Roman empire and on the other to consider it as a mere joke and fun. Walter Benjamin (2009, p.125) is correct as he succinctly narrates that "comedy does not destroy or support something. The strict joke is the imposition of repression". Suppression of the oppressed was the primary objective of tyrant Roman Emperors who had invented various torturous methods for amusement.

Habitually, we pinpoint deficiencies, discover faults, and mimic the imperfections of disadvantaged and underprivileged people. German Romantic writer and humour theorist Jean-Paul has exquisitely compared humour to a disguised Priest who weds every couple. We should study ideas of radically subjectivist thinkers Kant and Jean-Paul for discovering a connection between humour and laughter. They exhibit utterly objective views of twenty-first-century ethology and neural services. Jean-Paul further states that not a single theory of humour ever formulated is wrong. (Kozintsev, 2012, p.vii).

Moreover, jesting is typically concerned with reality, whereas humour is related exclusively with exemplifications. Satirical exclamations defy the connotations, whereas humorous expressions confront the ways meanings are expressed. Kozintsev (2012, p.147) says, by making an ironic statement, the speaker mentions or echoes something with which he/she disagrees; by creating a humorous account, the speaker mentions something which in his/her view makes no sense.

Humour in Literature (POEM)

Humour forms in human nature
Irrespective of your visible stature

Humour motivates, refreshes the brain
Helps wipe out depressive stain

Chaucer incited a medieval sense
Shakespeare keeps us in suspense

Humour is a priceless treasure
Subtract pain, receive pleasure

Dickens edited morning chronicle (1834)
Everyday life and everyday people (1836)

Posthumous papers of pickwick club (1836-37)
London theatres his comical hub

Horseback riding and brisk walks
Noteworthy are his literary talks

Arduous troubles of Oliver Twist
Dickens produced a superb gift

You must also read Jonathan Swift
His Gulliver's Travels are adrift (1726)

Witting style in modest proposal (1729)
Plenty of time at his disposal

Tale of tub in seventeen o four   (1704)
Deadpan satire read no more

(Composed by Dr Nazir Ahmad,
March 31, 2021,/ Sha'ban 17, 1442 Hijra, Wednesday]

Wits and Puns (POEM)

Wittiness spurs and releases dopamine
Extracts bodily pain from the spine

Worries diminish with comics pun
Anxieties perish with rousing fun

If you are filled with mental fatigue
Pick up a book of comical read

Moving jokes is a tiredness pill
Gladly take you to top of the hill

Watch a jack lemon movie for wit
Laughter makes your sides split

Perish your disquiets bit by bit
These are wonders of puns and wit

Takes your anger away for a while
Move your lips with a rhythmic smile

Relaxation descents with a hilarious joke
Enjoying smoking without a smoke

Life is filled with sorrows and struggles
Light funniness is a tablet for troubles

[Composed by Dr Nazir Ahmad,
March 21, 2021/ Sha'ban 7, 1442 Hijra, Sunday]

Comedians are matchless human classes divergent from other members of the society because they perform acts of daftness, silliness, and absurdity for indoctrinating joy and buzz into the lives of spectators. They are a living marvel and actuality, inspiring jolliness, stimulating gaiety, and disseminating gratification. Enid Welsford (1935) has documented the history of fools and clowns from early primitive England. She comments that the jokes operate upon the juncture of literature. They are partially responsible for drawing attention towards emancipation and the development of human sovereignty. Humour is a specific spectacle referring to 'What we call Comedy (Potter, 1954, p.25), but equally important is the role of natural comedians who hesitate to disclose nudity and hollowness behind disguises because they are fashioning emptiness.

Telling Jokes

Telling jokes are universal natural human phenomena surpassing boundaries and space. Once Mark Twain chirped, politicians and diapers must be changed often and for the same reason'. It could amuse many readers but might be significantly hurtful to those who are honest, candid, and noble in their practices and public obligations. Mike Yarwood, an English Impressionist, Comedian, and Actor (Years active 1966-1995) entertained millions of viewers by impressive impersonation of famous British dignitaries, politicians, sports personnel, and eminent entertainers.. Mike Yarwood's incredibly well-written books are "Just Joking" and "Impressions of My Life." Humour elicits from impersonators' bodily movements, facial expressions, and oral utterances. Jim Davidson, an English stand-up comedian, actor, and Roadshows performer, presented sudden insightful integration of controversial ideas that disturbed people's sentiments. Jim smirked about fat birds, fannies, and knobs, but often managed to swim against the tide of prevailing values and fashion. The audience sometimes did not appreciate his jokes, even dissenting with his tone and substance. For instance, he would say, "Book the wife in on Monday morning," I beg your pardon, Madam, but I can't think of anyone who … you twice". It was offensive brand humour, but he did lots and lots of charity shows for the army, and others around the country. One of the most entertaining humorous characters was Alfred Hawthorne Hill famously known as BENNY HILL, an English Comedian and a great joker of his time. He provided mind-blowing entertainment on British Television. A couple of jokes would suffice to elaborate on the performance of a remarkable humourist. For example, he would say, "Have you noticed that all the people in favour of birth control are already born" and then he utters that "Why would I make one woman so miserable when I can make so many women very happy."

In times of distress and gloom, when people are daily embracing the loss of their close relatives and loved ones, a bit of light humour might not do any harm, though cannot minimise despondency and joylessness. We have been surrounded by the lockdown in the United Kingdom, Spain, Germany, Italy, and France, owing to Corona Virus-19. Fortunately, there is hope now after the availability of vaccine. Optimistically, vast majority of British population would receive the vaccination by the end of July 2021. Most people can get back to work and start enjoying social life, visiting friends and families, eating out and restoring relationships.

Many entertainment programmes, comic festivals, and similar venues were cancelled at short notice to avoid the spread of the virus. All Auckland Live Comedy Fest' due to be held on April 30, 2020, was cancelled, and other comedy venues such as Bruce Mason Centre, The Cloud, Shed 10, Aotea Centre was closed down till further notice. Currently, the UK has the fifth-highest number of mortalities and infected cases after the USA, Brazil, India, Mexico, and the U.K. Despite the virus's gravity, a courageous group of Stand-up Comedians of Arab heritage gathered at the London stage to present a live performance to a live audience on March 5, 2020. It was "Corona Comedy: Arab Women Comics Laugh in the Face of Adversity" in East London, Rich Mix Venue. Its chief organiser El-Saqqa described the comedy show "Really a

Miracle" under the perturbing climate. A consecutive 6th "Arab Women Arts Now" hosted by stunningly charming Lebanese-British comedian Isabelle Farah pulled a massive crowd from all sectors of the London community.

OK, funny and timely jokes of Swiss-born Leila Ladari of Tunisian descent, Serine Ayari, Belgian resident of Tunisia, Bahranian-British Jenna al-Ansari Leila Alj, a Moroccan beauty, created an exciting atmosphere at this stressful time in human history. Ayari came on the stage informing about her arrival from Belgium and stated that her comedy originates from a personal perspective. She was not going to please the crowd, which she does not support. Some jokes in Belgium can get us in trouble, and we have to follow the prescribed rules, unlike England. Then appears Moroccan mirthful comedian Leila who describes herself "a bit of a bitch" and cracks a joke, "I enjoy coughing in public places and watching the panic unfold around me," we have the best couscous. We have sunshine, but we cannot shout about women's rights in Morocco. She says I have lived in Chicago where "no one knows where Morocco was." Next came Maria Shehata, an Egyptian-American Stand-up comedian who has lived in Los Angles and now settled in London. She looks gorgeous and dazzling in her humorous anecdotes as she says, "I miss LA a lot, but it is nice being around smarter people for a change." The show was a success, and everything closed.

Austria has a rich history of comedians like Farkas and Waldbrunn, Kreisler, Kraner, Dorfer, Hader, and Resetarits. Okello Dunkley established Vienna's Funniest Stand-up Comedy that holds tri-monthly shows. He says the Austrians do not laugh at everything. The Austrian people share German-Swiss culture, do not abruptly laugh, and rarely giggle. The humour delves towards the macabre but avoids direct insults because most jokes are very sober and restrained. The comedians such as Reginald Barris hold "Vienna Chuckles" since 2016, attracting both native Austrians and a vast proportion of migrants. The Salzburg Festival of Theatre and Music is one of the most famous cultural events that enables comedians to entertain the public, telling jokes and creating a humorous environment.

Graphic Humour

Humour can be verbal in-jokes or visuals such as graphical sketches, cartoons, caricatures, and animations. One of the significant dimensions of cartoons is that it successfully conveys visual communication, hilarious signals, and funny gestures. Inattentive browsing of comic books reveals diverse facets of pictures, graphs, and sketches, sometimes misunderstood by a common man but meticulously interpreted by thoughtful readers and heedful observers. It largely depends on the watchful eyes of the vigilant person who can diligently decode the information. An assiduous artist draws cartoons assigning precise facial expressions testing the readers' ability to envisage their conclusions. In such challenging scenarios, a few words or funny phrases beside the depictions help explicitly extricate the meaning behind the cartoons. In live television shows, comedians express facial emotions with different intensity levels to maximise audience pleasure and excitement. In printed cartoon books and magazines, the accurate geomatical drawings perform this function to a lesser degree, albeit supplemented by humorous textual matter.

Images of humans, animals, and objects engraved on rocks, stones, and cave walls have ancient roots. During my visit to Petra, Wadi Rum, and mountains around the Dead Sea in Jordan, the present writer witnessed several specimens of such historical portrayals, evolving ancient tales and traditions of inhabitants. While at Wadi Rum, the writer notably observed "vast areas of dunes neatly piled up against the mountains, offering a splendid view. Equally spectacular are rocks arches displaying incredible sight. The colour of rocks turns yellow when the Sun begins to sink below the horizon. Numerous impressions of animals, e.g., horses and camels on the mountains, have been painstakingly etched into the stones by tribesmen and Bedouins as signs of their heritage and tribal identification. Other inscriptions on the rocks of Wadi Rum are the Thamudic and Nabatean engravings" (Ahmad, 2016, p.133)

Some of the surviving manuscripts available in the British Museum (British Library London in which the present writer studied between 1973-1981) did contain artworks and graphics alongside text. Comic and caricature used to be a significant part of writing before the invention of printing. The detailed description of partially illustrated earliest printed books can be found in the current writer's work, "History of Arabic and Persian Printing" (2015).

William Caxton, an Englishman, printed the first book in English in 1473, initially written in French entitled "The Recuyell of the Historyes of Troye." The printing paved the way for the inclusion of drawings and graphic images to illustrate the textual matter of books. However, it was not until 1755, Koikawa Harumachi, a Japanese caricaturist, published 'Master Flashgold's Splendiferous Dream" comprising photos, drawings, and artworks ridiculing the ruling elite and the Japanese society. His influence was so significant that the comic characters and humorous images began to appear in commercial advertisements. William Heath was an extremely popular droller comic who produced in 1825, 'Glasgow Looking Glass,' profoundly exemplified magazine exhibiting a satirical view of British politics and the social lives of the public. The third well known Swiss comic artist was Rodolphe Topffer, who in 1833, demonstrated artistic skill in his book 'Historie de M. Jabot.'

"The Adventures of Mr Obadiah Oldbuck' with plenty of quainter sketches and photos was published in 1842 in the United States. Highly admired and greatly praised British illustrator George Cruikshank who had the honour of adding graphics to Charles Dickens' 'Oliver

Twist,' superbly produced 'The Life Of Mr. Lambkin" containing incredibly wittier animations, photos, and sketches.

In 1849, an American comic book, 'Journey to the Gold Digging,' was published by two brothers James and Alexander Read in California. There was a consistent flow of comical magazines in the USA and Europe. German cartoonists, French caricaturists, and Italian animators persistently entertained book lovers and magazine subscribers through their hilarious works of artistic beauty and satirist splendour.

Siegel and Shuster's "Superman" in 1938 steered the era of the Golden Age of Comic Books. The Silver Age of Comic Books commenced in the 1930's with the Flash in Showcase in 1956. From the 1950s onwards, detective comic, underground comic, alternative comics accompanied photos, drawings, and colour sketches. Comic books in Britain include "Ally Slopers' Half Holiday" (1884), Beano and Dandy (1934), and Tiger (1954). In the 1970s and 1980s, humorous journals and books speedily proliferated due to increased public demand, growing liberalism, and better purchasing power. Humour magazines frequently included partially revealing pictures of female movie stars, models, and fashion designer simulations. Hilarious imitations, replications, and mock-ups with witty quotations tremendously increased the sale of popular entertainment journals.

Cicero proclaimed, 'I believe that a witty man converses about anything more easily than about wit itself'. If a person attempts to describe a joke, the spirit of that joke evaporates as steam escapes from electric cattle or a high tide returning to the ocean. My assumption is affirmed by Monro (1951), who says, 'any attempt to analyse humour seriously is doomed to fail.' Humour relies on implicit and unspoken understanding rather than realistic comprehension. Humour can evade and outwit social modesty and social politeness. Positive jesting can penetrate our feelings and bring relief to our emotions. Humour is often based on inferred social bonds, undeclared bigotries, tacit intolerances, and silent biases. However, kidding cures the sick comforts the sad, and gives pleasure to amusement seekers.

Humorous events and slapsticks shows are avenues of youth and adult entertainment, permitting opportunities for informal human interaction, allowing intimate banters, and creating chances for the formation of durable connections. Humour, from the perspective of social psychology, exerts a pleasurable influence on teenagers' moods and dispositions. Conclusively, on-campus and off-campus social link-ups, unwavering intimacies, and obstinate fondness significantly structure youth lives, making them delightful, exhilarating, and meaningful. Our positive emotions invoke pleasant thoughts, instigating tender feelings, and activate compassionate fondness for newly formed connections and tender relationships.

CONCLUSION

Emotions are a natural expression of human feelings in response to a beautiful gesture, a moving utterance, a biological signal, or a psychological experience. Sentiments can neither be structured nor manufactured but believed to be an unrepressed display of excitements, the unrestrained spectacle of impressions, and the automatic flow of passions. Historically, awe-inspiring speeches of intellectuals Thomas Carlyle (June 1840, Abraham Lincoln(Nov. 1863), Sir Winston Churchill (June 1940), Recep Tayyip Erdogan (June 2018) profoundly impacted the emotions of the audience. Likewise, spiritually inspiring address of Jesus Christ (A.D. 30) at the Mount, divinely penetrating the last Sermon of the Prophet Muhammad [pbuh] (632 A.D.) at Makkah, and sacred speech of Pope Urban II (Nov 1095) at Clement, France have affected emotions of an ordinary people. Moving discourses brought tears into the eyes of unmoved individuals who passed on the contents to others.

Youth, in particular, are the most affected generations of all times across the globe. We have a massive task of equipping our teenagers with the characteristics of moral courage, spiritual understanding, emotional strength, and touching compassion. Our institutions are ordained to promote the intellectual, social, and ethical powers of youngsters. We empower broods to carve and create a unique place in society successfully. The book delineates on-campus hook-ups, emerging intimacies that vibrate youthful sentiments. Professor Hall's (1914) perceptions and William James (1884) insights trigger feelings. Our body is a crucible of emotional expressions and physical sensations that are irreducible atomic units of molecular chemistry. It is a cauldron of social norms, either inhibiting or displaying emotional experiences. Whenever an opportunity arises, we navigate and show a specific emotion. The vocal tone and facial nod are the familiar signals conveying an unuttered hint of warmth, acceptance, and enticement.

Emotion is a physiological feeling made up of psychological conditions as a consequence of impulses in the body that escort our conduct towards others. For instance, a student attaining the highest academic accolade would have an emotional experience of utter delight and purposeful gratification. Likewise, spiritual experiences cause ecstasy and rapture beyond the understanding of ordinary souls. Three theories stand out regarding emotions, namely: The Cannon-Bard (1927) Theory in which emotion and arousal co-occur; James-Lange Theory in which sentiment is the consequence of arousal; and Schachter & Singer Two Factor Theory (1962) in which both arousal and cognition combine to create emotion. William James (1884, p.190), contends, we feel sorry because we cry, we feel angry because we strike, fully supports James-Lange theory. Our emotional experience results in flushing when we are embarrassed. According to Schachter and Singer, intimate relationships have a higher level of arousal. This stimulation of feelings is due to the degree of attractiveness felt towards each other. When two youngsters share laughter, they experience healthy physical changes, relaxing muscles, and increasing pleasure. Laughter reinforces the immune system, lift mood, and abates pain, stress, and strain.

Sadness is one of the negative emotions with positive outcomes in daily lives. One of the advantages is that momentary gloom and despondency can improve courteous behaviour and politeness. World-renowned psychologists have proven that several supreme accomplishments of the human brain were primarily due to gloominess. Debauched moods have lasting rational concerns, but the impact is rarely permanent. Negative discernments improve faculty to perceive dishonesty and duplicity and differentiate between deviousness and candidness people.

Socio-moral violations, albeit inadvertently, do occur, eliciting smoke alarm, unease, and mistrust. These occurrences are the by-product of settings in which our teens grow, intermingle, and forge relationships. The parents set boundaries and imbed ethical standards for adolescents to evaluate others' motives, intentions, and inclinations. In some cultures, emotions are socially validated judgements, permitting unconstrained exploration. Physical intimacy is the reaching out from inside within the epigenetic framework of closeness. However, the lack of moral education and the implication of excessive use of Twitter, YouTube, Facebook, and the likes carry consequences of enormous proportion. Our minds, feelings, and emotions should neither be suppressed nor constrained but expressed freely. Sometimes, the undesirable mood had motivational implications ascribed to the anticipated states of the brain. Feel is the gasoline just as sense is the firewood that will make the youth ablaze, activate emotional strength, stimulate reading habit, instigate learning appetite, inflaming interpersonal passion, and encourage new adventures. The child is capable of establishing an equitable, free and fair world.

We learn from each other, share knowledge, thoughts, ideas, and ideals. We learn from civilisations, cultures, traditions, and role models that shape our character, personalities, and atmosphere. Even humorous episodes, comedian's puns, and photographic depictions stir human perceptions. Fifteen beautiful poems in this book amply stimulate sensitivities, kindle epitomes, and enflame romantic threads. Self-evaluation is an invigorating emotional experiment, reviving memories, refreshing social connectivity, and recanting pleasant occurrences In life. This academically conceived book is attention-grabbing, engaging, and fun.

PLATES

Excited Emotions: Girl holding an egg

Expressive Laughter: Girl laughing out loud

Frustrated Emotions: An annoyed girl

Sibling Emotions: Brothers and sister together

Scenic Emotions: Sister and brother on an adventure

Child Emotions: A happy girl won a Star Award

Happy Emotions: Youngsters having fun

Collaborative Emotions: Boy & Girl learning together

Academic Interactions: Students in a classroom

Warm Emotions: Two girls hugging

Emotional Pleasure: Enjoying summer break

Reading Interactions: Two brothers reading

Emotional Achievement: Girl passed her exam

Paternal Emotions: Father and son

Family Emotions: Family enjoying togetherness

Humorous Interactions: Graphic on a wall

Affectionate Emotions: Mother holding daughter

Expressive Emotions: Daughter imitating mother

Emotional Discipline: Telling a Child off

Smiling Emotions: Happy Parent with her daughter

Upset Emotions: Girl feeling upset

Romantic Emotions: A happy couple
(Istanbul, Turkey. October 2020)

Emotional Love: Couple showing affection

Group Emotions: A cheerful family & friend's day out
(Istanbul, Turkey. October 2020)

Friendly Emotions: A happy coffee shop manager
(Birmingham, West Midlands. September 2020)

Relaxing Emotions: Reading Sacred Land of Jordan book while afloat on Dead Sea
(Jordan, 2018)

**Professional Emotions: University Professors
Meeting at Habitat**
(Jeddah, Saudi Arabia. December 2020)

**Grateful Emotions: The Author Gifting his book
"Challenges of Raising Youth"**
(KAUST, Saudi Arabia. January 2021)

LIST OF PUBLICATIONS BY THE AUTHOR

1. Science & Technology: A select bibliography. London: Southwark College, 1975.

2. Building Technology: an annotated bibliography of critical path analysis. Surrey, England, Crown Books, 1976.

3. Man-Powered Flight: Its History and Progress. Surrey, Crown Books, 1977.

4. Structure of Education and Libraries in a Developing Society. Lahore: Sang-e-Meel, 1983.

5. Academic Libraries. Lahore: Qadriya Books, 1984.

6. University Library Practices in Developing Countries. London; Boston, Melbourne, Kegan Paul, 1985.

7. Indexing Newspapers: Subject Analysis. Birmingham: NAAF Tec, 1991.

8. The Illumination of Heart. Birmingham: ACS Publications, 2001.

9. Virtuous Life of Imam Ali: The gateway of knowledge. Birmingham: Radiant Valley, 2010.

10. Karwan-e-Zainab bint Batool. Birmingham: Radiant Valley, 2011.

11. Sufferings of the Sacred Family: Karbala Atrocities, Birmingham: Radiant Valley, 2012.

12. Karb-e-Hafsa. Lahore: Nida-e-Haq, 2012.

13. Manzoomat Dr Nazir Ibn-e-Zainab. Birmingham: Radiant Valley, 2013.

14. History of Arabic and Persian Printing. Birmingham: Radiant Valley, 2015.

15. Collection of Poems.[Allah ka Qurb] Birmingham: Radiant Valley, 2016.

16. The Sacred Land of Jordan. West Midlands: Radiant Valley, 2017.

17. The Refinement of Spiritual Potential: illumination of soul and mind. West Midlands: Radiant Valley, 2018.

18. Challenges of Raising Youth: Nurturing teenagers in a Digital World. Birmingham: Radiant Valley, 2020.

19. Emotional Wellbeing: Emotional Attachments Shape Our Lives. Birmingham: Radiant Valley, 2021. [Printing in Progress]

20. Literary Poems: Emotional, cultural, social, psychological, and holiday sonnets with Turkish, Jordanian, Welsh & Swiss Stanzas [to be published in 2021]

21. Family Memoirs: an Illustrated biography with Poems and Photos. Birmingham: Radiant Valley, [to be published in 2022.]

REFERENCES

Acitelli, L.K. (1987). Intimacy as the proverbial elephant. E(Ed.) D. Perlman and S.W. Duke (Intimate relationships: development, dynamics, and deterioration. Beverly Hills: Sage. (pp.297-308).

Adler, A. (1964) Social interest: a challenge to humanity. (J. Linton and R. Vaughan, tr.) New York: Capricorn Books.

Ahmad, Nazir (1975). Problem of discipline in college libraries. New Library World, London. October Issue 1975.

Ahmad, Nazir (1983). Libraries in Society. Lahore: Sangi-Meel Publications.

Ahmad, Nazir (1984). Oriental presses in the world. Q. Books.

Ahmad, Nazir (2015). History of Arabic and Persian printing. Birmingham: Radiant Valley.

Ahmad, Nazir (2017). Sacred land of Jordan. Birmingham: Radiant Valley.

Ahmad, Nazir (2018). Refinement of spiritual potential: illumination of mind and soul. Birmingham: Radiant Valley.

Ahmad, Nazir (2020). Challenges of raising youth: nurturing teenagers in a digital world. Birmingham, Radiant Valley.

Ahmad, Nazir and Ahmad, Adeel Nazir (2020). Cyber aggression: impact, awareness and protection. International Journal of Cultural and Social Studies, June 2020, 6(1); 32-41.

Ahmed, Sara (2008). The cultural politics of emotion. New York: Routledge.

Alcock, John (2005). Animal behaviour: an evolutionary approach. (8ᵗʰ ed.). Sunderland, MA: Sinauer Associates.

Alexander, Richard D. (1986). Ostracism and indirect reciprocity: the reproductive significance of humour. Ethology and Socio-biology, 7(3/4); 253-270.

Allen, Victor (2020). How even a short walk can give your memory a boost. Daily Mail, (London), September 10, 2020. P.29.

Alleyne, D., and Solan, I. (2019). Leveraging the Caribbean diaspora for development: the role of network effects. In M. Elo and I. Minto-Coy (eds). Diaspora networks in international business. Pp.55-77.

Andrews, Michael W. and Rosenblum, Leonard A. (1994). The development of affiliative and agonistic social pattern in differentially reared monkeys. Child Development, 65(5): 1398-1404.

Argyle, M. (1988). Bodily communication. London: Routledge

Aristotle (1941). The basic works of Aristotle. (ed.) Richard McKeon. New York: Random House.

Arnett, J.J. (1994). Sensation seeking: a new conceptualisation and a new scale. Personality and Individual Differences, 16: 289-296.

Aron, A. and Aron, E.N. (1986). Love is the expansion of self: Understanding attraction and satisfaction. New York, NY: Hemisphere.

Asare, M., and Danquah, S. A. (2015). The relationship between physical activity, sedentary behaviour, and mental health in Ghanaian adolescent. Child Adolescent Psychiatry Mental Health, 9: 11.

Atweh, B. and Clarkson, P. (2002). Some problematics in International Collaboration in mathematics education. In Mathematics Education in the South Pacific, edited by B. Barton, K. Irwin, M. Pfannkuch, and M. Thomas, 100-107. Proceedings of the 25th annual conference of Auckland: MERGA.

Augsburger, D (1988). Sustaining love: healing and growth in the passage of marriage. Ventura, California: Regal Books.

Bakhtin, Mikhail (1984). Rabelais and his world, translated by Helene Iswalsky. Bloomington: Indiana University Press.

Bar'el, Zavi (2007). Danger, female cartoonist. Haaretz Daily Newspaper, 13 March 2007.

Bataille, George (1991). Nonknowledge, laughter, and tears: a critical Review

Bateson, G.D., Jackson, J. Haley, and Weakland, J. (1956). Towards a theory of schizophrenia. Behavioural Science, 1(4); 251-64.

Baumeister, R.F., Bratslavsky, E. (1999). Passion, intimacy and time: passionate love as a function of change in intimacy. Personality and Social Psychology Review, 3: 49-67.

Bechterew, Wladimir Michailowitsch Von (1894). Unaufhaltsamcs Lachen Und Weinen bei Hirnaffektionen. Archiv für Psychiatrie Und Nervenkrankheiten, 26: 791-817.

Belsky, J., and Pensky, E. (1988). Marital change across the transition to parenthood. Marriage and Family Review, 12 (3/4); 133-156.

Benamou, P.H. (2006). Erotic and sadomasochistic foot and shoe. Behavioural Study, 22: 43-64.

Benitez, Mary Ann (2018). Those at risk tend to be disadvantaged and face discrimination, and also find their studies difficult. South China Morning Post, 24 September 2018.

Benjamin, Medea (2013). Egyptian female cartoonist pokes fun at fundamentalists: counterpunch, 29 March 2013.

Benjamin, Walter (2009). The origin of German tragic drama, tr. John Osbourne. London: Verso. Pp.125-126.

Benolt, D. Coolbear, J. and Crawford, A (2008). Abuse, neglect, and maltreatment of infants. New York: NY Academic Press.

Bensman, J and Lilienfeld, R. (1979) Between public and private: the lost boundaries of the self. New York: The Free Press.

Benson, P.L. (1997). All kids are our kids: what communities must do to raise caring and responsible children and adolescents. 2nd.ed.

Benson, P.L., Scales, P.C., Syvertsen, A.K. The contribution of the developmental assets framework to positive youth development theory and practice. In: Lerner, R.M., Lerner, J.V., Benson, J.B. (2011) editors. Advances in Child Development and Behaviour. 41 (1).197-230.

Berk, H. (1989) Neuroendocrine and stress hormone changes during mirthful laughter. American Journal of Medical Sciences, 298; 390-396.

Berlant, Laurent (2000). Intimacy: a special issue. In Lauren Berlant, ed., intimacy. Chicago: University of Chicago Press. 1-8 (6)

Berzoff, J. M., and Hertz, P. (2008). Inside out and outside in (2nd Edition wd.). Lanham: Jason Aronson.

Birnbaum, G.E., Reis, H.T., Mizrahi, M., Kanat-Maymow. Y., Sass, O., Granovski-Milner, C. (2016). Intimacy connected: the importance of partner responsiveness for experiencing sexual desire. Journal of Personality and Social Psychology, 111; 530-546.

Birren, F. (1972). The significance of light. American Institute of Architect Journal, August 1972; 27-30.

Birren, F. (1977). Color it colored. Pregressive Architecture, September 1977; 129-133.

Bogle, Kathleen A (2008). Hooking up: sex, dating and relationships on campus. New York: New York University Press.

Bolges, E.A. (1999).Grounded theory analysis of emotional pain. Psychother Research., 9; 342-362.

Bowen, Murray (1978). Family therapy in clinical practice. New York: Jason Aronson.

Bowlby, J (1969). Attachment and loss: vol.1. Attachment. New York: Basic Books.

Brackett, C.W. (1933). Laughing and crying of preschool children. Journal of Experimental Education, 2; 119-226.

Bradshaw, Carolyn, Kahn, Arnold S., Saville, Bryn, K. (2010). To Hook up or Date: Which Gender Benefits? Sex Roles, 62; 661-669.

Brannigan, C.R., and Humphries, D.A. (1972). Human non-verbal behaviour, a means of communication, In N.G. Blurton-Jones (Eds), Ethological studies of child behaviour (pp.37-64). Cambridge: Cambridge University Press.

Brown, BB, Prinstein, MJ, eds. (2011). Encyclopaedia of adolescents. New York: Elsevier.

Bryant, Gregory A., Daniel, M, Fessler, R.F. et al. (2018). The perception of spontaneous and volitional laughter across 21 societies. Psychological Science, 29(9): 1515-1525.

Bryant, J., and Zillmann, D. (1988). Using humour to promote learning in the classroom. Journal of Children in Contemporary Society, 20(2); 49-78.

Burner, J. (1985). Models of the learner. Educational Researcher, 14(6); 5-8.

Cal, Qing., Chen, Snead., White, Sarah J., Scott, Sophie K. (2019). Modulation of humour ratings of bad jokes by other people's laughter. Current Biology, 29(14)

Callard, Felicity and Papoulias, Constantina (2010). Affect and embodiment, In Susannah Radstone and Bill Schwarz, eds. Memory: histories. Theories and debates. New York: Fordham University Press. 246-262. (247)

Calvert, W.C. (1949). The effect of the social situation on humour. (Unpublished Master's Thesis), Stanford University, California.

Campbell, A (2008). The morning after the night before: Affective reactions to one-night stands among mated and unmated women and men. Human Nature, 19; 157-173.

Cannon, W.B. (1927). The James-Lange theory of emotion: a critical examination and an alternative theory. American Journal of Psychology, 39; 106-124.

Carey, John (1973). The violent effigy: a study of Dickens's imagination. London: Faber and Faber.

Carling, J., and Schewed, K. (2018). Revisiting aspiration and ability in international migration. Journal of Ethnic and Migration Studies, 44(6): 945-963.

Carlyle, Thomas (1836). Sartor Resartus. London.

Carothers, J.C. (1948). A study of mental derangement in African and an attempt to explain its peculiarities, more especially in relation to the African attitude to life. East African Medical Journal, 25;197-219.

Cashin, W (1985). Improving lectures. IDEA Paper no. 14, Centre for Faculty of Education and Development, Kansas State University.

Cassidy, J (2001). Truth, lies, and intimacy: an attachment perspective. Attachment and Human Development, 3(2); 121-155.

Catalano, R.F., Berglund, M.L., Ryan, JAM, Lonczak, H.S., Hawkins, J.D. (2004). Positive youth development in the United States. Research findings on evaluations of positive youth development program. Annals of American Academy of Political and Social Science. 591(1): 98-124.

Cavna, Michael (2011). Amid revolution, Arab cartoonists draw attention to their cause: the Washington Post, 3 July 2011.

Chapman, Anthony .J. (1975). Eye contact, physical proximity and laughter: a re-examination of the equilibrium model of social intimacy. Social Behavior and Personality: an international journal, 3(2), 143-155.

Chapman, Anthony J. and Foot, Hugh, C. (eds) (1977). It's a funny thing, Humour.

Chesterton, Gilbert Keith (1906). Charles Dickens: a critical study. New York: Dood Mead and Company.

Clinebell, H.J. and Clinebell, C.H. (1970). The intimate marriage. New York: Harper & Row.

Clore, G.L. and Byme, D. (1974). A reinforcement-affect model of attraction In T.L. Huston)Ed.) Foundations of interpersonal attraction. (pp.143-170). New York: Academic Press.

Coles, Nicholas A, Larsen, Jeff T, Lench, Heather C. (2019). A meta-analysis of the facial feedback literature: effects of facial feedback on emotional experience are small and variable. Psychological Bulletin, 145(6): 610-651.

Conard, Dan and Hedin, Diane (1981). National assessment of Experiential Education: summary and implications. Journal of Experiential Education, 4(2): 6-20.

Cook-Sather, A., Bovill, C., and Felten, P. (2014). Engaging students as partners in learning and teaching, A Guide for Faculty. San Francisco, Northern California: Jossey-Bass.

Cooley, C.H. (1914) Social organisation: a study of the larger mind. New York: C. Scribner's Sons. (originally published 1909)

Correll, Christoph U. (2002). Police Officers' dilemma: using ethnicity to disambiguate potentially threatening individuals. Journal of Personality and Social Psychology, 83; 1324-1329.

Coulter, Kresti. (2020) My first year of open marriage. Elle Fashion Forest, February 2020: 72-76.

Cousins, Norman (1979). Anatomy of an illness. New York: Bantam,

Coutts, R.L. (1973). Love and intimacy. California: Consensus Publishers.

Craik, Kenneth H., Lampert, Martin D., Nelson, Arvalea J. (1996). Sense of humour and styles of everyday humorous conduct. Humour, 9(3/4); 273-302.

Crane, T., Temple, V. (2015). A Systematic review of dropout from organised report among children and youth. European Psychological Education Review, 2: 1-18.

Critchley, Simon (2000). On humour. London: Routledge.

Crowe, M. (1997). Intimacy in relation to couple therapy. Sexual and Marital Therapy, 12; 225-236.

Dahms, A.M. (1972) Emotional intimacy: overlooked requirements for survival. Boulder, Colorado: Pruett Publishing Co.

Dandeneau, M.L. and Johnson, S.M. (1994). Facilitating intimacy: interventions and effects. Journal of Marital and Family Therapy, 20(1); 17-32.

Davis, D. and Perkowitz, W.T. (1979). Consequences of responsiveness in dyadic interaction: effects of probability of response and proportion of contact-related response on interpersonal and attraction. Journal of Personality and Social Psychology, 37(4); 534-550.

Davis, M.S. (1973) Intimate relations. New York, Free Press

Dew, J., and Wilcox, W.B. (2011). If Momma ain't happy: explaining declines in marital satisfaction among new mothers. Journal of Marriage and Family, 73; 1-12.

Dignam, D (1995) Understanding intimacy as experienced by breastfeeding women. International Health Care for Women, 16(5); 477-485.

Ding, G.F. and Jersild, A.T. (1931). The laughter and smiling of preschool children. New York City: Teachers College, Columbia University, New York. (manuscript). 33p.

Douvan, E. (1977) Interpersonal relationships: some questions and observations. In …………G. Levinger and H.L. Raush (ed).Close relationships: perspectives on the meaning of intimacy. Amherst: University of Massachusetts Press.

Du Bois, C. (1974) The gratuitous act: an introduction to the comparative study of friendship patterns. In E Leyton (ed) The Compact selected dimensions of friendship. Toronto: University of Toronto Press.

Duchenne de Boulogne, G.B. (1862). The mechanism of human facial expression (R.A. Cuthbertson, Trans.). New York: Cambridge University Press.

Duck, S. (1973) Personal relationships and personal constructs: a study of friendship formation. London: John Wiley and Sons.

Dunbar, Robin. (1996). Grooming, gossip, and the evolution of language. New York: Norton.

Dworkin, Andrea. (1974). Woman hating. New York: Penguin Books.

Edmonson, M.S. (1987). Notes on laughter. Anthropological Linguistics, 29; 23-24.

Eibl-Eibesfeldt, I. (1989). Human ethnology. New York: Aldine De Gruyter

Eliot, T.S. (1921). Hamlet and his problems, "in the sacred wood: essays on poetry and criticism". New York: Alfred A. Knopf. (7)

Ellsworth, Phoebe C. (1994). William James and emotion: is a century of fame worth a century of misunderstanding? Psychological Review, 101(2) 222-229

Erikson, EH. (1959). Identity and the life cycle: selected papers. Psychological Issues, 1: 1-171.

Erikson, Erik (1950). Childhood and society. New York: Norton.

Fisher, M.S. (1997). The effect of humour on learning in a planetarium. Science Education, 81(6);703-713.

Fisher, Maryanne.L., Worth, K., Garcia, J.R., and Meredith, T. (2012). Feelings of regret following uncommitted sexual encounters in Canadian university students. Culture, Health, and Sexuality, 14; 45-57.

Fletcher, Susan Willis. (1884). Twelve months in English prison. Boston: Lee and Shepard Publishers; New York: Charles T. Dillingham.

Flowerdew, J. Li, D., and Miller, L. (1998). Attitudes towards English and Cantonese among Hong Kong university lecturers. TESOL Quarterly, 32(2); 201-231.

Foon, Eleisha (2020). New Zealand young people facing silent pandemic of psychological distress. Rnz.co.nz/news/national/425172/new-zealand-young-people-facing-silent-pandemic-of-psychological-distress.

Ford, Brett, Lam, P., John, O.P., Mauss, I.B. (2018). The psychological health benefits of accepting negative emotions and thoughts: laboratory diary and longitudinal evidence. Journal of Personality and Social Psychology, 115(6): 1075-1092.

Frances, S.J. (1979). Sex differences in nonverbal behaviour. Sex Roles, 5;519-535.

Fredrickson, Barbara L. (1998). What goods are positive emotions. Review of General Psychology, 2(3); 300-319.

Freud, Ann (1969). Adolescence as a developmental disturbance. In G. Caplan and S. Lebovici (eds.). Adolescence, pp.5-10. New York: Basic Books.

Freud, Sigmund (1905). Jokes and their relation to the unconscious. In J, Strachey, A Freud, A. Strachey and A. Tyson (trans.) The standard edition of the complete psychological works of Sigmund Freud VIII. London: Hogarth Press.

Freud, Sigmund. (1949) Civilisation and it's discontent. London: The Hogarth Press.

Fromm, E. (1955) The sane society. New York: Rinehart and Co.

Frost, Liz. (2001). Young women and the body: a feminist sociology. New York: Palgrave.

Fry, W.F. (1963). Sweet madness: a study of humour. Palo Alto, California: Pacific Books

Fry, W.F. and Rader, C. (1977). The respiratory components of mirthful laughter. Journal of Biological Psychology, 19; 39-50.

Fullen, M., and Langworthy, M. (2014). A rich seam: How new pedagogies find deep learning. London: Pearson.

Gala, A. Celeste. Understanding emotional intimacy: a review of conceptional istation, assessment and the role of gender. International Social Science Review, 77 (3/4); 151-170.

Garcia, J.R., and Reiber, C (2008). Hook-up behaviour: a biopsychosocial perspective. The Journal of Social, Evolutionary, and Cultural Psychology, 2; 192-208.

Glasser, William (1992). The quality school: managing students without coercion. New York: Harper Collins.

Glenn, P. (2010). Interviewer laughs: shared laughter and asymmetries in employment interviews, Journal of Pragmatics, 42; 1485-1498.

Glick, Schiller N., and Salazar, N. B. (2013). Regimes of mobility across the globe. Journal of Ethnic and Migration Studies, 39(2): 183-200.

Goethe, Johann Wolfgang Von (1872). Elective affinities. New York: Henry Holt and Company.

Gordon, H.L. (1936). An inquiry into the correlation of civilisation and mental disorder in the Kenyan Native. East African Medical Journal, 12; 327-335.

Greef, A., and Malherbe, H. (2001). Intimacy and marital satisfaction in spouses. Journal of Sex and Marital Therapy, 247-257.

Grimaldi, Joseph (2008). Memoirs of Joseph Grimaldi. London: Pushkin Press.

Gross, J.J. and Levenson, R. W. (1993). Emotional suppression: physiology, self-respect and expressive behaviour. Journal of Personality and Social Psychology, 64(6): 970-986.

Habti, Driss, and Elo, Maria (eds) (2019). Global mobility of highly skilled people. Multidisciplinary perspectives on self-expatriation. Vol.16.

Hall, G.S. (1904). Adolescence: Its psychology and its relations to physiology, anthropology, sociology, sex, religion and education. Vol.1 & Vol.2, New York: D, Appleton & Co.

Hall, George Stanley and Arthur, Allin (1897). The psychology of tickling, laughing, and the comic. American Journal of Psychology, 9: 1-41.

Harker, L and Keltner, D. (2001). Expressions of positive emotion in women's college yearbook pictures and their relationship to personality and life outcomes across adulthood. Journal of Personality and Social Psychology, 80, 112-124.

Hatfield, E. and Walster, G. W. (1978). A new look at love. Lantham, MA: University Press of America.

Hatfield, Elaine., Hutchinson, Elizabeth.S.S., Bensman, Lisamarie., Young, D.M., and Rapson, R.L. (2012). Cultural, Social, and Gender influences on casual sex: New Developments. In Jan M. Turner and Andrew D,

Mitchell (Eds). Social Psychology: New developments. Hauppauge, NY: Nova Science.

Hemmter, Mary Louise, Ostrosky, Michaelene, Fox, Lise (2019). Social and emotional foundation for early learning: a conceptual model for instruction. School Psychology Review, 35(4); 583-601. http://www.arlington.k12.ma.us/

Hensher, Phillip (2011). Charles Dickens: the comic crusader. The Daily Telegraph, 21 December 2011.

Heymans, Gerardus (1896). Asthetische Untersuchungen in Anschlussan die Lippsche Theorise des Komischen. Zeitschrift für Psychologie Und Physiologie der Sinnesorgene, 11: 31-43.

Hher, N, Molstad, S. and Donahue, R. (1999). Using humour in the college classroom to enhance teaching effectiveness in "dread courses". College Student Journal, 33(3); 400.

Ho, K.Y., Li, W.H., Chan, S.S. (2015). The effect of power and income disparity on the psychological wellbeing of Hong Kong Children. Public Health Nurse, 32(3): 212-222.

Hobbs, Thomas (1651). Human nature Reprinted In William Molesworth (ed.) The English works of Thomas Hobbs of Molesbury, Vol.4, London: John Bohn, 1840: 1-76.

Hollington, Michael (2012) Dickens and the circles of modernity. P.134

Hollingworth, Harry Levi (1911). Experimental studies in judgement: judgement of the comic. Psychological Review, 18: 132-156.

Homans, G.C. (1950) The human group. New York: Harcourt and Brace.

Homans, George C. (1951) The human group.(The Sociology of Behaviour and Psychology). Ch.6: Human Behaviour and social process. Oxon, Routledge

Homans, G.C. (1974) Social behaviour: Its elementary forms. New York: Harcourt Brace Jovanovich

Huang, Eustance (2020). The future is elsewhere for Hong Kong's youth as the outlook is bleak. CNBC. 31 May 2020.

Izard, Carrol E (1971). The face of emotion. New York: Appleton-Century-Crofts.

Izard, Carrol E. (2009). Emotion theory and research: Highlights, unanswered questions and emerging issues. Annual Review of Psychology, 60; 1-25.

Izard, Carrol E., Stark, K., Trentacosta, C., Schultz, D. (2008). Beyond emotion regulation: emotion utilization and adaptive functioning. Child Development Perspective, 2: 156-163.

James, Henry (1865). A review for the nation; reprinted in The Critical Heritage. Pp.469-473.

James, William (1884). What is emotion? Mind, 9(34): 188-205.

Jensen, Eric (1998). How Julie's brain learns. Educational Leadership, 56(3); 41-45.

Johnson, HarrietM. (1993). The art of block building. New York: The John Day Company. 47p.

Johnson, Kjerstin (2009). Hanaa Hajjar: Saudi Arabia's female political cartoonist. Bitchmedia 25 November 2009.

Jones, H.E. (1935). The galvanic skin reflex as related to overt emotional expression. The American Journal of Psychology, 47, 241-251.

Kant, Immanuel (1790). Kritik der Urteilskraft. Berlin: Lagarde.

Katariina Salmela-Aro, K.A.-E. (2006). Couple share similar changes in depressive symptoms, and marital satisfaction anticipating the birth of a child. Journal of Social and Personal Relationships, 781-803.

Keltner, D (1995). Signs of appeasement: evidence for the distinct display of embarrassment, amusement and shame. Journal of Personality and Social Psychology, 68; 441-454.

Keywood, K. (2000). More than a woman? embodiment and sexual differences in medical law. Feminist Legal Studies, 8: 319-342.

Khiari, Nadia (2011). Facebook Willis from Tunis. 29 November 2011.

Kilpatrick, W. (1975). Identity and intimacy. New York: Delacorte Press

Kimber, Birgitta, Sandell, Rolf and Bermberg, Sven (2008). Social and emotional training in Swedish classrooms for the promotion of mental health: results from an effectiveness study in Sweden, Health Promotion International, 23 (2): 134-143.

Kohn, A. (1993). Punished by rewards: the trouble with gold stars. incentive plans and other bribes. Boston: Houghton Mifflin.

Kozintsev, Alexander (2012). The mirror of laughter, trans. From Russian into English by Richard P. Martin. London: Transaction Publishers.

Kraeplin, Emil (1885). Zur Psychologie des Komischen, In Wilhelm Wundt (ed.), 128-160.

Kraut, R.E., and Johnson, R.E. (1979). Social and emotional messages of smiling: an ethnological approach. Journal of Personality and Social Psychology, 37(9), 1539-1553.

Landis, C (1924). Studies of emotional reactions II General behaviour and facial expression. Journal of Comparative Psychology. 4 and 5; 447-510.

Langer, S.K.(1967). Mind: an essay on human feeling. Baltimore, MD: John Hopkins University Press.

Larson, H.J. (2018). The biggest pandemic risk? Viral misinformation. Nature, 562; 309.

Lee, E.S. (1966). A theory of migration. Demography, 47-57.

Lennon, S.J., Lillethun, A. and Buckland, S.S. (1999). Attitudes towards social comparison as a function of self-esteem: idealised appearance and body image. Family and Consumer Science Research Journal, 27(4): 379-405.

Lerner, R.M. (1978). Nature, nurture, and dynamic interactionism. Human Development, 21: 1-20.

Lerner, R.M. (1981). Adolescent development: scientific study in the 1980s. Youth and Society, 12; 251-275.

Lerner, R.M. (1982). Children and adolescents as producers of their own development. Developmental Review, 2: 342-370.

Lerner, R.M. and Busch-Rossnagel, N.A. (1981). Individuals as producers of their development: a life-span perspective. New York: Academic Press.

Levine, S. (1991). Psychological intimacy. Journal of Sex and Marital Intimacy, 17 (4); 259-267.

Levinger, G. and Raush, H.L. ed. (1977) Close relationships: a perspective on the meaning of intimacy. Amherst: University of Massachusetts Press.

Lewes, G.H. (1864). Life of Goethe. London: Smith, Elder & Co.

Lewis, J, M. (1989). How's your family? Rev. ed. New York: Brunner Mazel.

Lewis, M., Haviland-Jones, J.M. eds. (2000). Handbook of emotions. 2nd ed. Guilford; New York.

Libby, R.W. and Whitehurst, R.N. (1977). Marriage and alternatives: exploring intimate relationships. Glenview, Illinois: Scott Foresman.

Lieberman, A.F. and Van Horn, P. (2000). Don't hit my mummy/ a manual for child-parent psychotherapy with young witnesses of family violence. Washington D.C.: Zero to Three Press.

Lippert, T. K. and Prager, Karen J. (2005). Daily experiences of intimacy: a study of couples. Personal Relationship, 8(3): 283-298.

Lipps, Rheodr (1898). Komik und Humor. Eine psychologisch-asthetische Untersuchung (Bd. 6, Beitrage zur Asthetik) Leipiz: Voss.

Lucas, R. (1988). On the mechanics of economic development. Journal of Monetary Economics, 22; 3-42.

Ludovici, A.M. (1932). The secret of laughter. London: Constable.

Ludovici, Anthony M. (1933). The secret of laughter. New York: The Viking Press.

Malcolm, Andrew (2013) Dickensian laughter: essays on Dickens and humour. Oxford: Oxford University Press.

Martin, Eod A. (1983). Sense of humor as a moderator of the relation between stressors and moods. Journal of Personality and Social Psychology, 45: 1313-1324.

Martin, G.N. and Gray, C.D. (1996). The effects of audience laughter on men's and women's responses to humor. Journal of Social Psychology, 136; 221-231.

Martin, Lillian J. (1905). Psychology of aesthetics 1: experimental prospecting in the field of the comic. American Journal of Psychology, 16: 36-116.

Massumi, Brian (2002). Parables for the virtual: movement, affection, sensation. Durham: Duke University Press. 1-25. (3)

McComas, H.C, (1923). The origin of laughter. Psychological Review, 30; 45-56

Medhurst, Andy (2007). A national joke: popular comedy and English cultural identities. London: Routledge.

Mehu, Marc (2011). Smiling and laughter in naturally occurring dyadic interactions: relationship to conservation, body contacts, and displacement activities. Human Ethology Bulletin, 26(1); 10-28.

Mehu, Marc, and Dunbar, R.I.M. (2008b). Relationship between smiling and laughter in humans (Homosapiens): testing the power asymmetry hypothesis. Folia Primatologica, 79(5), 269-280.

Merves-Okin, L., Amidon, E., and Brent, F. (1991). Perceptions of intimacy in marriage: a study of married couples. American Journal of Family Therapy, 19 (2); 110-118.

Mikhailova, Ann (2020). Around 200,000 Hong Kong citizens set to move to the U.K. after citizenship offer. The Telegraph, 13 July 2020.

Milanich, Nara B. (2020). Who's is the daddy? Times Literary Supplement (TLS), London, Feb.2020, pp.4-5.

Mills, T.M. (1967) The sociology of small groups. Englewood Cliffs, New Jersey: Prentice-Hall.

Moneteiro, D., Cid, L., Marinho, D.A., Vitorino, A., Bento, T. (2017). Determinants and reasons for dropout in swimming: a systematic review, Sports, 5 (3) 50.

Monro, D.H. (1951). Argument of laughter. Melbourne.

Monteiro, D., Cid, L., Marinho, D.A., Moutao, J., Vitorino, A., Bento, T. (2017). Determinants and reasons for dropout in swimming: Systematic Review. Sports, 5(3): 50.

Morris, D. (1971). Intimate behaviour. New York: Random House.

Morris, Desmond (1978) The naked woman: a study of the female body. Vintage UK Random House.

Moss, B. F., and Schwebel, A.I. (1993). Defining intimacy in romantic relationships. Family Relations, 42; 31-37.

Moustakas, Clark, Callahen, Roger J (1956). Reflection on reflection of feelings. Journal of Social Psychology, 43; 323-331.

Muir, Claire (2018). Independent schools face up to a challenging 2018. [insider.co.uk/special-reports/independent-schools-scotland-leaders-tables-11899931]

Munro, Ian (2016). My emotional journey to the heart of headship. [tes.com/news/my-emotional-journey-heart-headship; accessed 3rd November 2020.

Munro, Ian (2020). Dollar Academy launches free, open access platform to increase subject choice for all Scottish pupils.'Dollar Discovers'. [https://www.dollardiscovers.org. dollaracademy.org.uk/news-and-events/news/dollar-discovers September 9, 2020.

Newcombe, Mildren (1993). The imagined world of Charles Dickens. Ohio: Ohio State University Press, p.230.

Nicolson, P. (2011). Loss, happiness and postpartum depression: the ultimate paradox, Canadian Psychology, 40(2); 162 189.

Nolan, J.A. (1960). Influence of classroom temperature on academic learning. Automated Teaching Bulletin.

Nussbaum, Martha (1990). Love's knowledge: essays on philosophy and literature. Oxford: Oxford University Press. 287-288.

O'Connor, E. and McCartney, K. (2007). Examining Teacher-Child relationships and achievement as part of an ecological model of development. American Educational Research Journal, 44(2): 340-369.

Oden, T.C. (1974) Game free: a guide to the meaning of intimacy. New York: Harper and Row

Olson, D.H. (1977). Insiders and outsiders' views of relationships: Research Studies, Close Relationships: Perspectives on the meaning of intimacy, (Ed.) G. Levinger and H.L. Rausch. Amherst: University of Massachusetts Press. (pp.115-135).

Orwell, George (1945). Funny but not vulgar. Leader Magazine, 28 July 1945. P.781.

Kelvinside Academy, Scotland. Outdoor learning blooms at Kelvinside Academy. Scottish Field. 1st October 2018. [Scottishfield.co.uk/living/education/outdoor-learning-at-kelvinside-academy-is-blossoming]

Paine, R. (1974) An exploratory analysis in middle-class culture. In E. Leyton ed. The Compact: selected dimensions of friendship. Toronto: University of Toronto Press

Palermo, F.L.D., Hanish, C.L., Martin, R.A., Fabes, and M. Reiser (2007). Pre-schoolers' academic readiness: What role does the teacher-child relationship play?. Early Childhood Research Quarterly, 22(4): 407-422.

Palisi, B.J. (1966) Ethnic pattern of friendship. Phylon, 27: 217-225.

Parsons, T. (1937) The structure of social action. New York: McGraw Hill Co.

Parsons, T. (1964). Social structure and personality. New York: Free Press

Patlak, M. (1993). Hair dyes dilemmas. FDA Consumer, 27(3):31.

Patten, Robert L. (1967). The art of Pickwick's interpolated tales. In ELH 34(3) 349-366

Pedersen, William.C., Putcha-Bhagavatula, Anila., and Miller, L. Carol. (2011). Are men and women that different? Examining some of the sexual strategies theory: (SST)'s key assumptions about sex-distinct mating mechanisms. Sex Roles, 64; 629-643.

Penhollow, Tina., Young, Michael., Bailey, William. (2007). Relationship between religiosity and "hooking up" behaviour. American Journal of Health Education, 38; 338-345.

Peterson, C and Seligman, M.E.P. (2004). Character strengths and virtues: a handbook and classification. Washington, DC: American Psychological Association.

Peterson, C., Park, N., and Seligman, M.E.P. (2005b) Orientations to happiness and life satisfaction: the full life versus the empty life. Journal of Happiness Studies, 6: 25-41.

Phelan, S.T. (2002). Fads and fashion: the price women pay. Elsevier Science, 138-143.

Potter, Stephen (1954). The sense of humour. London: Penguin Books.

Powell, J.P.A. (1985). Humor and teaching in higher education. Studies in Higher Education, 10(1); 79-90.

Prager, K.J. (1995). The psychology of intimacy. New York: The Guilford Press.

Provine, Robert R. (2002). The science of laughter. Psychology Today, 33 (6); 58-62.

Provine, Robert R. (1993). Laughter punctuates speech: linguistic, social and gender contexts of laughter. Ethology, 95; 291-298.

Provine, Robert. R. (1992). Contagious laughter: laughter is a sufficient stimulus for laughs and smiles. Bulletin of the Psychonomic Society of America, 30; 1-4.

Provine, Robert. R., and Fischer, K.R. (1989). Laughing, smiling, and talking: relation to sleeping and social context in Humans. Ethnology, 83(4), 295-305.

Proyer, Rene T., and Ruch, Willibald (2010). Editorial: Dispositions towards ridicule and being laughed at: current research on gelotophobia, gelotophilia and katagelasticism. Psychological Test and Assessment Modeling, 52(1); 49-59.

Ramey, J.W. (1976) Intimate friendship. Englewood Cliffs, New Jersey: Prentice Hall Inc.

Rapp, Albert (1948). The dawn of humor. The Classical Journal, 43(5); 275-280.

Ratelle, C. F., Carbonneau, N., Vallerand, R. J., Mageau, G.A. (2013). Passion in the romantic sphere: a look at relational outcomes. Motivation and Emotion, 37: 106-120.

Reis, H. T. and Shaver, P. (1988). Intimacy as an interpersonal process. In W. Duck (Ed.) Handbook of personal relationships: theory, research, and interventions. (pp. 367-389). John Wiley & Sons Ltd.

Reis, H.T. (1998). Gender differences in intimacy and related behaviour: context and process. In D.J. Canary and K. Dindis (Eds.) Sex differences and similarities in communication: Critical essays and empirical investigations of sex and gender in interaction (pp.203-232). Mahwah, New Jersey: Erlbaum.

Reisman, J.M. (1979) Anatomy of friendship. New York: Irvington Publishing

Ridley, J. (1993). Gender and couples. Do men and women seek different kinds of intimacy? Sexual and Marital Therapy, 8; 243-253.

Riley, M.W., Cohen, R., Toby, J., and Riley, J.W. jr (1954) Interpersonal relations in small groups. American Sociology Review, 19: 715-724.

Roberts, S.K. and Crawford, P.A. (2008). Real-life calls for real books: literature to help children cope with family stressors. Young Children, 63(5): 12-17.

Robinson, L.C. and Blanton, P.W. (1993). Marital strengthens in enduring marriages. Family Relations, 42, 38-45.

Rogers, C.R. (1957) The necessary and sufficient conditions of therapeutic personality change. Journal of Consulting Psychology, 21: 95-103.

Romer, P.M. (1986). Increasing return and long-run growth. The Journal of Political Economy, 94(5); 1002-1037.

Rosenbloom, Tova. (2009). Crossing at a red light: behaviour of individuals and groups. Psychology and Behaviour, 12(5): 389-394.

Rothbart, M.K. (1973). Laughter in young children. Psychological Bulletin, 80; 247-256.

Rottenstein, C., Laasko, L., Pihalaja, T., Kontinne, N. (2013). Personal reasons for withdrawal from team sports and the influence of significant others among youth athletes. International Journal of Sports Science Coach, 8; 19-31.

Ruch, W and Proyer, R.T. (2008b). Who is gelotophobic? Assessment criteria for the fear of being laughed at. Swiss Journal of Psychology, 67; 19-27.

Ruch, W., Proyer, R.T., and Weber, M. (2010). Humor as character strength among the elderly: theoretical considerations. Zeitschrift für Gerontologie und Geriatrie, 43; 8-12.

Russo, Mary. (1994). The female grotesque: risk, excess and modernity. London; New York: Routledge.

Rychlowska, M., Jack, R.E., Garrod, O.G.B., Schyns, P.G., Martin, J.D. and Niedenthal, Paula M. (2017). Functional smiles: tools for love, sympathy, and war. Psychological Science, 1259; 1-35.

Saarni, C and Harris, P. ed (1991). Children's understanding of emotion. New York: Chicago Press.

Sadrin, Anny (1993). Fragmentation in the Pickwick Papers, In Dickens Studies Annual, 22; 21-34.

Salovey, P. and Mayer, J.D. (1990). Emotional intelligence. Imagination, Cognition and Personality, 9; 185-211.

Scarantino, A. (2014). The motivational theory of emotions. In J.D. Arms and D. Jacobson (eds), Moral psychology and human agency. Philosophical essays on the science of ethics. Pp.156-185. Oxford University Press.

Schachter, S and Singer, (1962). Cognitive, social, and physiological determinants of emotional state. Psychological Review, 69; 379-399.

Schachter, S., and Singer, J. (1962). Cognitive, social, and physiological determinants of emotional state. Psychological Review, 69; 379-399.

Scharlemann, J, Eckel, P.W., Virginia, Catherine, Kacelnik, A and Wilson, Rick K (1999). The value of a smile: a game theory with a human face. (paper presented at the Annual Meeting of the American Political Science Association. September 2-5, 1999.

Scott, Alex. (2020). I am heaving therapy to beat trolls: adversity has always made me strong. The Sun, daily English. (London), 7 March, 2020. Pp 18-19.

Scott, J. (2005). Satire: from Horace to yesterday's comic strips. Clayton, Delware,: Prestwick House Inc.

Shaftsbury, Lord (1711). Characteristics of men, manners, opinions, times. quoted in Vice Gatrell, City of laughter: sex and satire in eighteenth century (London, 2006). P.169.

Shakespeare, William (1676). The Tragedy of Hamlet, Prince of Denmark. (written between 1599-1601 by Shakespeare). 6th ed. London: Published by Andr Clark for J. Martin and H. Herringman.

Shaw, George Bernard (1934). The Stalin-Wells talk. The New Statesman, 27 October 1934.

Shepherd, Richard Harne (ed.) (1937). The speeches of Charles Dickens. London: Michael Joseph Ltd.

Sherrow, V. (2001). For appearance sake: the historical encyclopaedia of good looks. Beauty and Grooming. Westport: Oryx Press.

Simmel, G. (1921) Sociology of the senses: visual interactions: In R. Park and E. Burgers ed. Introduction to the science of sociology. 3rd ed. Chicago: University of Chicago Press.

Smith, C.G. (1935) Spencer's theory of friendship. Baltimore: The John Hopkins Press

Speight, George (1955). The history of the English puppet theatre. London: George G Harrap ans Co.

Spencer, Herbert. (1860). The physiology of laughter. Macmillan's Magazine, 5: March 1860.; 395-

402.ssociation Corhum et le Centre de Recherche Interdisciplinaire sur l'Humour (Universite Paris 8, 2000)

Sternberg, R,J, (1986). A triangular theory of love. Psychological Review, 93: 119-135.

Sternberg, R.J. (1998). A balance theory of wisdom. Review of General Psychology, 2: 347-365.

Stora-Sandor, Judith (2000). A propose de l'Humour Feminin, Hmoresques. Armies d'Humour,. Rires au Fiminin, eds Judith Stora-Sandor and Elizabeth Pillet.

Sullivan, H.S. (1953) The interpersonal theory of psychiatry. New York: W.W. Norton.

Sutherland, P., and Badger, R. (2004). Lecturer's perceptions of lectures. Journal of Further and Higher Education, 28(3); 277-289.

Tan, Huileng (2020). Taiwan throws its weight behind Hong Kong citizens who want to resettle on the island. CNBC, 29 May, 2020.
Teychenne, M., Ball, K., Salmon, J. (2010). Sedentary behaviour and depression among adults: a review. International Journal of Behavioural Medicine, !7(4); 246-254.

Thackeray, William Makepeace The Book of Snobs.

Thompson. James. (1983). The end of libraries. The Electronic Library, 1(4); 245-255. https://doi.org/10.1108/eb044603

Thurston, R.W. (1991). Social dimensions of Satlinist rule: humor and terror in the USSR, 1935-1941. Journal of Social History, 24(3); 541-562.

Tidd, K.L. and Lochard, J.S. (1978). Monetary significance of the affiliative smile: a case for reciprocal altruism. Bulletin of Psychonom Sociology, 11; 344-346.

Titze, M. (2009). Gelotophobia: the fear of being laughed at. Humor: International Journal of Humor Research, 22; 27-48.

Tomkins, Silvan S. (2008). Affect imagery consciousness: the complete edition. New York: Springer.

Tomkins, Silvan.S. (1962). Affect, imagery and consciousness. Vol.1: the positive affects. New York: Springer.

Tomkins, Silvan.S. and McCarter, R, (1964). What and where are the primary affects? Some evidence for a theory. Perceptual and Motor Skills, 18; 119-158.

Turner, Lynn and Gordon, Lori H. (1995). Practical application of intimate relationship skills. Journal of Couples Therapy, 5(1-2): 37-53.

Twardosz, S (2005). Expressing warmth and affection to children. Center on the Social and Emotional Foundations for Early Learning. What Works Briefs. http://csefel.vanderbilt.edu/briefs/wwb20.pdf.

UNESCO (2018). African brain drain: Is there an alternative? The Unesco Courier, January-March 2018.

University of Surrey. Mothers nurture emotions in girls over boys, new study finds. Science Daily. 12 November 2014.

Waring, E. (1984). The measurement of marital intimacy. The Journal of Marital and Family Therapy, 10(2); 185-192.

Washburn, R.W. (1929). A study of the smile and laughing of infant in the first year of life. Genetic Psychology Monographs, 6, 403-457.

Watanabe, S. (1969). The brain from developing to developed countries. International Labour Review, 4: 401-433.

Watzlawick, P. (1983). The situation is hopeless but not serious: the pursuit of unhappiness. New York: W.W. Norton

Webb, M. A. (1985). The brain and educational opportunities in less developed countries. Eastern Economic Journal, 2: 145-155.

Weisfeld, Glenn E (1993). The adaptive value of humor and laughter. Ethology and Sociobiology, 14: 141-169.

Welsford, Dean Martin (1935). The fool: his social and literary history. London: Faber & Faber

Whyte, W.W. (1943) Street Corner society: the social structure of an Italian slum. Chicago: University of Chicago Press

Wilson, Glenn D., Rust, John and Kasriel, Judith. (1977). Genetic and family origins of human preferences: a twin study. Psychological Reports. 41: 659-660.

Wolf, N. (1990). The beauty myth. London: Vintage

Wolff, P.H. (1963). Observations on the early development of smiling. In B.M. Foss (Ed.), Determinants of infant behaviour (pp.113-138). London: Methuen.

Woolf, Virginia (1989). A sketch of the past In Moments of Being and other autobiographical writings, (ed.) J. Schuilkind. London: Grafton Books

Woolf, Virginia. (1929). A room of one's own, London: Hogarth Press.

Wormald, Mark (1999). Pickwick Papers. London: Penguin, p.xi-xii.

Wright, P., Henggeler, S., and Craig, L. (1986). Problems in Paradise? A longitudinal examination of the transition to parenthood. Journal of Applied Developmental Psychology, 7(3); 277-291.

Wynne, L.C. and Wynne, A.R. (1986). The quest for intimacy. Journal of Marital and Family Therapy, 12(4); 383-394.

Zhang, Q. (2005). Immediacy, humor, power distance and classroom communication apprehension in Chinese college classrooms. Communication Quarterly, 53(1); 109-124.

Zive, A. (1988). Teaching and learning with humor. Experiment and Replication, Journal of Experimental Education, 57(1); 5-15.

Zuckerman, M. (1995). Behavioral expressions and psychobiological bases of sensation seeking. New York: Cambridge University Press.

ABOUT THE AUTHOR

Parental affection, timely attention, tenacious guidance, and precise social management help youngsters keep on track despite life hindrances, hurdles, and obstructions. Time is a precious commodity, and self-discipline is invaluable for a teenager to succeed and carve a place in the intellectual sphere. The journey is arduous, demanding time management, a degree of self-restraint, and moderation in a socially alluring atmosphere. An academic expedition is challenging in a competitive world. Excellent school teachers, inspiring university professors, and pleasant study mates make the learning exciting and exhilarating.

One has to be stoutly ambitious to surmount difficulties and overcome diverse concerns to achieve higher accolades. Best teachers and cordial class fellows both in Manchester and London facilitated shared learning and group activities. Interestingly, student social clubs were practically knowledge co-construction hubs, holding debates on literary and scholarly significant subjects. Meaningful conversations reflected mannerism, respect, and gesticulation among members of the student unions. Occasional giggles, mild laughs, and harmless jokes rejuvenated the Manchester Polytechnic social club environment. The Polytechnic later became Manchester Metropolitan University. A few names stand out in the academic pursuit, such as Tim Baxter, Barry Mills, Michael Sharkey, Barry Cheale, Ian

Goldie, and Mrs. Patricia Coleman. They were vigorous participants in extracurricular undertakings. While studying at Manchester Metropolitan University, Dr. Ahmad benefited from awe-inspiring lectures by Professor Alan Duxbury, Professor Alan. G. Pate, Professor K.W. Neal, and Professor Keith Lund.

Having earned Post-graduate MCILIP from Manchester Metropolitan University, Dr. Ahmad served as a Research Assistant in the School of Oriental and African Studies, University of London. He gained admission at University College London for an intensive MPhil Degree programme. He had the opportunity of studying under Professor Ronald Staveley, Professor B.C. Vickery and Professor James. D. Pearson. In monthly postgraduate seminars, doctoral students were invited to give talks on topics ranging from research strategies, human ideals, the significance of archives, to understanding principles of psychology and philosophical doctrines. Dr. Nazir presented a paper in the presence of Professor Bernard Lewis, Professor Ronald Staveley, Professor J.D. Pearson, B.C. Bloomfield, K.C. Buller, B. Wallace, and Mr. Driskel, entitled " Psychology of Interpersonal Communication", receiving encouraging feedback and scholarly guidance for producing other research papers. At the university level, professors invigorated all students to help each other, share knowledge and research findings for the common good and mutual benefit. After the successful acquisition of an MPhil degree, Dr. Nazir Ahmad subsequently earned a place for Doctoral studies at the University of London. He pursued his studies and research with relentless resilience for four and a half years, and finally, the University of London awarded him a Ph.D. degree.

Fortunately, I received intellectual guidance from Professor Simon Digby of Oxford University, and Keeper of the Ashmolean Museum who invited me twice for a decent lunch at his residence and also facilitated my access to Bodleian Library collections. Academic support came from James Thompson, Chief Librarian of Reading University, who later wrote in British Book News, a review of my book published from London. He rightly commented about pre-emptive new technologies that 'libraries may disappear like the dinosaurs or they may adapt and survive'.

Barry Cambray Bloomfield, Director of British Library Collections was extremely helpful in directing my research for higher studies at University of London. Scholastic advice from Barry Bloomfield was a turning point in my career when I presented concurrently to him, two letters, one an offer of a position at the National Library of Australia in Canberra, the other an admission letter for MPhil Studies at the University College London. Barry asked 'what do you want'? A piece of advice was the reply because both opportunities had an equal fascination for me. Stay here and complete your higher degrees, proclaimed Barry, suggesting bright prospects gleam over promising young people.

Although I did not take up the job at the National Library of Australia, Canberra due to my admission in

University College London, I built up rapport with Peter Saunders, Diplomat and Director of Information and Research Services, Australia House, London. I completed two scholarly projects under his supervision and still exchange views and greetings to this day while he resides at Seacomb Heights, South Australia. Likewise, I keep in touch with my compassionate former colleagues Professor Dr. Bob Usherwood of Sheffield University and Barry King, Director of Age Concern, West Sussex.

In my professional career, I served London Borough of Sutton, Southwark College London, Rutherford School, Paddington, SOAS Library, University of London, and then for a couple of years, King Faisal University, Dammam, Saudi Arabia. While working for the Inner London Education Authority, I attended an interview at the Saudi Embassy, London, for the post of a Professor at King Abdul Aziz University, Jeddah, Saudi Arabia. Accepted the offer and proceeded to Saudi Arabia for teaching both undergraduate and Master's degree students for fifteen years. Some of those bright students have now become professors in various Saudi universities. It is pleasing to remember the traditional Saudi hospitality, friendly atmosphere and wonderful colleagues such as Professor Dr. Abdul Jalil Tashkandy [now retired], Professor Dr. Muhammad Amin Marghalani, Professor Dr. Hasan Al-Sereihy, and Professor Dr. Muhammad Jafar Arif. The sense of humour showed by Dr. Abdul Ghafoor Bukhari, Dr. Atif Qattan, and Dr. Sharaf Al-Jeffry enlightened the department. Among my best former students are Dr. Faisal Al-Haddad, Director of Strategic Studies, King

Abdul Aziz University, Jeddah, Dr. Jabreel Al-Arish, Dean and Professor, King Saud University, Riyadh, and Fahad Abdul Fattah, Library and Information Director, King Faisal Specialist Hospital and Research Centre, Jeddah, Saudi Arabia.

On behalf of my colleagues, I conducted semester exams when they were away on academic assignments. I taught female Master's degree students via CCTV, allowing them remote access to ask questions over the phone. In addition to my academic commitments, I rendered educational guidance, admission facilitation and maintained liaison with U.S. and British Universities for securing acceptance in doctoral programmes for our top student scholars.

While at Manchester Metropolitan University, I had specialised in the indexing, abstracting, and information retrieval discipline. Given my expertise, one of my colleagues Professor Dr Hashim Abdu Hashim (who was also Director-General of the Okaz Organisation, publishing an Arabic and English' Saudi Gazette' newspapers), engaged me for the task of indexing Saudi Gazette- an English daily. I dexterously indexed the backlog, devising thesaurus, assigning subject headings, and producing 25-volumes covering the twenty-five-year period from 1976-2000.

In my MPhil studies at University College London, one of the significant assignments was the "Psychology of Student Behaviour in the Classroom," which had provided me with an insight into the significance of sustaining a learning environment for university students. I applied my social psychology skills at King Abdul Aziz University classroom settings, keeping my students engaged, smiling with little harmless puns, and making the learning a pleasurable experience. My lectures were envisioned to be a subjective manifestation of knowledge, gleaned from reading, research, and strengthened by the needs of courses. I used multilingual Arabic-English proficiencies to facilitate absorption and retention for mostly Arabic speaking students.

At Southwark College London, I collaborated with Don W. Wendon, Director of Information and Learning Resources, to plan and prepare a comprehensive User Instruction programme for both pure sciences and Humanities students. We partly implemented Ralph Waldo Emerson's notion of 'urging colleges to appoint Professors of Books' (1840) to imbue in students the spirit of scientific enquiry, search strategies, and information retrieval capabilities. In cooperation with Professor H.G.L Davis, Head of Science department at the college, I prepared a series of lectures on research methods and taught research methodologies to final year physics, biology, and chemistry students. While serving at King Faisal University Dammam, I devised a research methods course in collaboration with Abdullah Driskell (formerly Michael Driskell), who was the Chief of the Medical Library. It was a series of lectures we both delivered at the beginning of each semester to medical students.

I have written many research articles published in professional journals of Europe, Turkey, the U.S.A., Australia, and South Asia. I have authored more than twenty books in the field of emotional psychology, youth nurturing and social media, digital learning, Islamic literature, library and Information management, and composed a comprehensive collection of English poems.

E-Mail: drnahmad3@hotmail.com
1443 Hijra/2021